Enterprise and Cu

This book addresses the fundamental questions concerning the economic reinvigoration of society through policies aimed at encouraging the development of small enterprises. Governments in Europe, the rest of the industrialised world and developing countries are increasingly including small enterprise development as a central feature of economic and social policies. Nowhere was this more evident than during the 1980s in Britain, as the Conservative government sought to establish an enterprise culture. However, despite an impressive growth in the numbers of people turning to self-employment, there is little evidence that British society has become more entrepreneurial or that the pursuit of enterprise has become part of the national culture.

In *Enterprise and Culture*, the author argues that the failure of small enterprise policy is not just a question of economics but is also caused by psychological and cultural factors. The book demonstrates that the individualism at the centre of enterprise culture policies is itself the main impediment to the successful growth and development of small enterprises. The book also questions whether it is appropriate to give the amorphous figure of the 'entrepreneur' such significance in economic development policy. The author contends that vibrant and progressive capitalism is a highly social enterprise and requires more collective approaches to its future development if the economic rewards are to benefit local communities and society as a whole.

Enterprise and Culture is a uniquely wide-ranging, insightful and well-informed critical evaluation of the economic and social project of creating an enterprise culture.

Colin Gray is Director of External Affairs at the Open University Business School and Deputy Director-General of the Small Business Research Trust. His publications include *Small Business in the Big Market* (1992) and *The Barclays Guide to Growing the Small Business* (1990).

Routledge Studies in Small Business
Edited by David Storey

Enterprise and Culture

Colin Gray

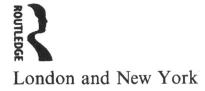

London and New York

First published 1998
by Routledge
2 Park Square, Milton Park, Abingdon, Oxon, OX14 4RN

Simultaneously published in the USA and Canada
by Routledge
270 Madison Ave, New York NY 10016

Transferred to Digital Printing 2007

© 1998 Colin Gray

Typeset in Times by BC Typesetting, Bristol

British Library Cataloguing in Publication Data
A catalogue record for this book is available from the British Library

Library of Congress Cataloguing in Publication Data
A catalogue record for this book has been requested

ISBN10: 0–415–16185–1 (hbk)
ISBN10: 0–415–43958–2 (pbk)

ISBN13: 978–0–415–16185–5 (hbk)
ISBN13: 978–0–415–43958–9 (pbk)

Publisher's Note
The publisher has gone to great lengths to ensure the quality of this reprint
but points out that some imperfections in the original may be apparent

Contents

Figures

Tables

Introduction

The word 'enterprise' is somewhat overused, if not abused, these days by politicians, so much so that it has undergone something of a grammatical shift. From its original introduction from French as a noun to describe commercial undertakings between people, it broadened to become almost a synonym for a business or firm. Its figurative use to describe the energy, ingenuity and application of people who successfully work in businesses or firms, or even generally show skill at overcoming problems, has now transformed a fairly useful noun into an adjective. Rather abstract concepts such as 'spirit' or 'culture' and more banal fiscal policy terms such as 'allowance' or 'loan' can apparently now be made more concrete and commercial by appending 'enterprise' to them as an adjective. Language, however, is central and fundamental to a nation's culture and it is by no means clear that ordinary people have yet learned to use the word in this new way.

I have no deep-rooted objection to this transformation. On the contrary, I am sure that one of the strengths of English as the language of international business and trade is its flexibility and its healthy disregard for the limiting constraints of too formal a grammar or lexicon. Indeed, you may find some fine examples of disregard for grammar in this book. For me, the interesting point about this transformation of the word 'enterprise' is that the change reflects some very real economic and social shifts that have taken place in Britain and elsewhere. I will leave aside for the moment the origins of 'enterprise' in a world where business was dominated by trade between merchants (there is some discussion of this in the book). The years after the Second World War have seen policies supporting the growth of large enterprises give way under the pressures of economic restructuring, global competition, new patterns of work and technological change to those that support more strategic commercial alliances and seek to strengthen 'enterprise' as an element not only in national economies but also in national psyches.

These important matters are explored and discussed in detail in this book. Indeed, its broad purpose is to examine to what extent public policy can influence or shape popular attitudes and cultural values concerning work and such personal matters as ambition, expectations and business behaviour. The more specific focus of the book is on how effective the batch of policies aimed at increasing self-employment and small business development in Britain, since the early 1980s, have been in creating an 'enterprise culture'. The more fundamental questions of whether these policies have been properly targeted or whether they have actually transformed Britain's economic fortunes are also directly considered. However, the book is as much about whether this form of social engineering can work as it is about the application of particular policies during the 1980s. It may be useful to consider a real-life example. British Steel provides a good instance of the cultural and economic processes I have just mentioned.

The British Steel Corporation started life in an honourable British tradition – as a huge nationalised enterprise put together by the first Wilson government in the mid-1960s as Britain's champion in the highly competitive global steel industry. Excess capacity, increasing competition from abroad and the worldwide recession that followed the oil price rises of 1973 found British Steel (and the entire British economy) in deep crisis by the mid-1970s. Under Sir Charles Villiers, who took over the chair of British Steel from Sir Monty Finniston in 1976, and later under Ian MacGregor who took over from him in the wake of the steel strike of 1980, British Steel shed some 70 per cent of its workforce, more than 140,000 people. By 1987, the corporation had climbed back into profit and today is once again an important player in international steel markets. The concern of this book, however, is not with big business success but with the challenges of creating dynamic smaller enterprises. The last important decision that Sir Charles Villiers took at British Steel in June 1980 was to close the Consett steel works.

However, Consett was not doomed to wither away completely. Recognising the extent of the crisis in the steel industry, British Steel had set up BSC (Industry) in 1975 as a body charged with responsibility for regenerating areas hit by steel plant closures. The aim was to create new job opportunities by encouraging new small firms to start in premises developed from the redundant British Steel sites. This scheme encapsulates most of the features and expectations of what later came to be known in the mid-1980s as the 'enterprise culture'. Three years after the steel works was closed, a certain Roger McKechnie approached BSC (Industry) with a plan to produce well-packaged flavoured corn crisps as an adult snack food. Twelve years later, Roger and his three partners were able to sell their enterprise, Derwent Foods, and its world-beating Phileas Fogg brand for £24 million. Roger reportedly picked up £7 million personally for his hard-won and innovative success: a clear triumph for the new enterprise culture. Indeed, when I attended the 1993 Institute of Small Business Affairs annual conference in Harrogate, Roger was one of the keynote speakers as a prime example of a successful entrepreneur, which he undoubtedly is.

However, it is the purpose of this book to look behind the scenes to find out if a truer and more durable tale exists to explain this type of success rather than the simple view that it is all down to the individual and the onset of a new enterprise cultural The aim is to uncover the factors that should be taken into account in policies designed to promote the more widespread establishment of enterprises of this type and, ultimately, an overall increase in prosperity and creativity. First, we need to examine the institutional and structural factors such as the state of the economy, the business cycle, the regime of regulations, access to capital, supply of the right kind of labour and so on.   en we can critically examine the personal and cultural factors that accompany the success of new enterprises such as the founder's motivation and personality, the decision to seek a self-employed career, work experience, teamwork, the role of small firms in their communities and so on. Finally, we can come to some understanding of the role that interventions such as training and education, financial incentives and public recognition may play in developing more successful enterprises to the benefit of our wider communities and the economy as a whole. The main focus of this book is on the middle area but the key issues of all three areas will be examined.

To return now to the particular case of Roger McKechnie and Derwent Foods, a number of interesting elements emerge which suggest that providing premises in old steel works and encouraging people to get on their bikes to seek new employment or start new small businesses may not be enough to encourage the replication of this success story in other fields. Let us look at Roger more closely. He left university to join Procter and Gamble as a marketing trainee, left and found a job with Tudor Foods, rising over nine years from marketing manager to become the managing director. In 1981, Associated Biscuits (the parent of Tudor and owner of Smiths Crisps) asked him to take over Smiths. He had already had his ideas for producing adult snack foods turned down and the move would have entailed a relocation which he was not inclined to accept, so he refused and left: clearly a lucky decision, as history demonstrated. But Roger was not just a man off the street seeking to start a small business in an old steel works. He had education, excellent marketing and management training, and plenty of high-level responsibility and management experience in a relevant field. There was also an element of being pushed and suffering some degree of work frustration. However, the most important success factor seems to have been Roger's knowledge of his market and the research he put into identifying what he felt to be the right product. This reflected his extensive experience and enabled him to control his risks.

He managed to control his financial risks. Without doubt, the support and finance he received from BSC (Industry) was welcome, but so too were a government regional grant and finance from Britain's biggest venture capital organisation 3i (Investors in Industry) which took a 25 per cent stake. Indeed, Roger did not start as a single individual but began with three partners, all of whom helped to spread the risk and provided their own experience. To obtain their £500,000 start-up capital they had to produce a well-considered, viable business plan. This further controlled the risk.

And the support extended beyond the realm of business. Roger had decided to resist moving to Smiths for family and community reasons; this meant, in turn, tremendous emotional and psychological support from those quarters. Thus, even though the actual decision to start required courage and confidence, all the manageable risks had been addressed and controlled to the extent that fate allows. This picture of a successful entrepreneur is quite at odds with the popular myth of the loner starting in a garage to emerge several years later as an industrial giant; it is also at odds with the realities encountered by thousands of unemployed people encouraged by enterprise culture policies to turn to self-employment. I have never met Roger McKechnie in person but, from his story as it has appeared in various articles, I have a clear picture of enterprise at work, of an entrepreneur, but not of a typical self-employed person or small business owner.

In this book, I am trying to examine critically the broader economic and personal psychological factors at work behind the scenes of the enterprise culture policies and the sort of small firm development that such policies are likely to produce. Many of the empirical data referred to are publicly available, mostly from government sources or international agencies. The more specific studies are usually based on surveys conducted by the Small Business Research Trust (SBRT), an independent educational charity that has been actively researching small firms in Britain since 1984. I have had the privilege of being the deputy director general of the SBRT since 1985, an experience which has brought me into contact with a constant flow of fresh information on the small firm sector, with most leading small firm academics, with influential small firm lobbyists and, above all, with countless small firm owners and managers. Indeed, it was not by chance that I chose the story of British Steel and Phileas Fogg adult snacks in order to highlight some of the key issues in entrepreneurial development covered in this book. Sir Charles Villiers was the first chairman of the SBRT and an enormous influence. One of the early reports published by the SBRT was on the job-generating record of the BSC (Industry) converted steelworks sites (the net balance was positive but most of the new firms would have started anyway, very few were founded by former steel workers and even fewer were as successful as Derwent Foods).

I also owe a debt of gratitude to the other people who helped to found the SBRT for many of the ideas and insights in this book; Graham Bannock (research director of the Bolton Report and a successful economic consultant in the small firm field), Stan Mendham (one of Britain's most tenacious small firm campaigners and the present chairman of the SBRT) and John Stanworth (director general of the SBRT and held by many to be Britain's first small business professor). Colleagues at the Open University Business School (where I am responsible for the open-learning materials and course for small businesses), fellow members of the board of the Institute of Small Business Affairs and the people who keep small but lively Camden Enterprise in the business of helping new and established local enterprises have all informed the ideas presented in this book (wittingly or otherwise). Gratitude also to Formez (the Italian state agency that used to be responsible for developing small and medium enterprises in the underdeveloped economy of southern Italy, the *mezzogiorno*) for providing me with many opportunities to evaluate their programmes that tried to introduce the vibrant entrepreneurial culture of northern Italy into the different cultures and structures of southern Italy. Finally, a sort of amorphous thanks must go to countless people I have learned something from as a researcher, as a humble self-employed freelance journalist and as a manager of my own small radio news agency.

The ideas presented in this book, however, are my own and I take responsibility for them. It opens with a consideration of the historical and political context that gave birth to enterprise culture policies, and moves on to consider the enterprise culture model of small firm development itself in more detail, then the evidence on how effective these policies have been in encouraging entrepreneur-led development in Britain. Alternative models are then considered before a closer look at the importance of culture in this sort of development process and the importance of individual and social psychological factors in cultural and enterprise development. The book closes with a consideration of how the different, and sometimes conflicting, individual and broader socio-economic forces might be combined to produce development policies that stand a chance of benefiting not only individuals but also local communities and entire economies. As the book started life as a more serious academic work, its origins may sometime creep through in places but I hope it remains readable. Above all, I hope it provokes some thoughts and even some new ideas.

1 The politics of 'enterprise'

Policies designed to promote pro-business attitudes and a stronger spirit of enterprise in Britain – in short, the creation of an *enterprise culture* – are among the most recent of many attempts by successive post-war governments to stem Britain's seemingly relentless economic decline. As each set of policies has failed to stem the slide, new sets of policies which rejected the old were introduced. Even many of the macro-economic monetarist policies of the first Thatcher government were thrust aside as Nigel Lawson, the Chancellor, and Lord Young, the Secretary of State for Trade and Industry (or 'Enterprise' as he preferred to call his department), pursued a growth policy of encouraging 'enterprise'. What marks out *enterprise culture* policies as unique, however, is not the rejection of previous policies but the reliance on personal motivation, attitude shifts and behavioural change – basically psychological concepts – as both instruments and targets of economic policy. In particular, enterprise culture policies explicitly envisage the regeneration of the British economy as flowing from the creation of new, innovative commercial enterprises which are expected to perform two key economic roles: the improvement of economic efficiency and competitiveness, and the attraction of inward capital investment (both resulting from a sustained supply of new advanced products and services).

The role and determination of individual motivation and behaviour in the processes and structures of economic development are matters of debate. Given the different social, political, economic and cultural factors involved, the issues are complex and simple solutions hard to find. However, one clear point of common reference has to be recognised. Economic and industrial policy in Britain in the twentieth century, no matter which political party has held power, has been about improving the efficiency of the capitalist system and no attempt to understand entrepreneurial development, the encouragement of entrepreneurs or the promotion of an enterprise culture can ignore this central point. It is also important to stress that accepting this point does not entail an acceptance of the currently prevailing *neo-classical* model of economic and individual behaviour.

Although the various industrial and economic policies pursued by Conservative British governments since 1979 have been wide-ranging and reflect a strong and fairly coherent ideological position, their main overall policy target in 1983–91 – the fostering of a more entrepreneurial spirit in British business life (the *enterprise culture*) – has been politically linked more to the growth of the small enterprise sector rather than to the promotion of large enterprises. Since the publication of the Bolton Report (Bolton, 1971), the official inquiry into the post-war weakness of Britain's small firm sector, the role of small businesses in the national economy and public consciousness has grown, steadily during the 1970s and rather dramatically during the 1980s. However, this recent growth in Britain's small business sector has been extremely uneven, the economic consequences are unclear and the permanence of the political-economic changes remains uncertain. What does seem beyond dispute is that small business growth since the early 1980s reflects a genuine and fundamental socio-economic shift not only in Britain but also elsewhere in the industrialised world. The extent of this shift, its true beneficiaries and the exact nature of the economic mechanisms which brought it about are, however, matters for debate.

The causes of Britain's variable industrial performance have been publicly discussed and disputed for more than a century. Britain has been a net exporter of capital since Victorian times and there are firm economic reasons for expecting an industrial decline as a result of falling domestic investment. Yet the belief is often expressed that Victorian Britons were more enterprising than present-day business owners. It is now clear, however, that the social and economic structure of eighteenth- and nineteenth-century Britain created the conditions for the country's global dominance during the latter half of Victoria's reign rather than some special British 'entrepreneurial' quality which foreigners lacked. For instance, capitalism began to emerge from mercantilism at about the same time in Britain, France, Italy and Germany, but countless wars and revolutions stunted its development on mainland Europe for the best part of seventy years, indicating that 'entrepreneurship' is not a *sufficient* condition for advanced economic development (lack of severe, if not violent, social disorder may be another equally important prior structural condition).

This is not to suggest that individual capitalists and adventurers had no role to play in Britain's success or that they did not display qualities enabling them to succeed, but more that the prevailing socio-economic structures gave rise to the opportunities and channels for certain active and enterprising people to express and satisfy themselves. A central theme of this book is that psychological characteristics are not independently sufficient causal factors but they are necessary for a proper understanding of the processes of economic development. Individual expectations and behavioural patterns are themselves functions of (and contribute to) the social, economic and, therefore, cultural structures that open or constrict economic outlets for action by certain types of people. The further implication is that different characteristics or strengths will be at a premium during different stages of economic development. The personal qualities demanded of a successful Georgian or Victorian entrepreneur may be quite different from those of an entrepreneur in the new millennium.

This means that there are at least two reasons why it may be misleading to speak of 'entrepreneurial personalities' in the context of economic development even if, for the sake of argument, it is conceded that it is possible to identify 'active and enterprising' behaviour as a personality trait. First, it is apparent that some enterprising people from a bourgeois business and other backgrounds may well seek careers as independent business owners and be described as entrepreneurs, yet equally enterprising people from the same backgrounds or, say, bourgeois academic, petit-bourgeois bureaucratic or industrial working-class backgrounds are more likely to seek their occupational satisfactions through equally demanding careers more valid in their own eyes (and sometimes yielding higher financial rewards). Second, it appears that the socio-economic structures which foster entrepreneurial opportunities are created and maintained by fairly non-entrepreneurial people (for instance administrators, planners and other bureaucrats). If so, economic development may be more a function of supposedly non-entrepreneurial behaviour, with different business skills coming to the fore at different stages of the process. David McClelland (1961), whose influential idea that national economic development depends on enterprising and achievement-oriented attitudes in society, is seen as providing important psychological underpinning for enterprise culture policies. McClelland indicated that innovative managers with budget responsibilities in large firms could also be considered entrepreneurs. Nowadays, where the major political parties appear to subscribe to a *managerial* rather than an enterprise culture, it may be more appropriate to refer to successful managers in both small and large enterprises as capable, efficient or even enterprising, but not entrepreneurial.

Entrepreneurship – in the sense of individual decision makers introducing successful innovations – may not even be a *necessary* condition for sustained economic development and is highly likely to require different personal qualities for success in different industries. It makes more sense to view individual business success in terms of skills and abilities necessary to achieve certain outcomes rather than in terms of behavioural or personality traits. As mentioned above, it seems clear that notions of what constitutes entrepreneurial behaviour may need to be constantly adapted as economic development progresses. During the closing stages of the Victorian era it was Britain's stranglehold over world shipping and insurance, plus *de facto* protection in imperial markets, which meant that the free trade policies advocated by British capital and pursued by successive British governments produced formidable economic benefits despite a declining industrial base. Foreign traders used British ships and insurance to facilitate their own trade with each other yet often found it difficult to penetrate the large internal trade of the British Empire. Who were the entrepreneurs: the risk-taking traders, who undoubtedly made more than adequate profits, or the secure custodians of world trade who accumulated fortunes?

It was not until after two world wars and the disintegration of the Empire that Britain's economic performance began to mirror its industrial decline. In retrospect, it is now clear that the British economy was displaying all the symptoms of old age. Indeed, many economists and politicians at the time did begin to voice their concerns but there was a considerable lag before Britain's economic weakness penetrated public consciousness. To some extent, the political and economic dominance of the United States in the industrialised world for much of the post-Second World War period obscured the internal causes of Britain's economic decline. Indeed, the United States was held up – and is held up today by some – as a role model of a successful economy. Over the past twenty to thirty years, however, new role models have emerged, with the spectacular resurgence of the Japanese and German economies and the appearance of fast-growth economies in eastern Asia. During this period, global competition has intensified and Britain's economic weaknesses have been ever more cruelly exposed. The first response in Britain, and elsewhere in Europe, was to see successful international competition as a function of size. The European solution was to expand existing European agreements controlling the iron, steel and coal industries into the Common Market. Caught in a post-imperial time-lag and increasingly in its 'special relationship' with the United States, Britain first decided to go it alone and create its own mega-corporations.

The Industrial Reorganisation Corporation, the mergers that formed GEC, British Leyland, British Steel Corporation and a host of nationalised industries were all a result of the 'build it big' strategy. The creation of big national corporations, however, was not the solution to Britain's economic problems either in the short term or in the longer term. The glamour of the post-war US multinational began to wear thin as a role model for burnt-out Britain. Interest in Japan and Germany as successful economies increased from a broad impression of them as general role models to a more particular appreciation of the factors that brought them success. This general change from fairly uncritical, impressionistic thinking to more analytic appraisal took two broad courses – both heavily infused with cultural and psychological concepts.

The first was a historical tendency which looked back to the qualities of the founders of the industrial revolution, the 'golden age' when Britain was at the forefront of technological innovation and seen as the workshop of the world. Ideologically, this era tends to be lauded by proponents of the enterprise culture policies as the heyday of neo-classical ideas and 'proof' that a sturdy *individualism* lies at the heart of entrepreneurial innovation and national vigour. A second, more competitive tendency wanted to identify and analyse the secret strengths of Britain's commercial rivals with the aim of emulating and then surpassing them. Consequently, great effort has been spent in demonstrating that, for one reason or another, the Japanese, Germans and Americans work harder or more efficiently than the British. Others have concentrated on how rivals *manage* their enterprises more efficiently. Better and more appropriate educational and training systems were – and are currently – another favourite. Yet one feature that stood out in the late 1960s was that the more successful economies had larger and better-developed small business sectors than Britain's.

The Committee of Inquiry set up by the Wilson government and chaired by John Bolton (1971) found significant weaknesses, though also a strong resilience and shared values, among Britain's small enterprises during the 1960s, perhaps partly as a result of the prevailing 'big is best' policy. As a benchmark to inform the issues discussed in this book, it is helpful to be reminded of the main small enterprise weaknesses found by John Bolton's committee. A strong desire to retain personal autonomy and independence, plus a linked widespread aversion to training and other forms of systematic management development, was a strong feature of the small enterprise sector. As these features characterise the small enterprise sector today, not only in Britain but also across Europe (Stanworth and Gray, 1991; Storey, 1994; ENSR, 1995), it is worth listing the main management weaknesses identified by Bolton:

1 raising and using finance;
2 costing and control of information;
3 organisation and delegation;
4 marketing;
5 information use and retrieval;
6 personnel management;
7 technological change;
8 production scheduling and purchase control.

Over the past twenty-five years, many of these problems have been extensively researched. For instance, problems with raising and using finance and with obtaining and applying information on costs and control, as much due to external constraints as lack of financial management skills, remain at the top of the list to this day. However, the nature of each problem and the enterprise challenges that each poses clearly change over time and in different regions, in some cases quite considerably. In fact, the information provided by Bolton was of policy interest more to regional development than to enterprise or broader economic development. The detailed and interesting picture of a distinctive small business culture was almost completely overlooked.

In 1979, the arrival of the first Thatcher government heralded a radical change of approach and a much more public role for small businesses. Various strands of thought – the nostalgic backward look to the 'bygone golden age'; the eclipse of the multinational as a model by the pioneering hi-tech firms; the part played by new small businesses in the economic re-generation of the German, Japanese and Italian economies; the impressive dynamism of the Pacific Rim; plus, above all, the changing class consciousness of the upwardly socially mobile – coalesced as a potent political slogan and credo, the *enterprise culture*. The important point to note here is the sudden introduction to public consciousness, despite the existence of fairly widely accepted existing models of economic development, of the *entrepreneur* and an *enterprise spirit* as key positive elements in the establishment of the new enterprise culture. Politically and philosophically, this new approach reflects a fundamental cultural divide in the body politic and represented the reassertion of what might be termed the *neo-classical* or *economic-liberal* ideology of the capitalist classes that had been pushed aside for the best part of fifty years. Essentially, this is opposed to collectivist and cooperative approaches to economic, political and social issues (increasingly termed the *communitarian* approach these days as it struggles to regain ascendancy) and, instead, holds that individual choices and effort are paramount.

A fundamental assumption is that individuals acting in their own self-interests will follow economic logic and that the net result will be economic efficiency and the Benthamite ideal of the 'greatest good for the greatest number'. The term 'neo-classical' was coined to emphasise the lineage of ideas back not just to Jeremy Bentham but further, to the 'father' of economics, Adam Smith, whose famous phrase 'the invisible hand' is often used as a slogan to support the claimed inherent allocative and distributive efficiency and fairness of the free market system. The use of the adjective 'free' is not by chance either. It relates to another fundamental assumption that markets would do their job in allocating resources and distributing goods and services efficiently and fairly if they were unfettered by (usually government) non-market interference. Critics would say that markets cannot be free because they are for those who have, and those who have not are excluded. The social and political aspect of the new approach was probably best summed up in Margaret Thatcher's famous reported dictum: 'There is no such thing as society, only families.'

It is not unfair to say that, during the 1960s and early 1970s, business people and the *business ethic* were perceived negatively among large sections, if not a majority, of the population (Bolton, 1971; Weiner, 1981). Collectivism was generally regarded in a favourable light whereas self-interested individualism – even when it was not naked self-interest or greed – was frowned upon. The new values of the enterprise culture were inviting a reappraisal of social attitudes and individual values across the complete spectrum of society. A second point to note is that the enterprise culture policies coincided – not by chance – with the widespread restructuring of economies throughout the industrialised world. One of the main effects of global competition had been the intensification of two related processes: *vertical disintegration* and *industrial concentration*.

Enterprises often develop in a fairly entrepreneurial way through the organic growth of their business into new territories or new products, or through a process of *vertical integration* – the acquisition of other firms linked to their own main business, either suppliers (backwards integration) or customers/distributors (forwards integration). The opposite process, *vertical disintegration*, refers to the break-up, voluntary or otherwise, of large corporations vertically integrated along the length of their own particular chains of production and distribution (and often into other less obviously related fields). The process of vertical disintegration, which has seen corporations strip back to their most profitable core activities and sub-contract or hire the relevant services previously provided in-house as they are needed, has been one of the main factors behind the formation of new small firms during the 1980s. Services formerly provided internally (such as design, maintenance, personnel, security, transport and so on) became externalised – sometimes to the old units newly independent through management buy-outs or sometimes to existing specialist sub-contractors. Some of the founders of these new 'spin-off' firms were experienced business managers who started sound businesses, and some even behaved in an entrepreneurial manner. Most were not in a position to provide well-sought-after specialist or *core* services and eventually joined a steady stream of other redundant workers, encouraged by enterprise policy self-employment promotion schemes, in a growing *secondary* sector comprising precarious small firms or self-employed providing *peripheral* goods and services. Some found their way to other forms of employment.

The second process, *industrial concentration*, is one of reintegration whereby cash-rich, slimmed-down corporations begin to expand within their core activities by acquiring other smaller successful firms which operate in their own line of business or in a new business area which the predator wants to enter. The aim is to acquire a dominant market share and significant reductions in costs through economies of scale and scope, which usually involves 'rationalising' the new workforce and further increasing the size of the secondary sector of the labour market by making more workers and managers redundant. This process was vividly described by Karl Marx who saw it as part of the cyclical crises of overproduction to which capitalism was prone. Marx's analysis of the workings of capitalism were taken up by the Austrian economist Joseph Schumpeter who turned the point of the analysis on its head, however, and preferred to talk of a process of 'creative destruction' which was both fed by and created new entrepreneurs. As the cyclical process of concentration followed by disintegration represents a failure of the free market mechanism, reactions to its effects also reflect the fundamental political divide between the neo-classical and the collectivist approaches. Ironically, both views can be traced back to Adam Smith.

Both these global tendencies, vertical integration and industrial concentration, require a reasonably compliant workforce – either crushed and dispirited or bought off through a share of the benefits of successful global competition – and both hold considerable implications for small business development and entrepreneurial opportunity. Although there were many domestic political reasons for the fall of the Callaghan government, there was no doubt that the new Thatcher government was elected not so much on a platform but more on a springboard of radical reforms in industrial relations (to deal with issues raised by the 1978–9 'winter of discontent'). Supporters of enterprise culture policies would view many of these reforms as the removal of unnecessary constraints on the labour markets. Their opponents see this as a reassertion of the unequal power relations that exist in the unfettered free markets of primitive capitalism. Once again, there is a fundamental split between an individualist, economistic approach and a broader, more social, collectivist view of political responsibility. This is by no means a British phenomenon. Poujade in France and the Christian Democrats in Italy also tried, with some initial success, to appeal to the cultural values of small enterprise managers and mobilise them as a political force in support of individualist policies.

The strategic interests of larger enterprises, however, demand much more cooperative business behaviour from local small and medium enterprises, if vertical integration and industrial cooperation are to work to their competitive favour in the global arena. This is the approach supported by the European Union and by most national employers' associations. Faced with this contradiction, the populist small enterprise movements ran out of political steam. Indeed, the Thatcher government's attempt to impose the poll tax, the ultimately individualistic property tax, as a supposedly 'business-friendly' tax, led to a revolt among large numbers of small enterprise (and other) people and is widely regarded as the cause of Margaret Thatcher's downfall. In Italy, successful small enterprise owners and managers in Europe's small enterprise heartland of Emilia-Romagna were often supporters of the Communist Party rather than of the Christian Democrats. The cultural forces at work are clearly much more complex than the simple economic processes or political divides would suggest.

A third important factor that is greatly influencing the shape of global competition and worldwide economic restructuring is the growing applications of information and communication technologies. Although this raises important questions about future patterns of employment, new small businesses, entrepreneurs and entrepreneurial competition, it is not so politically contentious as the two processes of large enterprise development just discussed. The invention, development and, above all, the application of new technologies open many doors of capitalist opportunity to quick but educated entrepreneurs, offering well above average rates of profit to successful firms. Economists as diverse as Karl Marx, Alfred Marshall, John Maynard Keynes and Milton Friedman all agree that successful business growth depends on the use of capital, and that capital is irresistibly drawn to the highest rates of profit which are often linked to applications of new technologies. It may well be that the entrepreneurs of the future will be those founding new enterprises in the core, technologically advanced spheres of the economy while non-entrepreneurial small firms and the self-employed become central elements of the secondary sector. Previously undreamt-of new products and services are entering the market in increasing quantities. This represents a huge opportunity for certain technologically oriented small enterprises and certain enterprising business people but, ulti-mately, the large corporations which have pared themselves to the bone in anticipation of entering the new age will move in when they feel the time is ripe.

The economic, political and social forces mentioned in this chapter form the backdrop to enterprise culture policies and also set the bounds within which those policies could operate. As also suggested, the concerns over management issues which also surfaced in the mid-1980s now look as if they have superseded the enterprise culture model as the framework for eco-nomic development. The space for successful small and, especially, medium-sized enterprises may well begin to contract rapidly. Indeed, the tempo of takeover activities by larger firms of certain types of small and medium-sized enterprises (SMEs) has been increasing across Europe as the integra-tion of the Single Market intensifies. Still more to the point, there are even stronger signs that the 1980s tide of enterprise culture is on the ebb as the economic structure of global competition becomes more evident.

The British economy has seldom experienced a more turbulent period than that of the 1980s. Once renowned as the workshop of the world, Britain has seen more than 2 million jobs shed from the manufacturing workforce over the past fifteen years and unemployment hitting peaks estimated at 5 million during the early 1980s. Even continuously 'adjusted' official un-employment statistics (due to a series of bureaucratic reclassifications whole segments of people without jobs were removed from the official tally but 3.5 million people were still registered unemployed during the mid-1980s) make it clear that the British economy has not experienced such dis-location since the 1930s. At the same time, self-employment grew to record levels, as it also had in the 1930s. Critics naturally pointed to the hastily adopted monetarist policies of Margaret Thatcher's Conservative govern-ment as the chief cause. However, the government's supporters were able to hold up the sorry record of successive post-war governments in failing to halt Britain's century-long economic decline. They could claim that the sharp crisis was really due to a number of rather nasty economic chickens from earlier periods coming home to roost.

Whatever the truth, the strict macro-economic policies of monetarism soon gave way to more psychologically inspired policies including massive increases in financial motivators to the business sector and a high-profile publicity campaign to improve public attitudes towards business. Unemploy-ment declined during the late 1980s only to resume its upward spiral in 1990 as high interest rates slowed the economy without having an immediate impact on already high inflation. Although since then, interest rates and inflation have tumbled and the policy shift under the Major government was towards a more managerial approach (most evident in the prominence now given to human resource management, skills training and initiatives such as Investors in People and the management quality standard, ISO 9000), it is the enterprise culture years of the 1980s to the early 1990s that is the focus of this book. Throughout all the different swings of this ten-year economic cycle, the main government policy objective has been to free market constraints and encourage an *enterprise culture* – initially as a general pro-business policy but eventually as an affirmative policy encouraging the formation of new small businesses. However, another prominent thread that has persisted through public policy has been the creation of successful innovative firms. In this sense, the term 'enterprise' takes on an even more significant meaning and the clear focus of policy is targeted even more tightly on the role of a fairly mysterious figure, the *entrepreneur*.

There are many different definitions of the entrepreneur. Elizabeth Chell and her colleagues (1991) cite Hebert and Link's (1988) list of a dozen theoretical 'themes' that provide different definitions, and there are many others. However, it is the maverick Austrian economist Joseph Schumpeter's (1934) theories of economic development which provide our definition of the entrepreneur and much of the theoretical basis for this book. Schumpeter's definition of an entrepreneur as a person who initiates some form of change in order to gain an advantage over the competition provides the most widely accepted, empirically useful and theoretically grounded technical specification (Brockhaus, 1982; Kirzner, 1973, 1982; Silver, 1984). This definition highlights the creativity, novelty and high activity that characterise entrepreneurs in contrast to employees, the unemployed and most other small and large business managers. The entrepreneur (as the source of the changes leading to economic growth and progress) is placed at the centre of economic development in such a way as to provide useful criteria for analysing the impact of enterprise culture policies. Schumpeter, however, made it very clear that entrepreneurs are fundamentally successful capitalists and, by implication, it follows that the theoretical and political objective of enterprise culture policies is the reinvigoration of British capitalism.

Therefore, entrepreneurial behaviour can be researched and measured as that appropriate for the founding and management of successful, competitive and growing small enterprises. This means that entrepreneurial behaviour must be regarded as directed and intentional. Profits, innovation and effective organisation can be treated as features of entrepreneurial businesses. Essentially, Schumpeter (1942) accepted Marx's analysis of capitalism but adopted the viewpoint of the capitalist rather than the proletariat. Agreeing with Marx that profits are the measure of capitalist success, Schumpeter was more sociological in holding that entrepreneurs were motivated to improve their social standing by using business success to enter or maintain their position in the dominant capitalist class. Consequently,

Schumpeter recognised that skills in managing social relations are the key to business success and that entrepreneurs can have legitimate personal aims other than profit maximisation. However, this was not the line taken when enterprise culture policies were introduced in the mid-1980s.

The policies rested explicitly on traditional economic views of the world, often called the neo-classical approach. The underlying assumption is that problems occur in the economy because factor markets are obstructed in some way from operating freely. However, as we shall see, the whole notion of there being a need to remove barriers to entry for entrepreneurial firms seems questionable. Rather, it is the non-entrepreneurial firms that generally need help in overcoming barriers to entry. Despite this seemingly obvious point, it is interesting to see how the Department of Employment (1986) White Paper, a seminal enterprise culture policy document, is dedicated to the aim of implementing the neo-classical view, as the following quotation clearly shows

> Regulations and licences tend to build up a cosy industry insulated from outside competition. The difficulty and costs of entry for new firms may be high and the stimulus of competition may be lacking. Indeed that explains why some firms take a relaxed attitude to regulations: they may even benefit from an entrenched position. But new growth is stifled and the consumer suffers. So lack of concern within an uncompetitive industry is no sign that all is well. State control breeds corpulent firms.
> (Department of Employment, 1986: 2, Section 1.10)

It is clearly no exaggeration to assert that neo-classical assumptions lie at the theoretical heart of enterprise culture policies. Consequently, the comment above about the lack of any obvious need to protect entrepreneurs from barriers to entry becomes highly significant. The policy target of the enterprise culture model is to encourage the development of more entrepreneurial firms and a more entrepreneurial approach within existing firms. Yet, if enterprise culture policies have the net effect of encouraging the growth of non-entrepreneurial firms, the model may be deeply flawed both theoretically and empirically. The expectations and goals of the ordinary people who run Britain's small enterprises appear to have been left out of picture. On the face of it, there was a potentially dangerous assumption that only new small firms are entrepreneurial. Furthermore, as we have just seen, there was also a strong strand in the enterprise culture brigade that saw the small firm's role as that of helping large enterprises to become more efficient and flexible. The working habits and cultures of existing small enterprises appear to have been pushed to one side by the early enterprise policy makers. As the following chapters will show, psychological theory offers better prospects for understanding the cultural and economic behavioural implications of small enterprise development and the motivational issues of entrepreneurial success.

2 The 'enterprise culture' model of development

Spearheaded by a series of fundamental changes to fiscal policy and industrial relations legislation, the development of an enterprise culture has been specifically linked to the birth of new small firms and the enlargement of the private sector. Despite consistently strong evidence that the German, Japanese and Southeast Asian economic 'miracles' spring from cooperative working practices (if not always from collectivist social policies), enterprise culture policies in Britain have also been characterised by attempts to foster *individualism* as the dominant ideology. Apart from a fairly wide-ranging privatisation programme and the extension of the notion of the market into such areas as health and education, government policies have aimed at reducing so-called *supply-side* constraints in factor markets, promoting private competition in areas previously in the public sector and encouraging the unemployed and newly redundant to start their own businesses.

RATIONALE OF THE ENTERPRISE CULTURE MODEL

According to the *enterprise culture* model, the public sector is inherently inefficient, and private firms, spurred on by competition and the fear of failure, are not only more efficient in themselves but also boost overall economic development by enriching the range of products and services available. A stage model of development, whereby successful small firms grow into the large corporations of the future, is implicitly (and often explicitly – 'from acorns to oaks!') fundamental to the economic rationale of enterprise culture policies. Economic progress is said to depend on sharp, efficient and dynamic small firms providing a constant flow of new ideas and products, thus supplanting older, moribund firms. However, previous policies are held to have placed an increasing number of barriers in the way of budding 'entrepreneurs', preventing them from attaining satisfactory profits, the search for which is fervently believed to be the driving force of their innovative endeavours and a just reward for their efforts and the risks they take. Indeed, according to the proponents of the enterprise culture development model, earlier public policies had substituted government intervention and support for individual effort, and thereby actually dampened the latent entrepreneurial drive which is an integral part of 'human nature'. The emphasis on *individualism* is fundamental. According to the logic of the enterprise culture model, this means that overly dependent attitudes (on the state or collective action) must be confronted, the profit motive actively encouraged and structural barriers to starting up profitable small firms removed. The psychological implications of these policies rests on the underlying enterprise culture assumption that a latent entrepreneurial spirit is 'part of human nature' and that the profit motive is sufficient to ignite this spirit.

However, neo-classical economics are more concerned about the market behaviour of firms (as abstract entities) than about their owners. The size of the firm holds no particular importance except where the comparative efficiency of small business usage of the factors of production or questions of economies of scale in relation to larger firms are of interest. Yet, even though the different motivation or even business efficiency of the owners of firms receives little attention, the neo-classical approach, in outlining models of optimal behaviour in certain situations (for example, under monopoly, oligopoly and other forms of imperfect competition) or in establishing a theory of the ideal firm, can offer a series of additional criteria for assessing business behaviour.

For instance, if the firm's production is understood to be the way it combines inputs to produce its output of goods and services, its production performance can be assessed against the managers' stated expectations. Economists often talk in terms of production (or business) plans instead of expectations even though such plans are a rarity in most small businesses (perhaps less so in entrepreneurial businesses). Indeed, this is how accountants, bankers and investors usually do monitor a firm's performance. There is little evidence that many small firms either produce or, even less likely, use formal plans to guide their operations. Where they are used, the firms tend to be larger and more professionally managed. However, it is interesting that growth does seem to be connected with the adoption of a more planned approach by enterprise managers.

As already mentioned, the rationale for placing the small firm at the centre of the new 'enterprise policy' can be traced back to the late 1960s, when it was realised that Britain had the smallest proportion of small firms among the leading industrialised economies. The subsequent official inquiry into the state of the small enterprise sector in Britain, chaired by John Bolton (1971), confirmed both the weaknesses (see the list on p. 10) and the relative importance of the sector to the British economy. Bolton's findings were influential in justifying some aspects of 'enterprise policy' during the early 1980s. For instance, Graham Bannock (1981), the research director of the Bolton Report, reported that the

> principal economic importance of small firms lies in their responsiveness to change and since change is what is required if economic growth is to be

resumed, it is desirable that more rather than fewer resources should be channelled into small businesses.

Despite two deep recessions directly connected with recent 'enterprise' policies and little convincing evidence supporting the underlying assumptions of the enterprise culture, the basic policy still has plenty of supporters. For instance, the very first paragraph of the executive summary of a recent report on the 'enterprise challenge' by the Advisory Council on Science and Technology (ACOST, 1990) sets the scene by stating:

> The growth of smaller firms is a vital element in the wealth creation process. Experimentation and growth are central mechanisms in a competitive enterprise economy, and it is for the government to ensure that small firms operate effectively and vigorously.

Ignoring the rather paradoxical view of the scientists that government should play a central role despite repeatedly asserted government views to the contrary, the Cabinet Department welcomed the ACOST view of economic development by agreeing that SMEs

> have a crucial role to play in bringing about a dynamic and competitive economy. They have a significant role in innovation, and are a major source of new competition and new employment opportunities . . . the minority which do grow rapidly have a particularly important role to play; among other things they have the potential to become the new large firms of tomorrow.

These two statements neatly encapsulate the basic hopes and assumptions that underpin policies aimed at creating an enterprise culture. Enterprise culture policies have included a wide-ranging privatisation programme, measures to encourage various people – especially the unemployed – to start their own businesses, fiscal measures including tax cuts for the 'wealth creators', and an advertising and publicity campaign partly aimed at drawing attention to various policy measures but, much more importantly, also aimed at transforming social perceptions and attitudes towards the world of business and self-employment. Consequently, it is entirely legitimate to view enterprise culture policies as an attempt at social engineering.

Large enterprises have long recognised the motivation of both workforce and management as key factors in corporate success. Attempting to apply these lessons from the private sector to the task of reversing Britain's long-term economic decline, policy makers have spent more than a decade attempting to create the so-called 'culture of enterprise' in Britain. Apart from a tendency to seek a 'market solution' to most social problems and a number of profound changes to industrial relations law, the spearhead of this policy has been the promotion of self-employment and new small businesses. Its main thrust, however, has been an attempt to motivate change through 'top-down' exhortations from leading politicians, opening certain doors of opportunity and blocking others. Perhaps the most succinct official government summary of enterprise culture policy objectives can be found in *Building Businesses . . . not Barriers* (Department of Employment, 1986), the important deregulation policy White Paper presented to Parliament by the Secretary of State for Employment in May 1986. On the inside of the front cover, the prime aim of the Department of Employment was stated to be: '. . . to encourage the development of an enterprise economy. The way to reduce unemployment is through more businesses, more self-employment and greater wealth creation, all leading to more jobs.'

The main policies for achieving these aims were listed under four key areas:

1 promote enterprise and job creation in . . . small firms, self-employment and tourism;
2 help businesses grow and jobs multiply by cutting 'red tape';
3 improve training arrangements;
4 help the young and those out of work for some time to find work, training or opportunities.

The case for deregulation, a fundamental enterprise culture policy, was supported on the following grounds:

> Removing unnecessary burdens is particularly important for people starting new firms and taking on their first employees. They are faced by a formidable array of regulations on direct and indirect taxation, social security, health and safety, planning, consumer protection and trading standards. . . . New business start-ups are the essential source of jobs in the future.

Two of the assumptions of enterprise policy in particular – first, that self-employed small business managers are entrepreneurs and, second, that the absolute growth in the number of these small firms will boost national economic performance – are contentious and, as we shall see, the balance of evidence is against them. There is also a third implicit assumption in the application of the policies, which also appears to be without firm foundation: that exposure to basic management training will remove personal skills weaknesses and, as a consequence, lead to the formation of more entrepreneurial small firms. Yet even if theoretical and empirical support for the enterprise culture approach is found wanting, it is worth noting that the practical, theoretical and motivational issues of small enterprise development raised by the model are extremely important. With the collapse of eastern Europe's command economies and as many as one-third of western Europe's 18 million or so firms in 1991 expected to have disappeared by the end of the century as a result of the Single Market, governments have been increasingly keen to develop innovative products, create demand and avoid a return to mass unemployment through the growth of dynamic small firms. In France and Italy, which have strong small firm populations and traditions, governments of all political persuasions have supported policies of direct intervention to assist small family and artisanal firms, and conservative Germany adopts similar policies in an effort to stem unemployment among the large immigrant and east German populations. The emphasis, however, is less on the individual and more on social groups (family firms, ethnic or cultural sectors, depressed regions and so on) and on encouraging efforts through organisations such as chambers of artisanal firms. In Britain, the Labour government has adopted 'social enterprise' policies linked to regional development like those prevalent in continental Europe, a position similar to that held by many Liberal Democrats.

There is now a consensus on small enterprise development as a policy target across Europe and within the European Commission. What distinguishes the enterprise culture approach is its strong rejection of public intervention in direct support of firms (usually on the grounds of avoiding market distortions) and the dominance of *individualism* in its underlying ideology, with emphasis on the primacy of individual effort and success. Although the focus of this book is on the processes that are likely to lead to entrepreneurial behaviour, the ultimate validity of the enterprise culture development model is clearly an important issue. If the enterprise culture model is based on false assumptions, resulting policies and strategies are also likely to be misconceived and to provide a poor test of whether entrepreneurial behaviour can be encouraged and sustained through public policy. The enterprise culture model is also extremely interesting theoretically because it is essentially a *psychological* model of economic development that views attitudinal change as the key to economic progress and economic liberalisation as the key to the desired attitudinal change.

The psychology of the enterprise culture model, however, appears to rest on the rather dubious assumption that there are significant numbers of people with entrepreneurial personalities or qualities who are held back from founding successful enterprises by barriers that prevent the proper functioning of free markets. It is more reasonable to assume (an assumption strongly supported by the evidence presented in this book) that most existing small business owners and potential new entrepreneurial small business founders are unlikely to exhibit or develop a growth-oriented approach to business unless it meets their own personal and social development goals. In many ways, the quest for a universal 'entrepreneurial personality' leads us into a cul-de-sac (which we will discuss in more detail later). To ascribe career choice and subsequent performance to a set of defining personality traits weakens intentionality and the likelihood of there being any significant training effects. This line of inquiry is almost impossible to operationalise in research terms because it reduces to a rather meaningless search for the 'correct' bundle of traits or regular behavioural features. These are generally only identified after the defined entrepreneurial behaviour and give few clues to the prior conditions. The search for the entrepreneurial personality also can distract attention from an analysis of the processes that lead to the founding of entrepreneurial businesses. Just as the career choice to enter one of the professions can appeal to many different personalities, regardless of whether there is a 'medical personality' or a 'lawyer's personality', so the factors leading to the career choice to set up a successful small business are sidelined if the process is said to depend mainly on the personality of the founder even if certain behavioural features can be seen as beneficial to success in a particular field.

There are such manifestly different management needs for different businesses in different industries, regions and sizes that it is difficult to accept the notion of one, identifiable entrepreneurial personality. Whether or not an 'entrepreneurial personality' exists, however, one central assumption of the enterprise culture model will be examined critically later in the book. This is that political-economic constraints of the 'dependency culture' prevent people with the right aptitudes (by inference, those with 'entrepreneurial personalities' and appropriate skills) from maximising their economic gains by forming their own enterprises. However, as we shall discover, people 'dependent' on unemployment and other benefits do not generally start growth-oriented enterprises. It appears that the best 'customers' for enterprise training courses are probably people already gainfully employed but keen to escape organisational constraints and take responsibility for their own business decisions. At this point, we can look at another central enterprise culture policy assumption: that one good reason for encouraging lots of people to start up their own businesses, even if they are one-person shows, is that entrepreneurial small firms will provide the new larger enterprises of the future. This is the 'oaks from little acorns' argument that sees small enterprises moving through several stages of development as they are transformed into professionally managed corporations that provide innovative products and services, and more jobs.

STAGES OF ENTERPRISE DEVELOPMENT

It is strongly implicit in enterprise culture policies – best symbolised by Lord Young's 'changing' the name of the Department of Trade and Industry to the Department of Enterprise (while his successor Michael Heseltine preferred to be called the President of the Board of Trade) – that enterprise development is more than just business development and is specifically about the promotion of new, innovative, 'leading-edge' businesses. However, the original enterprise culture policies were clearly aimed at encouraging the creation of new enterprises, particularly among the large numbers of unemployed thrown onto the labour market by economic restructuring. As we shall see, these are not the best candidates for the role of starting innovative, sustainable enterprises and, indeed, most of those who were attracted to start their own business remained as self-employed sole-traders. A body of critical comment and research grew which questioned the new start-up 'acorns to oaks' thesis as extremely economically wasteful and inappropriate (Storey, 1994). It was strongly argued by many critics that a sort of 'saplings to oak trees' policy would be more effective, with the focus on existing small enterprises. To be effective, enterprise development should address: (1) real structural barriers to small enterprise development; (2) management weaknesses that inhibit most small business growth; (3) the motivational and skills mix that most encourages innovation and proactivity.

This section examines the focus of enterprise culture policies in relation to the development of already existing small businesses. These became a policy target only when the non-entrepreneurial nature of the self-employed and of most new start-ups became inescapably apparent to policy makers in the late 1980s. A closer examination of the stage models of business development that underlie enterprise culture policies will be used to demonstrate that these three development objectives have not been addressed effectively. Indeed, there are sound practical, psychological and cultural reasons why few existing small firms are likely to satisfy enterprise culture expectations. Thus, a fundamental problem for policy makers is that their stage model of small business development is deeply flawed because very few firms appear to take growth and the accumulation of capital seriously. Indeed, most self-employed do not even take the first step and employ another person. Even among well-established small enterprises which do have the experience and resources to contemplate further growth, actual expansion and even the desire to expand appear to be driven by external structural factors in the economy, especially the business cycle, rather than a compelling need to grow. Before considering some of the more interesting and relevant stages of growth models, it is interesting to see (in Table 2.1) the differences in attitudes towards growth among the respondents to two SBRT quarterly surveys, the first during the depths of recession in 1991 and the second during 1996 when some small enterprises were experiencing growth and many felt the economy had turned.

Many of the growth-averse firms in both periods indicated that they had already reached their preferred size and had no need or desire to increase capacity, whereas many of the growth-oriented firms expected only marginal

Table 2.1 Small enterprise attitudes to growth, 1991 and 1996 (percentages)

	1991	*1996*
Growth-oriented	37	33
Growth-averse	38	37
Exit/retire/sell	25	30
(Sample total	1,718	753)

Source: NatWest/SBRT, *Quarterly Survey of Small Business in Britain*, 7(3), 12(4).

increases in staff. Also, many of those who had set certain growth targets in 1991, especially those in catering and services, had done so with the intention of selling their enterprise as a going concern. Over the five-year period, many of those who had wanted to sell their businesses and retire had done so. By 1996, others were in a position to change their objectives to fit their own life-cycle. For many small enterprise owners, their firm and assets are also expected to provide their pension. Very few small or medium-sized enterprise owners seem to have the intention of developing into very large enterprises (including entrepreneurial types like Roger McKechnie mentioned in the Introduction). The most interesting feature of these findings, however, is that the proportion who remain averse to the notion of growth has remained stable through the different phases of the economic cycle. On the face of it, the stages-of-growth aspect of enterprise culture policies does not seem appropriate to the small enterprise sector as a whole.

Nevertheless, a small minority of small enterprise owners clearly are motivated to go on to greater things. It also seems that some enterprises take off unexpectedly. Although there are indications, as we shall see, that growth-oriented firms differ significantly from the majority of small enterprises, it is important to understand the stages of growth that enterprises go through and the challenges that each stage poses to the owners and managers of the enterprise. Some of the earlier models were influenced by the stages-of-development model championed by the US economist Walter Rostow (1962). These tended to be very mechanistic and ignored many management and organisation issues. For instance, a manager-oriented five-stage model, which used a series of crisis points to chart the firm's progress from *small youth* to *large maturity*, was developed by Greiner (1972), who identified managerial problems with each stage:

1 creativity provides the impetus to growth and leads to a crisis of leadership;
2 growth is through direction, which leads to a crisis of autonomy;
3 growth is through delegation, leading to a crisis of control;
4 growth is through coordination, provoking a crisis of red tape;
5 growth is through collaboration.

Greiner's model seems open-ended and ill-defined in its later stages but it provides a series of choice points and introduces the idea that growth or non-growth involves the owner's volition and intentional participation. Furthermore, the stages do represent well-recognised problem areas for enterprise development but it is important to note that, apart from the first stage, all subsequent stages involve collective action and explicitly reject the individualism that is so central to enterprise culture ideology. It is also worth noting, however, that many small firm owners and self-employed share this individualism as part of their own self-concepts and, as we shall see, even growth-oriented owners tend to be directive in their management styles and suspicious of delegating responsibility, albeit less so than growth-averse owners. Developing this idea that the owner's attitudes and decisions have to be balanced against the social imperatives of team work, Neil Churchill and Virginia Lewis (1983) described a five-stage model (with a sixth *bale-out* stage for reluctant growers) linking management style, organisational structure and the firm's strategy to successive stages:

1 existence – directly managed by the owner personally, simple organic structure;
2 survival – more complex structure with some delegated tasks, supervised by the owners;
3 success – functional management has appeared and the owner is concerned about maintaining profitability but also concerned about whether future growth is a personal aim;
4 take-off – having decided on growth the firm acquires a more divisional management structure (with or without the original owner);
5 resource maturity – internal systems and complexity reveal a firm that is concerned about obtaining the maximum return on its investments.

The Churchill and Lewis model is more flexible and recognises the dilemma facing many successful small firm owners when they are forced to choose between their personal preference for individual control and their firm's development needs for more strategic goals. However, this model essentially retains a big-business approach and, as the findings of the surveys mentioned in relation to Table 2.1 indicate, the effects of individualism and non-economic motivation so strongly present among the smaller enterprises are reflected in aversion to growth and may inhibit the desire to pass through many of these stages. Many small enterprises opt for a non-growth approach and intentionally decline to move to the next development stage. A simple four-stage development model for the transition from an entrepreneurial firm to a more professionally managed enterprise was developed by Eric Flamholtz (1986):

1 new venture;
2 expansion;
3 professionally managed business;
4 consolidation.

Flamholtz explains clearly what is involved in each stage and suggests that the firm's transition from stage (2) to stage (3) could well involve a change in owners. For enterprises whose owners have no wish to grow or increase the size of their staff, yet who get caught in a growth trajectory because of a buoyant business cycle or lucky choice of product, there is clearly a need for a different type of model. Specific decision points were used by Sue Bates and Peter Wilson (1989) to develop a *choice-point* as a useful tool in delivering enterprise training to growing small enterprises of this type.

Their four-point model is more focused on the earlier stages and is very owner-oriented:

1 awareness of the need for strategy – without conscious recognition of the need for an explicit strategy there will be little systematic, formal management development;
2 a willingness to loosen control – growth will be more likely if the owner delegates other management functions;
3 recognising the limits to the owner's competencies – a management team is more likely to be developed if the owner recognises his or her own limits;
4 recognising the value of external agents – an effective management team is unlikely to be constructed until the owner accepts that external intervention can be beneficial.

Both these models describe the main management and organisational problems associated with growth of new or small enterprises. They also identify areas where public policy or training initiatives could be useful in the general development of enterprises that either want to grow or want to improve their business or management effectiveness. Development models share a common understanding that business development involves a shift away from the owner's personal objectives (as a producer) towards objectives and organisational forms more socially determined by the need to compete effectively in their chosen markets (customer-driven). For small business owners who feel their independence or self-esteem is threatened by this process, there are basically two options: either to sell their business to more professional or entrepreneurial managers or – generally the preferred option – to freeze the development of their business at a stage where personal control is maintained. As the responses from small enterprise owners in Table 2.1 show, both options are quite common. Indeed, Schumpeter predicted that the majority of enterprises cease any pretence at entrepreneurial growth once they feel secure, which can occur at fairly modest levels of earnings.

Given the increased complexity involved in managing increased transactions costs and monitoring performance as levels of hierarchy develop, it is not surprising that even the small firm owners who do perceive that they have adequate ability are nevertheless reluctant to move on to succeeding stages. It appears that, in fact, very few new enterprises ever grow to a stage where they employ more than twenty employees (Gallagher, 1991; Storey and Strange, 1992). Therefore, a major problem for enterprise culture policies is that very few enterprises appear to conform to the stages-of-growth model. Even more worrying for the policy makers intent on changing popular attitudes and business behaviour is the indication that training appears to have had little effect in increasing the number of enterprises successfully moving through each stage of growth.

ENTERPRISE TRAINING

To encourage the growth of entrepreneurs in Britain, enterprise culture policies have basically relied on mass training programmes as their preferred instrument of intervention. In fact, the development of enterprise training as a policy instrument dates back to 1977, under a Labour government, with a pilot of the New Enterprise Programme involving thirty-two unemployed managers. The aim of helping them to become self-employed and start sustainable enterprises that employed other people was at that time an innovative departure from other vocational training schemes which aimed to provide skills to enhance the employment prospects of the unemployed. The numbers of enterprise trainees continued to rise but it was not until the second Thatcher government ushered in the enterprise culture era that numbers shot up dramatically, jumping from 7,870 in 1984/5 to 26,294 in the following year and just under 60,000 a year later.

Allowing for slight variations in teaching methodologies and target populations, enterprise training courses share the common training objectives of inculcating sufficient management skills to enable trainees to start or develop their own businesses. Occasional remarks from various Small Firms Ministers also implied a rather strong psychological dimension, in that proponents of enterprise culture policies also felt that exposure to business ideas on these enterprise training and awareness courses would lead to a shift in public perceptions of business as an occupation. Initially, the publicly stated aim of enterprise training was to encourage a net increase in the formation of new firms, though it became clear to many observers that the underlying policy target was a net reduction in the massive unemployment spawned by the collapse of large manufacturing industries during 1979–81 when the first Thatcher government came to power (Johnson, 1991). During the mid-1980s the emphasis was almost exclusively on start-up enterprise training, until it was recognised that existing small firms had more potential to generate extra jobs (Johnson, 1989). From the late 1980s until the early 1990s, when the Training and Enterprise Councils (TECs) and Local Enterprise Companies in Scotland (LECs) took over local responsibility for enterprise training, a number of national training programmes were designed for existing small firms and other specific groups.

Without each of the many enterprise training programmes being described in detail, generally they fall into two broad categories: basic management skills training for start-ups (people about to become self-employed, about to start their own business, and who have recently done so) and management improvement for existing firms (Gray and Stanworth, 1985; Blythe *et al.*, 1989). As already mentioned, the Manpower Services Commission (MSC, now DfEE) introduced a range of enterprise training programmes in the 1970s and many more in the mid-1980s. Initially, the main programme was the New Enterprise Programme (NEP), a four-month instruction plus practical experience course designed for specially selected new start-ups with real growth and employment potential. Responding to criticism that existing firms would benefit more from management skills training than inexperienced start-ups, but could not afford the time for a full-time course, the MSC introduced Firmstart as a part-time NEP in 1985. Local training providers were contracted to run Firmstart programmes for existing small firms with problems and for firms just about to start trading. In 1986, a specially enhanced version of the NEP – the Graduate Enterprise Programme (GEP) – was introduced to encourage graduates to consider a career in self-employment. Many trainees who completed the course did not start their proposed business and many of those who did later used the experience to seek work as employees, a return to the vocational training aims of the mid-1970s.

In many ways, this approach reflects the emphasis increasingly adopted by management development thinking which, in turn, reflected the influence of human resource development ideas (Guest, 1987). The high expectations of training as an intervening variable in economic development, effective management and behavioural change were evident in the influential management development reports published in the mid-1980s (Mangham and Silver, 1986; Constable and McCormick, 1987). These reports led directly to the management competencies approach adopted by management development training programmes and by various enterprise training initiatives (though many of them came after the enterprise culture period). The ideological and intellectual justification for pursuing a training-led model of small enterprise and entrepreneurial development can be traced further back to the neo-classical economic model of the labour market. Reducing human behaviour to the pursuit of economic goals, labour market theory holds that labour supply and demand are determined by wage levels. Qualifications and actual levels of experience and skills (and the time taken to acquire these) strongly influence the patterns of supply and demand and the levels of actual and expected wages. Leaving aside the fact that employment costs are always higher than employees' earnings, the effects of differential entry qualifications for different jobs, imperfect information about job offers and conditions, and very strong barriers to labour mobility beyond certain geographic limits meant that the neo-classic model had to be adapted.

Gary Becker's (1964) *human capital theory* represents a more convincing attempt to explain the effects of education, training and experience on levels of earnings within the neo-classical approach that underlies enterprise culture policies. Becker holds that there are many separate labour markets, and that entry to those where a higher wage equilibrium prevails is a function of education (broadly defined to include appropriate training but often legitimised as formal qualifications) and experience. Thus, the prospect of higher earnings means it is economically rational for individuals to invest in appropriate training or in acquiring particular qualifications. However, small enterprise owners (except in the professions and other fields where qualifications are a legal requirement) relate their earnings and expectations of future earnings to structural shifts in the economy rather than to their own skills or formal qualifications. This suggests that most small firm owners, especially if they are mainly motivated to achieve non-economic goals such as independence or the attainment of a certain lifestyle, would need to be strongly convinced that training will lead to a quite appreciable increase in earnings before they would be prepared to invest their precious time in acquiring new management skills. If they are already earning close to their target levels, they are likely to conclude, probably correctly, that any increases in earnings are likely to be marginal. Indeed, many entrepreneurs may have calculated that the opportunity costs of attending training (the costs of lost working time) may already be too high to justify investment in that area. In other words, there are sound a-priori theoretical grounds to be sceptical about the attractions of enterprise training to potential or budding entrepreneurs. Nevertheless, despite fairly strong evidence that the expected economic outcomes of human capital theory (increased earnings coming from additional investment in training and education) do not hold in the secondary sector (King, 1990), a series of awareness and training programmes continue to be designed with the aim of helping people found new small businesses and of providing the newly self-employed, and weak existing small businesses, with basic business skills.

3   The state of small enterprises in Britain

The purpose of this chapter is to describe the self-employed and small enterprise sectors as recorded through publicly available sources of data, then to examine various industry, regional and size-of-firm effects in the recent growth of the small enterprises in Britain. As the patterns of recent small enterprise development emerge, it should become clear that concepts such as enterprise, small business and entrepreneurship are very general labels for a wide variety of individual and particular cases. Enterprises must take on different forms, and their owners and managers may be expected to display an equally wide range of personal abilities and temperaments, according to the different environments in which they operate. As with most sectors of the economy, there are common trends and many of the requirements of effective and sound management apply across most sectors and in firms of all sizes. However, small enterprises are not merely large enterprises cut down to size. Economically, they usually face much tighter constraints on their time and resources; more interestingly, they generally reflect the characters and expectations of their owners and managers much more directly than large organisations.

Because they are often much more exposed and volatile than larger enterprises (they tend to go in and out of business more frequently and find it easier to change the structure or nature of their business fairly quickly), accurate and up-to-date statistics on the whole small enterprise sector are hard to find. The most accurate official statistics on patterns of growth in the small firm sector are derived from registrations and deregistrations on Value Added Tax (VAT) registers operated by the Department of Customs and Excise and from annual Labour Force Surveys conducted by the Department for Education and Employment (DfEE). Other useful public sources of information are the General Household Survey and the British Social Attitudes Survey, both of which can be accessed via Essex University. Generally, these two large-scale surveys require further analysis in order to focus on the self-employed and small enterprises because these are peripheral to their main areas of interest. Additional national detailed data have been provided by the regular surveys conducted by the independent, non-profit Small Business Research Trust. Some of the SBRT data mentioned in this book come from its regular quarterly surveys conducted since 1984 and some from specific studies commissioned by the SME Research Group of the Open University Business School (OUBS). The Economic and Social Research Council's (ESRC) SME initiative and relevant national surveys conducted by small enterprise departments in universities and other institutions also provide useful information on the complexities, dynamics and patterns of development of small enterprises during the enterprise culture period (and beyond, where data exist, in order to examine any medium-term effects).

GROWTH OF THE SMALL ENTERPRISE SECTOR

There is no doubt that the growth of self-employment and of small enterprises in Britain was quite dramatic during the 1980s. In its 1996 annual report on small business, the Department of Trade and Industry (DTI) noted that the number of people in self-employment, excluding the agricultural sector (which tends to employ more people in mainland Europe than in Britain), had grown between 1979 and 1993 by 80 per cent in Britain compared with an average of 29 per cent in the whole European Union (EU). And the small enterprise sector looks set to be the focus of public policy for some time to come not only in Britain but throughout Europe. The sheer size of the sector makes it impossible to ignore. Of around 15 million firms in the EU (excluding farms) in 1993, 93 per cent had fewer than ten employees. These micro-firms, as they are termed in the EU, account for 32 per cent of EU employment, but slightly less (24 per cent) of total EU sales turnover (ENSR, 1993). However, there are differences between member states in the relative significance of small enterprises to their economies. Roughly half (7 million) the micro-firms are actually self-employed sole-traders without other employees (75 per cent of the self-employed are in this category in Britain). As we shall see, these very small firms are generally growth-averse and resistant to training and other support initiatives (Gray, 1994).

Although there are many interesting and highly profitable businesses run by people working on their own (many specialist professionals, freelance journalists, creative people and so on), we will take the view that a small enterprise is a social entity that combines the labours and energies of more than two people. In other words, an enterprise is an organisation that involves interpersonal dynamics and the scope to benefit from specialisation of labour. As a consequence, an enterprise has management needs and an economic potential beyond that of one or two individuals working on their own account. As Table 3.1 shows, however, these smallest firms and self-employed account for most businesses in Britain. Because of dormant companies, a raised VAT registration threshold, multiple VAT registrations (for different parts of larger enterprises) and a significant number of people with more than one self-employed job, it is hard to estimate the

Table 3.1 Enterprises and employees by firm size, 1979, 1986 and 1991

Firm size (staff)	1979			1986			1991		
	Number ('000s)	% of firms	% of total work-force	Number ('000s)	% of firms	% of total work-force	Number ('000s)	% of firms	% of total work-force
1–2	1,099	61	7	1,595	64	11	1,735	64	11
3–5	319	18	6	535	22	10	565	21	10
6–10	179	10	7	178	7	7	196	7	7
11–19	109	6	8	84	3	6	97	4	6
20–49	46	3	7	56	2	8	65	2	9
50–199	31	2	15	25	1	13	30	2	15
200+	9	–	51	8	–	46	9	–	42
Total	1,792	100	100	2,481	100	100	2,697	100	100

Source: Employment Gazette and Graham Bannock and Partners data as cited by Storey (1994).

actual number of enterprises. Even so, the best estimates of the total small firm populations by Graham Bannock and Partners for the DTI show significant growth in all sizes of small enterprises, and an increase in the proportion of the national workforce employed by them during the enterprise culture 1980s, but the growth concentrated in what we may loosely describe as the 'non-enterprise' self-employed and two-person firms. Table 3.1 shows the number of firms in each size band (measured in terms of salaried employees) and the proportion of the national labour force working in each band at three key points in the enterprise culture period – 1979, 1986 and 1991.

There was a significant increase, of about 60 per cent, in self-employment and the number of small enterprises during the enterprise culture years. This was accompanied by a notable shift from paid employment to self-employment. Unfortunately, the proportion of larger small firms and medium-sized enterprises (50–200 employees in EU terms), often seen as the source of innovative ideas and products and a vital link in the supply chains of larger enterprises, actually dropped over the same period. By 1991, Graham Bannock calculated that 55 per cent of all enterprises were sole proprietorships, 25 per cent were partnerships and just 19 per cent were incorporated (*NatWest Review of Small Business Trends*, June 1996). These broad trends in small enterprise growth need to be examined more carefully. There is a growing body of evidence that very few of Britain's millions of self-employed and small business owners should really be described as entrepreneurs in the sense of being innovative or even being interested in growth. As various *Employment Gazettes* (1986, 1991, 1992) have revealed, one feature of the enterprise culture years has been not only a growth in self-employment but, more particularly, a steady increase in the proportion of self-employed who do not employ any other people. A similar pattern was observed during the recession of the 1930s. It suggests that the move into self-employment was not an entirely voluntary career choice for many of Britain's new business owners (Binks and Jennings, 1986). This may help to explain why so few smaller firms seem willing to grow (Doyle and Gallagher, 1986; Gray, 1989; Gallagher, 1991; and Table 2.1 on p. 23).

The most widely used national source of data on enterprises, big and small, is provided by registrations to and deregistrations from Value Added Tax (VAT). Even though it is not strictly accurate to treat VAT registration and deregistration rates as exact equivalents of small enterprise start-up and failure rates (again, Graham Bannock reminds us that only around 44 per cent of all firms register for VAT), VAT registration–deregistration analysis provides the most accessible estimate of business formation and failure rates. Certain industries (food, printed materials, charities, baby clothes, etc.) are currently not required to register for VAT, registration turnover thresholds have risen so that fewer self-employed or micro-firms need to register, and firms may deregister for reasons other than failure. In practice, many smaller self-employed firms, including 15–20 per cent of respondents to SBRT surveys, operate below VAT thresholds and these smallest firms have higher deregistration and failure rates (Ganguly, 1985; Doyle and Gallagher, 1986; Gallagher, 1991). However, the main focus of interest here is on the small enterprises that employ people other than the owner and most of these will be included in VAT data.

Overall, the DTI (1996) reports that there was a net increase of 26 per cent in the stock of VAT registered enterprises over the period 1980–94, but of course this obscures different patterns during boom and recession and differences between declining and growth industries. After 1979, net VAT registrations show almost uninterrupted increases up to 1990/1. Since 1991, they have been difficult to monitor with complete accuracy because the VAT sales turnover threshold, above which registration becomes legally obligatory for most industries, rose far faster than the inflation rate, from £25,000 to £35,000. It has risen steadily ever since and each rise has seen some drop in registrations as firms leave the VAT 'net'. However, 1991 was also the nadir of one of the most severe recessions that enterprises in Britain have had to endure, and many deregistered because they had ceased trading. It is hard to separate the two effects. In 1991, the VAT stock stood at 1,716,000 enterprises under the old system and at 1,628,000 under the revised system – a drop of 88,000. By 1994, the VAT stock had slid to 1,572,000.

In spite of its shortcomings, the VAT register is comprehensive and remains the best barometer of changes in the population of enterprises in Britain. It provides, for example, a useful measure of the average life-cycles of different types of enterprises in Britain. Analyses of VAT registrations and deregistrations during 1974–82 and 1989–91 reveal wide variations in percentage failure rates across different industrial sectors within the first year of trading and within three years. The general pattern in Table 3.2 is

Table 3.2 Average VAT deregistration rates from initial registration by industry, 1974–82 and 1989–91

Industrial sector	1974–82		1989–91	
	Within 1 year	*Within 3 years*	*Within 1 year*	*Within 3 years*
		(% of total industry)		
Manufacturing	10	28	12	34
General services	11	30	15	42
Financial services	8	25	10	29
Retail	11	33	12	37
Wholesale	12	30	14	39
Construction	11	30	13	34
Transport	14	35	14	41
Motor trades	13	32	11	31
Catering	10	31	15	45

Sources: Ganguly (1985); SBRT (1992).

one of increased turbulence and higher deregistration rates from the 1974–82 period immediately prior to the launch of the policies specifically labelled as 'enterprise culture policies' to the tail end of the enterprise culture years.

Only the motor trades have not shown increased risk and turbulence over the enterprise culture period. In most other sectors, the short-term deregistration rates were higher by 1989–91 and much higher in the medium term. Catering, hotels and restaurants replaced transport firms as the riskiest sectors. Many of these variations are a function of firm size, with larger firms having more resources to weather economic storms and more room for manoeuvre. The higher risk and lower security associated with the distribution sector – transport (many single-lorry or single-motorcycle self-employed drivers), wholesalers and retailers – compared with financial services and manufacturing is evident and partly explains some of the differences in regional net new firm formation rates. The apparent smoothness of this steady expansion of the small enterprise sector is deceptive. Analysis of the 1974–82 VAT data identified the first eighteen months as the period of highest vulnerability for new firms (more than 40 per cent of all deregistrations), leading to cumulative deregistration rates of around 40 per cent within five years of formation, tapering off to around 60 per cent within ten years (Ganguly, 1985). By the mid-1980s, despite record small business growth, the DTI's *British Business* magazine (3 April 1987) reported that deregistration rates had worsened to 50 per cent within five years, and virtually 70 per cent of enterprises had deregistered within ten years of initial registration.

Nevertheless, a significant growth in self-employment and net increases in new firm formations were evident features of the British economy during the 1990s. Figure 3.1 shows the rise and decline in self-employment and registered unemployment, and the steady rise in VAT stock (all measured in

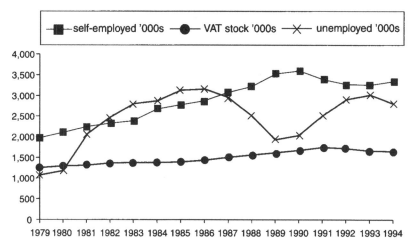

Figure 3.1 Growth in self-employment, unemployment and VAT stock, 1979–94

thousands). The quarterly Labour Force Survey (LFS) of some 65,000 respondents nationally is the best source of data on trends in employment, self-employment and unemployment. It uses slightly different industry and size categories from the VAT statistics but provides an essentially comparable and supplementary picture of the small enterprise sector and internationally comparable labour market data. The pattern of rapid, even spectacular, growth in self-employment since 1979 is immediately evident in LFS data presented in Figure 3.1 and is of clear comfort to the supporters of enterprise culture policies. These aggregated numbers, however, hide an increasing turbulence and a variety of sometimes conflicting underlying trends.

There has been a spectacular growth in self-employment (from 1.9 million in 1979 to 3.3 million in 1991) and a noticeable rise in the relative importance of small businesses in the economy (Bannock and Daly, 1990). There was no evidence, however, that these growing firms either employed many unemployed or were founded by them (Gallagher, 1991). Indeed, the aggregated unemployment figures hide a more complex picture. For instance, many young first-job seekers are included but other previously economically inactive people – such as women entering or re-entering the labour market, immigrants and so on – who would like a job are often not. Also, there are major differences between the short-term and long-term unemployed. More than 70 per cent of all unemployed find work within six months. However, the longer-term unemployed (in April 1988, at the height of the enterprise culture 'boom', roughly 650,000 had been unemployed for more than two years) tend to be older and find it harder to obtain work (*Labour Market Quarterly Report* (LMQR), July 1988). The vast bulk of confirmed redundancies occurred more than five years previously, during 1980–1, mainly in the manufacturing industries. In 1980, more than 80 per cent of the 493,700 confirmed redundancies were in manufacturing and in the peak year 1981, three-quarters of the 532,000 confirmed redundancies were in manufacturing, leaving 300,000 or so people unemployed for more than five years.

In general, the dramatic rise in both self-employment and unemployment in recent years, plus high churn (company birth and death rates) and low propensity to employ other people in most self-employed sectors, suggests that there are some linkages between the self-employed and the unemployed. Manufacturing industries have seen the most dramatic decrease in employment since 1979, slumping by more than 2 million from 7,107,000 to 5,055,000 in 1990. During the same period construction firms shed some 200,000 workers and transport industry employment dropped half a million, but employees in the financial services and miscellaneous services increased by around 1,200,000 each. Over the decade up to 1988, there were 1,322,000 net job losses in paid employment, partly countered by a gain of 959,000 self-employed, leaving a net loss of 363,000 jobs (*Employment Gazette*, 1988, 1991). The more serious, longer-term problem of youth unemployment, however, was highlighted by the fact that more than 2 million of the 3,431,000 total population of 16–19-year-olds in 1987 did not have a job (LMQR, July 1988). A great deal of the growth in both the unemployment and self-employment curves seems to have some common causes (though it is equally clear that there are also important differences between the two populations).

These wider social and economic changes will have effects on both VAT registrations and deregistrations but, on balance, it seems that the positive effects dominated. Table 3.2 gives some indication of the turbulence that underlies this seemingly steady and placid rise (and shows that the churn in registration and deregistration rates has increased markedly in recent years). However, even though the stock of VAT registered firms shows a slow upward rise until the slight dip in recent years, changes in policy and VAT registration requirements can have significant effects on registration and deregistration rates. For instance, following a sudden relaxation of monetary policy (the 'Lawson boom'), there was a net increase of 64,000 VAT registrations in 1988 due to a sudden leap in new registrations to 230,000 while deregistrations held to their trend of the past five years at around 165,000. By 1990, however, new VAT registrations slowed down while bankruptcies, firm insolvencies and VAT deregistrations hit record levels.

The important point about the patterns revealed in Figure 3.1, however, is not so much the net growth in enterprises but the signs of increasing instability in the labour market and the signs of real cultural and structural shifts in the nature of work for many people. After several years of falling unemployment (attributed to the enterprise culture by its supporters), February 1991 saw unemployment (as measured by the Labour Force Surveys method used throughout the EU) top 2 million once again, with the biggest monthly jump (150,000) in ten years, and 1993 saw 3 million again. The LFS data on the growth rate in numbers of self-employed show the dramatic growth since 1979 that we have already remarked on, but more variability than the VAT data. The early 1980s recession had mainly hit blue-collar jobs but in the late 1980s it was the turn of the middle classes, the largest source of entrepreneurs. Mortgage repossession of homes – as collateral and the basis of secured loans, the most important source of capital for new businesses – experienced a record rise during 1990 to 40,000 (up from 13,740 in 1989), and white-collar jobs in the business services were dropping by 70,000 a month (*Observer*, 3 February 1991). The British Venture Capital Association confirmed that the investments by British venture capitalists had fallen 20–30 per cent from 1989 levels by the end of 1991. By the end of 1990, one of Britain's largest accountancy firms – Peat Marwick McClintock – noted that company receiverships were up 120 per cent on 1989 (*Financial Times*, 7 January 1991) and another large firm of accountants – Touche Ross – revealed that company failures had increased 160 per cent from 1989 to 1990 (*Guardian*, 19 January 1991). Small wonder that some critics saw the enterprise culture as a temporary phenomenon.

Indeed, the rapid growth in self-employment in Figure 3.1 conceals underlying trends which do not seem particularly entrepreneurial. The most striking features are large increases in part-time employment and sole-trader (no other employees) self-employment. It seems that part of this trend is accounted for by a generally higher entry of women into the workforce. Three-quarters of Britain's 3.3 million self-employed are men, accounting for around 16 per cent of the total male workforce, but the 7 per cent (about 800,000) of self-employed women in the total female workforce represents a 140 per cent increase since 1979. The government's *Labour Market Quarterly Reviews* suggest that this trend is projected to continue. More than half of the 1 million new female entrants to the workforce during 1984–8 were more than 25 years old and had been occupied at home immediately prior to re-entering the labour market. One in five of female entrants to the labour force – around 200,000 – sought the opportunity to work for themselves as self-employed. However, many female 'self-employed' are often part-time workers operating from their own homes for a single employer. It is difficult to distinguish between labour-only sub-contracting 'self-employed' and casual part-time employees.

According to the SBRT's quarterly survey in the final quarter of 1996, owners and managers in Britain's micro-firms (fewer than ten employees) work on average a fifty-five hour week. However, the LFS reports that around 10 per cent of the self-employed work fewer than sixteen hours per week, rising to one-quarter (which includes 52 per cent of self-employed women) working fewer than thirty hours a week. In many cases this is more like casual labour than self-employment and certainly not an enterprise in any significant economic or social sense. The confusion is compounded because most agency and temporary workers do not see themselves as self-employed but continue to regard themselves as dependent employees despite a number of industrial tribunal rulings to the contrary. In 1984, the year which saw the greatest net increase in self-employment (a 12.7 per cent growth over the previous year to nearly 2.5 million), there were also 1.5 million temporary workers in various industries of whom only 15 per cent regarded themselves as self-employed. There were interesting industry differences. Only in the business services sector did a majority – 60 per cent of the small group of 'professional and related scientific' agency workers (including computer programmers) – count themselves as self-employed, contrasting with 6 per cent of the 120,000 seasonal, temporary and casual workers in the hotels and catering sector (Casey and Creigh, 1988).

By the end of 1990, the mass enterprise culture period seemed to have come to an end. More people were leaving self-employment than were entering, and during 1991 there was a net decline in self-employment (Daly, 1991). Furthermore, there are wide variations between the types of businesses started and their prospects not only for future growth but also for mere survival. With the shift in the implementation and delivery of small enterprise policy to the LECs and TECs, the emphasis also seemed to change to the management needs of existing local firms, with less of a focus on encouraging large numbers of people to turn to self-employment. Given the local and industry differences that will become apparent in the next section, this switch away from large numbers to a tighter focus seems sensible. There is one last point to make about the recent patterns of small enterprise growth in Britain which has a bearing on the impact of enterprise culture policies. As the number of small firms has grown, their average size has decreased, suggesting that the proportion of entrepreneurial small firms in Britain has been declining despite overall impressive growth in the sector. Furthermore, there are distinct industry, regional and size effects on patterns of small enterprise growth.

DISAGGREGATING THE SMALL ENTERPRISE SECTOR

It should have already become clear that it is misleading to talk about the small enterprise sector. It is too heterogeneous and the differences due to industry, size of firm and region are deep and significant. As many of these differences are due to cultural influences which simple enterprise culture initiatives are unable to affect to any marked extent, it is important to examine these differences in some detail. Looking first at the industry effects, the most notable feature of the growth in self-employment as recorded in Labour Force Surveys has been the huge increase in services which accounted for the largest proportion of the 1,331,000 net increase in self-employment in 1979–95. However, the increase was not smooth and it affected industries in different ways. Over the enterprise culture years 1981–90, the LFS revealed an overall 59 per cent increase in all self-employment but a net 4 per cent drop in the following year, 1990–1 (Campbell and Daly, 1992). Financial and business services grew an impressive 123 per cent over 1981–90 and other personal services by 109 per cent, but construction by only 18 per cent (though the structural change in employment relations in the construction industries was reflected in a 21 per cent net increase in self-employed building workers by 1987). Manufacturers only represented around 11 per cent of the net increase in self-employment over 1979–91, though that meant an 80 per cent increase in self-employment in the manufacturing industries (*Employment Gazette*, 1991). The increase in manufacturing self-employment, however, must be compared with the massive 2,063,000 drop in manufacturing employees, mainly from big firms, over the same period.

The key industries for the self-employed and small businesses are distribution, construction and manufacturing, although the self-employed and small business tend to occupy special segments there. For instance, in retailing the self-employed would include a large number of stallholders and small corner or village stores. Unless they can find a local niche which offers some protection from competition but usually limited prospects for growth, the self-employed and small business retailers face savage competition. Although the broad distributive/catering sector has grown steadily, small retailers were disappearing for most of the 1980s (VAT registrations down from 21 per cent of all firms in 1979 to 15 per cent in 1991). Despite a high failure rate, however, low barriers to entry mean a constant inflow of new entrants and the sector remains overcrowded (Ganguly, 1985; Curran *et al.*, 1987). Even from this brief outline of some of the key industry changes, it is clear that self-employment carries different meanings in different industries. A builder's labourer or a small stallholder has different relations with clients or customers from a computer consultant or specialist employment agency.

There are even more significant segment differences between the self-employed and small enterprises that employ other people. For instance, most of the self-employed in the construction industry are labour-only sub-contractors. Sometimes, skilled and semi-skilled craftsmen offer their skills as self-employed and, at other times, they form small businesses, often hiring other skilled workers. It seems fairly clear that the major cause of these impressive increases has to do with structural shifts in the economy as a whole and the construction industry in particular rather than any upsurge of entrepreneurialism. In the construction sector, more people shifted from employee to self-employed status and the shift was more balanced with 217,000 employees being replaced by 199,000 self-employed, a net 58 per cent increase of construction self-employed. In services, virtually one-third of the record 2 million new jobs during the enterprise culture boom years of 1979–87 were self-employed, a net increase of 52 per cent (*Employment Gazette*, 1988).

Although it is not designed as a business survey, the General Household Survey (GHS), with its annual national sample of more than 10,000 people, has proved to be a valuable source of national small business data. In the 1980 Survey, the two big industries for self-employed heads of household were construction (28 per cent) and distribution (27 per cent). Financial and professional services together accounted for 12 per cent of self-employed heads of household but only 5 per cent were in manufacturing. By contrast, heads of household who were small business owners employing up to twenty-five people were more likely to be in distribution (30 per cent) and manufacturing (11 per cent), though also well represented is construction (20 per cent) and the financial and professional services (9 per cent). This confirms the patterns described in Labour Force Surveys which reveal that only 2 per cent of the self-employed employ more than twenty-five people. Of those self-employed who do employ other people, the most popular industries were once again 'distribution, hotels, catering and repairs' (42 per cent), followed by construction (13 per cent) and business and financial services (12 per cent), but only 7 per cent were in manufacturing (Creigh *et al.*, 1986). The already mentioned trend towards self-employed status in the building industry and among certain business and technical professionals strongly suggests that entrepreneurship must vary in its technical and psychological requirements from one sector to another.

Indeed, if overall employment relations are changing on a sector basis, this means that the mere act of opting for self-employment cannot be taken as particularly strong evidence of entrepreneurial behaviour. In fact, small manufacturers are more business- and growth-minded and tend to be more promising candidates as entrepreneurs, but many of them would not be included in national self-employment statistics because they are attracted to the protection of limited liability through incorporation. The uncertain interaction between regulation and the demands of the marketplace certainly varies between industries but it also obscures the behaviour of entrepreneurial firms at an early stage in their existence behind the hurly-burly of business life in the small firm sector. For instance, there is some evidence that innovative small to medium-sized manufacturers are better than average job generators, though their role may be obscured by larger-scale manufacturing's shedding of more than 2 million employees since 1979 (Storey, 1986b; Keeble, 1987). Annual net new firm formation rates, however, bear no statistical relationship to annual real rates of growth of GDP. Aggregated net new firm formation rates reveal little information on the velocity of business births and deaths, the average size of firm in each sector or, most significantly, the quality and flair of management. The overall figures say very little about the entrepreneurial nature, or otherwise, of individual firms. Also, the industrial sectors are defined so broadly that high performances by, for instance, technology-based firms tend to be swamped by the often more stodgy performance of more traditional firms.

There are wide regional variations in economic performance across Britain (and elsewhere in Europe), which may be explained partly by local environmental and natural endowment factors but mainly by differences in industrial composition and concentration as well as differential access to capital (Mason, 1989). Regional economies with different economic structures can have quite different industrial profiles. The differences are most obviously highlighted in the concentration of old, heavy 'rust-belt' industries in the northern regions of England and south Wales compared with the growth of financial and professional services in the south-east. Regions with higher concentrations of industries at risk – such as haulage and retailing – are clearly at a disadvantage compared with regions that attract the higher-growth industries such as advanced manufacturing and business services, and they will, in general, present fewer entrepreneurial opportunities (especially if a 'like attracts like' influence is at work). If a strong growth in wholesalers, transport firms and associated services is an indication of healthy trading opportunities, then the southern half of England clearly offered attractive pastures for budding entrepreneurs. By contrast, the northern English regions – even though Hull and Newcastle should be benefiting from increased trade with Europe – have historically offered far fewer apparent entrepreneurial opportunities. The 'Celtic fringe' seems to have had fairly average growth during the 1980s although the manufacturing sector in Wales looks very robust (there was a lot of Japanese and Welsh Development Agency investment) and the Scottish financial sector has enjoyed spectacular growth.

Although each local economy has its unique structure, the four southern regions – south-east, south-west, East Anglia and west Midlands – seemed to form a distinct and privileged group during the mid-1980s boom. For instance, the new firm formation rate between 1980 and 1983 was seventeen per 1,000 employees in Greater London, twelve per 1,000 in the rest of the south-east, eleven per 1,000 in East Anglia, ten per 1,000 in the south-west and eight per 1,000 in the west Midlands, compared with Yorkshire's six per 1,000 and five per 1,000 in both northern England and Scotland (Ganguly, 1985). On average, 9 per cent of households have a self-employed head but during 1979-86 self-employment leapt 90 per cent in the south-west (where 12 per cent of household heads are now self-employed), 61 per cent in East Anglia and 58 per cent in the south-east, which accounts for 36 per cent of Britain's self-employed (*Regional Trends*, 1988). By 1985, the four southern regions contained 56 per cent of all businesses, 57 per cent of the self-employed and a higher rate of growth in terms of new firm formations and GDP (55 per cent of the UK total). A survey of the 1,000 fastest-growing unquoted businesses in Britain found that 44 per cent were in London and the south-east (Mason, 1989). More importantly, Mason and Harrison (1991) have demonstrated a clear link between successful start-up and growth rates and the local provision of capital from formal and informal (non-institutional sources such as private investors) sources, particularly in south-east England. The link between certain entrepreneurial firms, technology and capital goes beyond firms providing high-technology products and services. An interesting feature of the financial and business services sector as a whole is the widespread use of new technological applications, especially in information technology. The use of new technology is also a feature of modern, entrepreneurial manufacturers and distribution firms in non-technology sectors. Because technological awareness reflects exposure to education, this strongly implies that growth-oriented entrepreneurial and innovative firms are likely to have higher educational levels, certainly in technical and engineering skills but also, for services in particular, in academic skills than most self-employed and probably most employees.

ECONOMIC POTENTIAL OF ENTREPRENEURIAL SMALL BUSINESSES

There are two main economic goals frequently mentioned in support of small enterprise development policies whether of an enterprise culture type or of the various structural, interventionist types: (1) the generation of new jobs; and (2) the diffusion of new, innovative technologies. The most obvious political goal of enterprise culture policies has definitely been the reduction of mass unemployment even though there is nothing in any theory of entrepreneurship to support the notion that entrepreneurs are intrinsically interested in recruiting a large workforce for its own sake. By the end of Britain's enterprise culture decade, small enterprises employing fewer than twenty people were generating 0.5 million extra jobs net, slightly more than larger firms with their much larger labour forces (Daly, 1991). Businesses with fewer than twenty employees accounted for more than 96 per cent of all businesses and 36 per cent of all employment (or roughly half of all private sector employment). However, they accounted for a much smaller proportion of the national sales turnover (21 per cent). Furthermore, fewer than 5 per cent of the self-employed have more than twenty employees and more than 75 per cent of all self-employed in Britain do not employ other people.

In David Storey's Cleveland study (Storey and Strange, 1992) comparing a 1979 cohort of local small firms with a 1990 cohort (which included the 1979 survivors), it is interesting to note that the average size of small firm had dropped from twenty-six employees to just under nine. In fact, the proportion of sole-traders without employees has grown steadily over the years (from 60 per cent in 1980) and, during 1990, the steady increase in net self-employment went into reverse for the first time in twenty years. With the onset of recession, record levels of small business liquidations and personal bankruptcies suggested that much of the recent growth in small firms was either not particularly resilient or else in exposed, low barrier-to-entry industries. Indeed, an increasing number of self-employed admit they would prefer to work as someone else's employee, a similar phenomenon to the patterns of unemployment and self-employment during the recession of the 1930s (Daly, 1991). This raises important questions about the potential for growth and innovation of small enterprises and the role that management capabilities, expectations and styles can play in realising this potential.

In particular, the effects of scale and size of workforce (and resource base) mean that the links between firm size and growth need to be examined more carefully. It may be useful to glance again at Table 3.1 on p. 32. In the manufacturing sector, which includes a lot of dynamic and growing small firms, evidence suggests that the most dynamic employ between one and two dozen people (SBRT, 1986: no. 4). The best job creators among firms which sought enterprise agency support were those employing 11–20 people (BiC, 1987). Analysis of data from the credit rating agency, Dun and Bradstreet, indicates that, while British firms employing 11–19 are very active, very few are likely to grow into the 20–49 employee size band (Doyle and Gallagher, 1986). These findings were broadly confirmed by David Storey's (1986b) studies of manufacturing firms in Cleveland which revealed that, over the years 1965–76, only 14 per cent of small, single-plant firms registered any significant growth. However, this study suggests that the barrier to growth for small manufacturers may be slightly higher than twenty employees. Almost one in five firms with 10–24 employees registered growth and these firms had the lowest death rates. Just 8 per cent of firms with 25–49 employees grew, while only 7 per cent of firms with 50–99 employees did so, and they registered the highest failure rates. SBRT surveys also tend to find that the 10–24-employee enterprises emerge as the most significant employers of new staff. A similar picture appeared in the United States where an analysis of Small Business Administration data, involving thousands of small firms, indicated that young firms less than six years old employing fewer than twenty employees displayed the most dramatic growth (Evans, 1987b).

Findings from the Cleveland manufacturing firms and from similar studies also indicated that it is these dynamic small firms themselves which spawn other successful new firms. The founders of surviving small firms are more likely to have previously worked in another small firm than in a large firm. As much of the unemployment has been fed by redundancies from large firms, this implies that policies which promote redundant workers as a source of successful new firms are likely to fail (Storey, 1986b; Storey and Strange, 1992). Indeed, doubts have been expressed on the type of new firms being founded by the unemployed and their destructive impact on existing local firms (Gray and Stanworth, 1986; Binks and Jennings, 1986). The strong suggestion is that training resources should be concentrated mainly on encouraging dynamism and efficiency in existing firms rather than spread thinly in frequently vain attempts to nurture start-ups.

Analyses of data from the 200,000 or so firms covered by the credit rating company Dun and Bradstreet have suggested that many firms employing 10–20 employees expand rapidly but that few small firms are likely to pass beyond a twenty-employee 'barrier' (Doyle and Gallagher, 1986). Indeed, other studies confirm that firms with up to twenty employees have different patterns of development and that those of, say, 15–25 employees are very active but very few will expand (CBI, 1986; Storey and Johnson, 1987). These findings have recently been confirmed by separate analyses of Dun and Bradstreet data which revealed that firms employing 5–19 employees generated some 290,000 new jobs between 1985 and 1987 while those employing 20–49 people actually shed some 80,000 jobs (Gallagher, 1991).

At the individual level, the unemployed of the early 1980s were mainly middle-aged, male, semi- or unskilled workers from heavy industries who are neither inclined nor suited to self-employment. Clearly, transforming the work potential of these types of unemployed is beyond the powers of enterprise training. For them, casual work and part-time work represent two further low-level employment alternatives to self-employment although the distinction is so blurred as to be meaningless. Indeed, Labour Force Surveys reveal that part-time work, including part-time self-employment, boomed during the mid-1980s. Home working and other similar forms of casual labour account for much of the recent rise in female self-employment, which represented roughly 20 per cent in the total growth in self-employment during 1981–4 (Casey and Creigh, 1988). It is clear that the enterprise culture offers only limited and insecure employment options to the unemployed, whether as casual, part-time, temporary or self-employed workers.

The second main promise of small firm economic potential held out by the enterprise culture model lies in the development and diffusion of new technological innovations in products and processes, making them a source of the growth industries of the future. New technology is expected by many to revolutionise both productive capacity and productivity, and there is an underlying assumption that the growth of dynamic, small, high-technology manufacturers will boost new technological applications by other small and medium-sized firms. Certainly, manufacturers and business services connected with micro-electronics, information technology and bio-technology appear to enjoy the best potential for growth and provide the most exciting environment for the blossoming of entrepreneurial talent. Against the background of industrial decline in traditional industries, small, new-technology manufacturers have been net providers of new jobs in Britain with more than 11,000 new jobs created during 1980–4 in firms employing fewer than fifty people – swamping the 4,000 jobs lost in firms employing more than 1,000 people. In 1981, 11.5 per cent of the workforce was employed in high-technology manufacturing and by 1986 this proportion had crept up to 13 per cent (Keeble, 1987).

However, there is a widely held view that new technology, which permits small batch production and lower staff levels, actually benefits bigger firms much more than it does small manufacturers. Technologically innovative firms tend to be either very small or very big (Rothwell and Zegveld, 1982). Also, small high-technology manufacturers can be rather vulnerable, relying on a single product, while the larger innovating firms tend to have more heterogeneous product lines (Javanovic and Rob, 1987). However, these firms may be more receptive to training initiatives. New high-technology entrepreneurs tend to have a high educational level and they give way to management teams as their innovative firms grow from small specialist firms to larger enterprises (Oakey, 1987). So far, there is little evidence that small high-technology firms are better job creators than other small manufacturing firms (Storey *et al.*, 1987). Indeed, during the enterprise culture period, there was strong evidence that British technology-based firms invest far less on research than their European rivals; according to the measure of patents registered in the United States, British firms are losing out in global markets to Germany, where investment among firms of all sizes is many times higher (Patel and Pavitt, 1989). This suggests that successful entrepreneurs and innovators have more developed management skills and a stronger understanding of capital requirements.

The regional pattern of development in Britain cannot be ignored. In general, entrepreneurs are attracted to areas where there are already a lot of entrepreneurs. Whether this is because of some social imperative – a sort of entrepreneurial herd instinct – or because they are all drawn by the same economic and environmental attractions, this phenomenon is a feature of certain high-growth areas in Britain, Italy and the United States (Amin *et al.*, 1986; Keeble, 1987). Networking and the grouping together of complementary businesses seems to be a particular developmental pattern of successful technology-based firms. The openness to networking also suggests fairly well-developed social skills and it is interesting that new manufacturers are twice as likely to be small companies with employees rather than sole-trading self-employed (Curran, 1986). The main problems facing these firms are connected with growth: finding markets, the right employees, appropriate forms of finance, and so on. These fundamental differences and the regional, industrial and size variations above indicate that not only is the small firm sector extremely heterogeneous but also that there is little point in seeking a single 'entrepreneurial personality' as the main explanation of entrepreneurial behaviour because such behaviour is likely to vary from one situation to the next and from one 'type' of small firm manager to another.

BUSINESS BEHAVIOUR IN THE SMALL ENTERPRISE SECTOR

A useful source of data on small enterprise attitudes, behaviour and expectations is the *Quarterly Survey of Small Business in Britain* which was launched in late 1984 by the Small Business Research Trust, an independent educational non-profit organisation. The sample was originally drawn from the memberships of Britain's leading small business representative organisations and a number of other sources. Although the SBRT sample is not random, it has been possible to weight the responses to reflect the latest VAT registration distributions, and seasonal adjustments have improved the predictive value of the data which are fairly empirically accurate. One of the strengths of using the SBRT database is that there is an overlap of 400–800 respondents common to each survey. This allows the actual growth of respondent firms and some of their attitudes to be tracked over time. The attraction of being able to explore longitudinal effects is clear in Figure 3.2. There is no doubt that the self-employed and new small enterprises can provide significant employment opportunities but, as Figure 3.2 makes very clear, the job security of this form of employment is extremely vulnerable. The business environment is the key determining feature in the behaviour of small enterprises. Figure 3.2 tracks the balances (percentage of respondents reporting increases less those reporting decreases) as reported in SBRT quarterly surveys for actual annual performance in sales and employment, and the percentage reporting difficulties in attracting skilled labour.

As in Figure 3.1, the effects of recession, measured by falling sales, on expectations and on employment are immediately obvious in Figure 3.2. The 'boom' had peaked for small firms by the end of 1988 (confirmed by subsequent official statistics), with negative balances for employment occurring before the slump of sales turnover into negative balances. Employment balances have remained significantly lower than sales balances ever since.

quarters

Figure 3.2 Quarterly actual employment and sales, expected employment percentage balances among SBRT SMEs, 1988–97

Sources: NatWest/SBRT, *Quarterly Surveys of Small Business in Britain.*

These surveys do not include firms which have failed in the meantime, so it must be assumed that the shedding of labour by small firms and the precariousness of employment within them are more severe than the figure indicates. Indeed, it is clear that the recent increase in sales and emergence from the depths of recession have not boosted employment as firms are making use of slack capacity (though it is interesting that a residual demand for skilled labour continued during the recession and looks likely to leap once spare capacity is used up and general unemployment begins to drop). In fact, the large growth in self-employment during the 1980s took place in parallel with an even larger growth in unemployment which suggests that both phenomena may have common causes – socio-economic structural changes within Britain's economy and society.

As we have just seen, self-employment does not appear to offer an effective answer to unemployment, especially longer-term core unemployment and youth unemployment. However, the enterprise culture claims for small businesses as net creators of new jobs may have more substance. The services sector is now showing the fastest economic growth in terms of new firms but there is some evidence that small firms in the manufacturing and construction industries respond more positively to training and, proportionately, create more jobs (Gray and Stanworth, 1985; SBRT, 1986: no. 4). However, there is some debate about this because it can be very difficult to draw the line between some services and some manufacturing processes. Economists are increasingly drawing a distinction between services which are not portable but depend very much on being locally based and those which are like manufacturing in that they can move and be relocated virtually anywhere. For example, personal services like haircuts and car repairs cannot be telephoned to the client but financial services, marketing and even transport can be transacted anywhere. With many small assemblers, jobbing engineers and manufacturers of components and other semi-finished goods being increasingly drawn into tightly specified 'just-in-time' supply chains with larger enterprises, the service element of what they provide becomes almost as important as the products they make.

These net changes in different industries across the different regions reflect the broader structural changes taking place not only in the British economy but also more globally. The deregistration of older, less efficient businesses from VAT will have been even more severe than Table 3.2 reveals but there is no way of knowing from these data whether the new registrations represent more modern and efficient firms. Nor is there any way of gauging any cultural differences between regions that may impact upon new firm formation rates (such as a historic reliance on large-scale heavy industry in the north and stronger links with commerce in the south). However, it is worth pointing out that the above patterns of growth aggregate all small firms and self-employed and that entrepreneurial firms may exhibit different patterns of development. The important point to note from the perspective of this book and of entrepreneurial development, however, is the weakness of the industries – retailing, catering and transport – which are popular as new self-employed and small businesses because of their low barriers to entry (low initial capital, no entry qualifications, minimal workforce, etc.). Also there are plenty of models of existing businesses in these industries for newcomers to imitate. For these reasons, and from the previously mentioned high failure rates, it seems clear that the mere act of starting a new business is often very risky but not necessarily entrepreneurial. Indeed, patterns of growth in Britain's small firms sector led to the unavoidable conclusion that structural factors have been much more influential than subjective motivational factors in explaining recent trends (though not necessarily individual behaviour). As recent growth occurred mainly in industries where barriers to entry have always been comparatively low, and not in the more innovative sectors, there seems to be little basis in fact for one of the main promises of enterprise culture policies.

So far, the structural sources of differences between small firms – historic period, external economic environment, region, industry and size effects – have been discussed. These factors mainly affect the distribution and function of different types of small firm in the economy and, therefore, their business behaviour (including any growth strategy). However, non-structural factors, particularly those relating to the expectations of owners, managers and workforce, appear to have a greater influence on business behaviour. Sociologists have provided the most useful studies of these factors but these have mainly been descriptive. Ever since Weber (1930), one of the pioneers of sociology, the marginal origins of many entrepreneurs have been identified, and the success of immigrants and 'outsider' subgroups – such as Huguenots, Quakers, Jews and Nonconformists in the past, and East African Asians, Cypriots and Overseas Chinese more recently – has been extensively studied. Labour Force Surveys provide some evidence for Weber's theory but only to an extent. By 1989, much higher proportions of certain ethnic minorities were more likely to be self-employed than the 12.6 per cent national average. A high 21.2 per cent of Indians and 22.3 per cent of Pakistanis/Bangladeshis were self-employed (and there are indications that a sizeable proportion are the proprietors of incorporated enterprises). However, only 6.7 per cent of another socially marginal group, people of Caribbean origin, described themselves as self-employed according to the 1989 Labour Force Survey (*Employment Gazette*, March 1991).

The same data also suggest that groups originating in the Indian subcontinent are much more likely to employ other people (48 per cent of Pakistani self-employed and 42 per cent of Indians were employers, compared with only 19 per cent of Caribbeans). Family networks and support structures among Asian families appear much tighter than in the white or Caribbean communities. However, caution has to be adopted in interpreting these data: it should not be ignored that the vast majority of the labour force in all groups are neither self-employed nor small firm owners. Also, unemployment rates are much higher among ethnic minorities. Many Asian businesses are in fact low-income family retailing enterprises in the non-entrepreneurial convenience food or CTN (confectionery, tobacco and newsagency) sectors. Although there is some empirical and theoretical support for the notion that some entrepreneurs seek their business careers because other desired career paths are blocked, the 'marginal group' theory fails to explain why only a small proportion of people within the 'outsider' group start their own businesses and why most do not.

The 'marginal group' approach also fails to explain the success of small business founders who come from more mainstream groups, though Curran and Stanworth (1981) did find that certain entrepreneurs (mainly in the electronics and printing industries) started their own businesses out of frustration at not achieving promotion or due status, often because of a lack of formal qualifications. This strongly implies that other cultural or social factors, as well as blocked expected career trajectories, are needed to explain the career choice of self-employment in general and the successful attainment of a career as an entrepreneur in particular. Indeed, the fact that the phenomenon needs to be explained across different ethnic groups suggests that general social forces other than ethnicity must be at work. As we have already seen, other powerful sociological concepts with strong cultural overtones are those of family influence and of class. The implication of that analysis was that the self-employed and small business sector would be composed of different segments: the largest, a collection of various pre-capitalist, mainly self-employed occupations; the next biggest, petit-bourgeois retailers and small businesses attempting to survive the squeeze between capital and organised labour; the smallest, elements of the bourgeoisie seeking to maintain their class position or to accumulate capital at an extraordinary rate. Below them all and merging with the largest group is the so-called reserve army of labour, the dispossessed proletarians now termed the *secondary* sector.

While the concepts of family and class are quite separate, they are sociologically and empirically intertwined and their effects on entrepreneurial (and non-entrepreneurial) development are likely to be strongly interrelated. It is significant, therefore, that General Household Surveys and other studies have found that there is a significantly higher-than-expected tendency for the parents or close relatives of the self-employed to be also self-employed and for small firm owners to have parents who were managers – either in small businesses or in larger organisations (Bolton, 1971; Curran and Burrows, 1988; Bannock and Stanworth, 1990). Our view that there is often a clear distinction between most self-employed and small enterprise owners, similar to that made by Carland *et al.* (1984) about distinctions between small business owners and entrepreneurs, is strongly supported by the sociological evidence presented here. Small business owners are not merely the self-employed who have taken on more staff. There is a strong reluctance among both enterprise trainees and experienced business owners to shift from self-employment to small business management and vice versa. This may be a function partly of age, because small business owners tend to be older, with a median age in the 35–45 band, but appears to be linked to culture. Also, there are a growing number of part-time female self-employed who are more interested in managing conflicting work and family pressures than in developing a business. Catharine Hakim (1988) has pointed out that low-income secondary-sector self-employed women are displacing low-skilled (unemployed) males as chief breadwinners in many working-class families in economically decayed regions.

Hakim (1988) also pointed to confusion in the secondary sector where the low-skilled self-employed overlap with temporary, often seasonal, workers. Temporary workers rarely report themselves as self-employed to Labour Force Surveys, yet industrial tribunals hold that to be their status. As pointed out on p. 38, of 1.5 million temporary workers in 1984 only 15 per cent regarded themselves as self-employed (the main exception being highly skilled information-technology specialists in the *core* sector where 60 per cent reported themselves as self-employed). This gives a clear indication of the force of self-concept and (mis)perceptions (Casey and Creigh, 1988). It is clear from even a superficial analysis of the data on new firm formation in Britain that most of the recent growth in self-employment and small business is not particularly entrepreneurial in the commonly accepted sense of the term. Recognising the force of sociological evidence, policy research has now shifted its focus to explaining why certain founders of new firms survive and flourish and why others stagnate or fail. In enterprise training terms, the emphasis becomes one of encouraging the potential expanders and seeking to support likely success rather than boosting the absolute numbers of self-employed. Although the onset of deep recession in 1989 and the fragmentation of centralised research to meet the varying requirements of eighty-two (now eighty) Training and Enterprise Councils in England and Wales and twenty-four Local Enterprise Companies in Scotland means that it is harder to gather national data on this late switch in public policy interest, the focus on local economic issues and a deeper understanding of cultural background factors seem to offer the most fruitful potential for enterprise promotion policies.

4 Effectiveness of enterprise culture policies

The main aim of this chapter is to examine the effectiveness of enterprise culture policies according to their own stated objectives. Particular attention is paid to the major enterprise culture policy – enterprise training – and the main fiscal policy – the Enterprise Allowance Scheme (EAS). Before an examination of the empirical evidence concerning these two central policies, however, it is worth considering the theoretical underpinnings of the enterprise culture model more critically.

THEORETICAL ASSUMPTIONS

There are sound reasons for being sceptical about the assumptions that starting a business or becoming self-employed is in itself entrepreneurial or that the growth of the self-employed sector as a whole will generate more positive attitudes towards enterprise and promote more widespread entrepreneurial activities. Indeed, the evidence presented in this book in relation to career motivation, business objectives and growth orientation suggests otherwise. Furthermore, there appears to be little evidence that 'demand-side' government intervention necessarily stifles enterprise (one of the central criticisms levelled at previous development models by enterprise culture supporters). More importantly, there is even less evidence that the 'supply-side' type of enterprise policy intervention has encouraged entrepreneurship or that the growth in absolute numbers of small owner-managed units of production actually leads to economic development.

Despite a record growth in self-employment over the past ten years, Britain actually under-performed compared with rival economies during the enterprise culture period and immediately following it. Also, the greatest increase in new enterprise formation was among the self-employed and micro-firms employing fewer than ten people. These experienced the highest failure rates and suffered a decline in relative productivity, measured in output per employee, over the period (Bannock and Daly, 1990; Hughes, 1990). The net effect of enterprise culture policies, it would appear, has been to encourage the founding of large numbers of very small, relatively non-productive firms – possibly at the expense of slightly larger, potentially more productive small firms. Certainly, there has been a lot of comment in recent years about the relative weakness of not the small enterprise sector but the medium enterprise sector, with unfavourable contrasts made with Germany's medium enterprise sector (*Mittelstand*) in particular. Given the increases in unemployment during the 1980s as the failure rate of the weaker small enterprises also increased, enterprise culture policies appear quite inefficient. Indeed, there are strong suggestions that – as in the 1930s – the growth of self-employment is a symptom reflecting the pressures causing high unemployment rather than a desire for entrepreneurial growth (Binks and Jennings, 1986). Socio-economic structure plays a key role in explaining and predicting rises and falls in levels of unemployment and self-employment. Both phenomena seem linked to the level of government investment (expenditure as a percentage of GDP) which fell in Britain, quite early in the 1980s, to the lowest level in the European Community. Structuralists would say that the resultant shrinkage and disappearance of large firms led directly to a growth in both unemployment and self-employment. The mere act of starting a new firm or embarking on a self-employed career is not necessarily entrepreneurial. It is also clear that many small enterprises that do have employees are not managed as entre-preneurial businesses (even if many do secure a balance between business and domestic life quite effectively). The criticisms of the stage-of-growth models have been borne out empirically in the fact that so few small enter-prises grow into medium-sized enterprises, let alone are transformed into significantly large corporations.

GROWTH EFFECTS

In economic theory, it is assumed that firm growth is independent of firm size although this 'law' may only apply to firms that have attained the level of minimum efficiency. The economists' view on enterprise growth reflects the effects of different supply and demand conditions on different sectors at different points of the business cycle. Much of the evidence and discussion in this book supports the view that these structural effects do largely determine enterprise growth and that, therefore, policies aimed at stimulating enterprise growth need to be embedded in broader industrial or development policies. The minimum efficiency condition, however, sug-gests that, in general, growth may also be linked to the experience of the owners and managers, the collective experience of the enterprise itself as an organisation, and the acquisition of modern skills and practices through management development and staff training. Although there are strong intuitive reasons for believing that these factors do exert positive influences on enterprise growth, empirical evidence in support of these propositions is fairly equivocal.

In an econometric study of 20,000 firms in the USA, Evans (1987a, 1987b) found strong evidence to support the counter-proposition that firm growth decreases with age. Economic theory was not supported as growth decreased with firm size even though Evans found that the growth–size relationship is highly non-linear because it varies over the size distribution of firms. David Storey and his colleagues at Warwick University have searched for but found little convincing evidence that training improves the performance of small enterprises (Storey, 1994; Storey and Westhead, 1994); however, the SBRT's John Stanworth found a variety of improvements in growth-related business behaviour and performance resulting from close one-to-one, quasi-consultancy relations between trainers and owner managers (Stanworth *et al.*, 1992). These findings are reflected in the SBRT studies reported in this book (see Table 2.1 on p. 23) where there is strong evidence that managers' attitudes towards growth are a powerful intervening variable but one conditioned by external social realities. Further analysis of the SBRT data suggests there is a reasonably strong link between attitudes and actual growth. In Table 4.1, growth-oriented firms surveyed towards the end of the enterprise culture period in the third quarter of 1991 – even while suffering deep recession – achieved higher growth (measured as reported increases in actual sales over the past year, plus annual increases in either employment or investment) than firms with non-growth targets.

These studies also provided support for Schumpeter's view that even entrepreneurial small business owners are often only entrepreneurial during the initial start-up phase of their enterprise, preferring to restrict further growth so as to preserve their autonomy or to protect what they have achieved. As pointed out in the previous chapter and earlier, most small firms are services organised as sole-traders or partnerships with limited or no growth objectives. The SBRT survey conducted for the OUBS in 1995 revealed that very few small firms or self-employed people have the employment of other people as their main objective. Staff are often taken on only with reluctance and mainly in order to get particular jobs done or to handle increased workloads. In most cases, staff seem to be viewed as an expense rather than a resource. Consequently, there are doubts about the willingness of many small enterprise owners to delegate authority to other managers or

Table 4.1 Growth orientation and actual business performance, 1991 (percentages)

Performance	Growth-oriented	Growth-averse	Exit/sell/etc.	Total
Growing	27	12	12	18
Static	48	57	48	51
Declining	25	31	40	31
Total	100	100	100	100
Total number	648	660	411	1,719

members of staff, a crucial stage in most growth models. Indeed, we found differences between growth-oriented and growth-averse enterprise owners in attitudes to delegative or directive management styles. Some 300 of the same small enterprise owners had replied to the 1990 SBRT business and personal objectives survey, the 1991 SBRT growth survey and a 1993 OUBS survey that asked whether, on balance, they were directive or delegative (the question was posed as a forced choice between two positive statements to reduce any social desirability effects). Analysis of the data had already revealed the strong desire among small enterprise owners to maintain personal independence. Potential conflicts over loss of personal control at a particular stage of personal and business development can then be seen in their proper context of the owners' overall life ambitions. Owners keen to grow only as far as the real delegation choice point may, in effect, be saying that personal control is more important than creating a lasting organisation. The conflict between increasing organisational complexities related to size and the owner's personal motivations can be seen in Table 4.2 on delegation effects.

The overall reluctance of small firm owners to give up personal control inside their firms is clear. A directive management style is stronger among owners with 'lifestyle' as a business objective than among those with business/economic objectives. Growth models assume the development of more devolved management and it is not surprising that growth-oriented owners were found to be twice as likely to be delegative as growth-averse owners (although directive management styles dominate both groups). The average directive owner had twelve employees and the average delegative owner seventeen employees. By contrast, a forced choice question contrasting the acceptance of external equity with the desire to retain personal control – which also addresses a commonly raised problem concerning small enterprise growth – did not discriminate significantly between the two groups. There were no significant personal life-cycle effects on management styles. However, there were highly significant differences in relation to years of trading for the current business, with longer-established enterprises being much more delegative and participative in their management approach (possibly reflecting closer interpersonal bonds as the core workforce stabilises). Although in managerial terms, these issues are linked to growth and

Table 4.2 Business objectives by management style

Objectives	Directive		Delegative		Total (%)	
Business/economic	54		37		91	(30)
Security	63		30		93	(31)
Lifestyle	81		23		104	(35)
Other	9		3		12	(4)
Total (%)	207	(68)	93	(31)	300	(100)

(Chi-square = 13.98; d/f = 6; significance p < 0.03)

Table 4.3 Definitions of growth by firm size (full-time employees) (row percentages)

Staff numbers	Sales	Profits	Market share	Orders	Products	Staff	Sites	Other	Total	(Col. %)
Sole-trader	42	27	2	21	1	1	1	5	686	(27)
2–9	52	29	2	11	1	2	1	2	1,262	(50)
10–14	62	21	1	8	–	1	5	3	191	(8)
15–24	59	27	2	6	1	1	1	3	175	(7)
25+	59	32	–	4	–	2	–	3	203	(8)
Total	1,248	706	45	313	19	43	14	129	2,517	(100)
(%)	(50)	(28)	(2)	(12)	(1)	(2)	(1)	(5)	(100)	

Source: Open University Business School.

efficiency, there is evidence that small enterprise owners do not view growth in these terms. The responses to the special SBRT survey conducted in 1995 for OUBS indicate (in Table 4.3) that small enterprise owners are much more concerned with the direct financial implications when they themselves define growth.

There is a clear and statistically significant size effect present ($p < 0.0000$). More of the larger SMEs are likely to measure their growth in terms of sales and then profits, while the smaller SMEs and sole-traders have a significant tendency also to use the number of orders or contracts as a measure of growth. Very few of these SMEs operate in niche markets where share of the market is a significant business consideration. The most significant finding from a policy perspective, however, is the clear message that SMEs do not use employment as a measure of growth. It appears that they are reluctant employers, and regard new employees as an additional cost (not an investment). There is also little support for the view that SMEs are great innovators: an increase in new products is not seen by many as a sign of growth. However, this table gives little information on the stability of SME attitudes towards growth. Responses to all SBRT surveys strongly suggest that SME growth expectations are a function of external economic structural conditions. Since 1989, SMEs have reported 'low turnover and lack of sales' as their single most serious problem, so it is not surprising that sales volumes feature so prominently. The structural and size effects on SME growth intentions can be seen in Table 4.4 which summarises the responses of the same 902 SME owners to the 1991 SBRT quarterly survey question on growth intentions and their later responses to the 1995 survey question on how their firms were founded. This table thus also reflects cultural effects with growth motivation significantly ($p < 0.00370$) linked to origin of firm.

The constraints of individualism are seen in the strong growth aversion of SME owners who founded their firms themselves. In the depths of recession in 1991, the prime challenge for many was survival, not growth. However, SME owners who started as a team or with partners and those who bought their businesses are more growth-oriented and much more interested in selling their firms as going concerns in order to realise their investments.

Table 4.4 Growth intentions (1991) by how a firm was founded (row percentages)

	Self	*Family*	*Team*	*Bought*	*Other*	*Total*	*(Col. %)*
Positive	61	7	13	14	5	354	(39)
Averse	73	9	6	10	2	292	(32)
Unsure	67	8	14	9	2	132	(15)
Exit	50	8	16	23	3	124	(14)
Column total	578	69	103	121	31	902	(100)
(%)	(64)	(8)	(11)	(13)	(4)	(100)	

Source: SBRT.

By 1995, team starts were even more growth-oriented and more reluctant to sell their businesses, while single founders (and non-owner-managers) remained cautious. This supports other research indicating that team starts are more durable as businesses and offer stronger growth potential (Vyakarnam and Jacobs, 1993). It is clear that small enterprise owners do not share the same measurement concepts as enterprise policy makers (who virtually always couch growth in terms of new employment). Small enterprises make a large contribution to the net creation of new jobs compared with large firms (especially during periods of weak economic performance) but most of these new jobs come from relatively few firms (Storey and Johnson, 1987).

Clearly, attitudes towards growth and the processes of growth itself are very complex among the small enterprises, even those with the potential to grow. It seems reasonable to conclude that the vast majority of small enterprises do not go through the various stages of growth described in Chapter 2. However, it is also clear that a small minority of 'entrepreneurial', 'progressive' or 'serious' small enterprises do seem to follow the path described by the sort of stage models that underlie enterprise development theories. This is some comfort to enterprise culture supporters; however, there are strong theoretical grounds for being sceptical about the general applicability of such models. One evident weakness of stage models is that they generally do not provide an explanation of why an enterprise was founded in the first place and of the relation between the founding motivations and objectives on the one hand, and subsequent developments on the other. They also assume that a management learning process occurs and, almost inevitably, creates the conditions for the next stage of growth. Indeed, stage development models of growth are models of firm growth rather than models of individual entrepreneurial or even small enterprise manager development. However, we have to take into account the broader aims of the enterprise culture model before rejecting the stages-of-growth approach out of hand. As we have seen, active and entrepreneurial firms that achieve significant and sustainable growth are likely to be even more rare. It is reasonable to assume that entrepreneurial firms in transition towards significant growth and a more professional management structure will pass through certain important stages and that policy initiatives might help them to pass through each stage more successfully. However, the enterprise culture may not have been particularly effective in promoting these necessary transitions. We need to consider its effects on the target small enterprise and self-employed owners and managers over the period since it was introduced in the mid-1980s.

PERCEIVED IMPACT ON SMALL ENTERPRISE OWNERS

The poor educational backgrounds and problems with time management of many small firm owners suggest that their lack of ability may also represent a constraint for enterprise culture policies. Given the isolation and lack of peer comparison that individualism fosters, plus the general effects of fear of failure, they may well underestimate their own abilities. Furthermore, small business owners of this type will be prone to attribute their own limitations to external agencies beyond their control, and to reject growth or business development on pseudo-rational grounds. This has the effect of restricting their *perceived* opportunities (even when the range of actual opportunities may be wider). Indeed, as the recession deepened during the early 1990s, most respondents to SBRT surveys attributed their own poor performance to the absence of business opportunities (44 per cent of respondents) or cashflow/debtor problems (11 per cent) rather than to their own managerial abilities (0.2 per cent), even though marketing and debt control are management functions. Their responses certainly represented economic structural realities in many cases but serve to show how broad economic effects are mediated psychologically through individual perceptions to affect expectations, motivation and business behaviour. At the early stages of growth, when so much depends on the owner's perceptions and expectations, it is clearly extremely difficult for most small business owners to separate their own personal objectives from those they set for their businesses.

Since most small firms have only local horizons, a weak grasp of technological and business principles, and little desire to expand, many researchers have concluded that few small business owner-managers are either entrepreneurs or growth-oriented (Binks and Jennings, 1986; Storey, 1986b, 1994; Gray 1989, 1990; Stanworth and Gray, 1991). On the question of whether a growth in the number of the self-employed and small firm owners helps to change attitudes towards enterprises and entrepreneurs, there is strong evidence that this has not happened. Apart from the pattern of declining entrepreneurship since the mid-1980s, a survey of some 350 owners of small service businesses discovered that just over one-third of respondents were unable to explain what the term 'enterprise culture' meant to them, and that many of those who could use the phrases and concepts employed by the enterprise culture model felt that the notions did not apply to them. In other words, the very targets of enterprise culture policies basically felt alienated from the model and, in the words of the researchers (Curran and Blackburn, 1991: 27),

> the notion of the enterprise culture has clearly become reified in the minds of many respondents to assume the status of something which even when they discuss it, they feel has nothing to do with them, their economic experience or views. In a more extreme fashion, for many respondents it appears to be so outside their conceptions of themselves and their activities that it is literally beyond any comment at all.

Personal discussions with the researchers revealed that many of the small business owners understood the concepts of the enterprise culture perfectly clearly but felt that they applied to 'yuppies' and 'people in the City' rather than to themselves as active owners of small businesses. Consequently, the findings of British Social Attitudes (November 1990) should come as no surprise. During the 1980s, the enterprise culture appears to have made virtually no impact upon the broader public consciousness. If anything, seven years of enterprise culture policies, 1983–9, appear to have hardened attitudes both against cuts in government expenditure and against treating self-employment as a reasonable career. Over the seven years the proportion of people in favour of increased social spending leapt from under one-third (32 per cent) to well over one-half (56 per cent).

In 1983 just 5 per cent of employees were very seriously (12 per cent quite seriously) considering self-employment, compared with 70 per cent who took the idea 'not at all seriously'. By 1989, these percentages had hardly shifted – to 6 per cent 'seriously' (10 per cent 'quite seriously') and 73 per cent 'not at all seriously'. Therefore, there are strong reasons to doubt that personal business motivations can be manipulated collectively to serve the needs of public policy. Indeed, the implicit critique underlying the enterprise creation policy – that anti-entrepreneurial attitudes have been allowed to dominate social consciousness, leading to the demotivation of otherwise potential entrepreneurs – finds little support in the treatment of motivation in economic or psychological theory and less in the actual behaviour of the self-employed themselves or of small business managers. An influential study of small manufacturers in the north of England concluded that the probability of a start-up manufacturer employing 100 people within ten years was less than 0.5 per cent (Storey, 1986b). This suggests that it is virtually impossible to identify genuinely entrepreneurial firms at the start-up or early stages.

Despite the very small proportion of employees who claim to be actively seeking a self-employed career, Labour Force Surveys reveal that more than half (53 per cent) of new entrants to self-employment come from paid employment, with just 20 per cent entering from unemployment (and about 30 per cent from previous economic inactivity, such as students and women re-entering the workforce). This suggests that self-employment may well have an important role to play in the personal 'career paths' of certain groups of people but may not be an entrepreneurial end in itself. The upsurge of self-employment over the past decade seems to have been much more a function of economic restructuring. The formation of entrepreneurial small businesses appears to have been a function of actual opportunities in the British economy. In their comparative study of self-employment in Britain and Germany, where the entry to self-employment is much more regulated, Nigel Meager and his German colleagues (1992) found that economic restructuring and the contracting out of services had become new factors in the rise in self-employment as well as the traditional recruitment from the petite bourgeoisie. These different structural effects, as well as some cultural influences, explained most of the differences in the different patterns of growth in self-employment between the two economies.

In Germany, where there are fewer but larger small enterprises, more than 80 per cent of the new self-employed came from previous paid employment and just 6 per cent from unemployment. Their findings contrasted the *laissez-faire* approach of enterprise culture policies with the more regulated German approach, by pointing to the greater stability and higher survival rates of the German model despite the faster growth of self-employment in Britain. Their conclusion was that 'there is little or no evidence of the UK's self-employment growth having been fuelled by a major change in workforce attitudes towards self-employment and "enterprise"' (Meager *et al.*, 1992: 46).

The important point to note here is that active self-employment and entrepreneurial activity have always been and still remain very much the activity of a minority despite powerful attempts to introduce an enterprise culture. It is hard to avoid the conclusion that the tenets of the model run counter to most people's personal and work motivations, including the career motivations of most small enterprise owners. The Department of Employment (Hakim, 1989) found that the highest proportion (45 per cent) of the new self-employed cite as their main reason the desire to be *independent* in the sense of not being told what to do or whom to work for, rather than the chance to make their own business decisions. Roughly one-third mentioned various *push factors* (34 per cent), including unemployment, while a minority – less than one-quarter (22 per cent) – mentioned any other motive that could be construed as entrepreneurial. The findings of the surveys conducted for this book confirm the linkages between personal expectations, work motivation and actual performance (in terms of growth) among small firm owners of all sizes, with the clear indication that most small firm owners are and will remain very small because they want to for valid reasons of their own.

This means that less than 3 per cent of people entering the workforce during the 'enterprise culture years' were seeking to do so for entrepreneurial reasons – hardly a mark of success for the enterprise culture model. And, on the wider issue of economic development, there are few signs that the enterprise culture actually has delivered the goods. The growth of non-agricultural self-employment from 6.5 per cent of the working population in 1979 to roughly 13 per cent today is often cited as evidence that Britain is becoming more enterprising; but most of the new self-employed are part-time and fewer than one-quarter of all self-employed have employees (a *sine qua non* for the successful capitalist). Indeed, the trend during the 1980s showed a strong shift away from having employees, with sole-trading self-employment increasing from 59 per cent of all self-employed in 1980 to 74 per cent in 1990 (Creigh *et al.*, 1986; Hakim, 1988; Bannock and Daly, 1990). Larger small firms employing more than two dozen people offer the best prospects for economic growth and development, hence for sustained reduction in unemployment (Giannola, 1986; Storey and Johnson, 1987), yet they have declined in number under enterprise culture policies (Doyle and Gallagher, 1986; Bannock and Daly, 1990). Apart from specialist high-technology firms, which in any case suffer high turbulence and failure rates, there is little evidence that small firms account for more technological innovations than large firms. However, there is good evidence to suggest that larger firms are better placed to exploit such innovations, even though, taken as a whole, the entire new technology sector has actually declined over the enterprise culture years (Rothwell and Zegveld, 1982; Keeble, 1987; Oakey, 1987).

In a follow-up to his landmark study of attempts to develop an enterprise culture in the hostile environment of Cleveland, David Storey (together with Adam Strange) sums up the effects of the enterprise culture decade by concluding

> that the new firms established in the 1980s, although more numerous, are less likely to achieve significant growth than the new firms established during the 1970s. Many of the 1980s firms appear to have been established primarily for the 'lifestyle' benefits which business ownership provides. For almost half of new firm founders the prime lifestyle benefit is that of having a job at all.
>
> (Storey and Strange, 1992: 77)

This hardly accords with the high hopes of the enterprise culture in terms of wealth generation and innovation expressed by the Cabinet Office's scientific advisers or the Department of Employment deregulation White Paper (quoted in Chapter 2, p. 20). Indeed, now is the time to look more closely at those high hopes.

EVALUATION OF ENTERPRISE TRAINING

The Manpower Services Commission (MSC), which had responsibility for enterprise training in the mid-1980s, conducted internal assessments of the 1984/5 pilot courses for training in enterprise initiative. Six months after the end of the course, fewer than 60 per cent of the original start-up participants had started a business. However, for the existing small business participants on expansion courses, more than 80 per cent of the original participants were still operating their own business. There are few published figures on longer-term drop-out rates but research on similar courses suggests that non-completion and non-start-up present significant problems. Consequently, the quality and the focus of the training need to hit the mark if it is to make any impact on small business performance (Gray and Stanworth, 1985).

Figures provided in 1986 by the MSC to the Advisory Group on Enterprise Training (AGET), before it was disbanded in the middle of 1987, revealed that MSC courses for existing small businesses reached less than 1 per cent of firms registered in Britain. Even though the MSC planned a threefold expansion of its training provision for existing small firms, from

4,473 in 1985/6 to 13,121 in 1986/7, the new target figure was still less than 1 per cent of the estimated 1.4 million small firms in Britain. The large growth in the supply of a wide variety of small business training courses had not been matched by a similar flood of demand from small businesses. Most of the places on small business courses are taken up by the unemployed, the self-employed or newly started businesses. In fact, even on the MSC's projected figures for 1986/7, which saw more emphasis placed on courses for existing businesses, more than three-quarters (78 per cent) of almost 60,000 course places were for start-ups. In relation to the 160,000 new VAT registrations for that year, the MSC could claim, during the heyday of enterprise culture policies, to have trained more than one-quarter (28 per cent) of all start-ups in Britain if they all actually started and managed to establish their sales above the VAT threshold (an unlikely scenario).

Even though the total number of people on MSC courses in 1987/8 was around 105,000 (with just under one-half from already established businesses), this contact rate does not look so impressive when viewed in relation to the rapid growth of 1 million self-employed over the past decade or in relation to the 3 million people who were without work at that time in Britain. The poor participation rate, however, is not unexpected and is a feature of most small enterprise initiatives not just in Britain but in most of the European Union except, perhaps, Germany where the more formal approach and regulatory requirements generally lead to higher participation rates (Meager *et al.*, 1992).The usual reasons for low participation reported by small enterprise owners include lack of time, lack of appropriate courses or subject matter, inconvenient location and timing of training, lack of knowledge about what is on offer (information gaps), lack of resources and fear that trained staff or line managers will be poached by larger firms (Stanworth and Gray, 1991). These perceived and real barriers to training are felt most strongly by the smallest enterprises and the self-employed, the main targets of enterprise culture policy. The findings of the special 1988 survey conducted for the OU Business School by the SBRT revealed that firms below the twenty-five-employee mark have significantly more negative attitudes towards management training. The size effects on attitudes towards the benefits of business training, which have been a feature of a number of studies on small business management training, were clearly apparent. One-third (31 per cent) of the 1,468 responding firms employing fewer than five people stated that they had little or no interest in using training to boost their business performance.

These results are based on the total salaried workforce – both full-time and part-time. The size effects on attitudes towards business training are evident in the summary balance statistic (total positive respondents less total negative). Just under one-third of the respondents (30 per cent) were expanding in both sales turnover and staff. More than half (59 per cent) of these respondents were in favour of training. More than half (54 per cent) of those who

Table 4.5 Importance of training by firm workforce size, 1988

| Firm size (employees) | Positive | Attitudes towards training (% across row) | | Balance |
		Neutral	Negative	
1–4	28	41	31	−3
5–9	33	43	24	9
10–14	33	50	16	17
15–24	33	50	16	17
25–49	35	57	7	28
50–99	53	37	10	43

Source: Open University Business School.

had received no formal training themselves (36 per cent of the sample) believed that training would be useful for their business. A slightly higher proportion of those who had received training themselves also believed it would be useful in improving their business performance. Although cost factors and educational background clearly affect attitudes and decisions regarding training, it is also clear that there are strong structural effects at work reflected in clear regional and industrial differences. Firms in the distribution sector, providers of financial services and small manufacturers displayed the strongest interest.

It may be hard to make direct comparisons with other firms since, in fact, only a small proportion of the MSC trained start-ups registered for VAT. Interestingly, small firms on the longer-running MSC courses which apply stricter selection criteria in recruiting their participants appeared to survive and to perform better than other small firms. The MSC claimed an 80 per cent start-up rate with a less than 2 per cent failure rate after three years' trading for its New Enterprise Programme. An independent evaluation concluded that even with pessimistic assumptions the net training effects were positive (Johnson and Thomas, 1983). This bullish picture of the NEP firms was confirmed by a separate survey conducted by the Manchester Business School of more than one dozen NEP courses they had run over seven years, 1977–83 (Chisnall, 1986). More than half the respondents were breaking even within one year and by the end of the next year more than 80 per cent had passed the break-even point.

In 1985, in an effort to be more flexible and to meet small business training needs, the MSC introduced a part-time NEP called Firmstart. The Cranfield School of Management conducted a review of Firmstart courses in 1986–7 which found that the growth rates and arrival at break-even point did not differ significantly between firms which had and had not received training, but that the sales turnover and employment growth of the Firmstart firms were considerably higher (Saunders and Harries, 1987). Equally interesting is the Graduate Enterprise Programme (GEP), a sort of NEP for recent university graduates. Although the GEP firms are not big employers, their sales turnover appears to have grown fairly quickly and more than 85 per cent had passed break-even point within two years (Brown and Myers, 1987). Although these course evaluation studies suggested that clearly focused training does improve small business performance, the MSC was concerned that these targeted courses were too costly and began to withdraw its support. The government's preference for start-up courses – which were easier and cheaper to design and run (and which absorbed far more unemployment) – remained apparent despite evidence that existing businesses respond more usefully to training. This pressure to reduce unemployment rolls by boosting the growth of new firms and the expansion of existing ones led the MSC to measure enterprise training effectiveness by a crude accounting-type criterion – total cost of each course per participant – rather than by economic criteria such as total jobs created, impact of new firm on local economy, improvement to overall infrastructure, etc. Because it takes around four years for new firms to stabilise and find their feet, judgements based on economic criteria were felt to be too slow.

There is an immediate flaw in the enterprise training model in that most enterprise trainees are motivated by a need to avoid their own unemployment or to support a particular lifestyle rather than by a positive desire to start their own businesses. Most enterprise trainees were unemployed, compared with only around 22 per cent of all self-employed coming directly from unemployment (Hakim, 1989). Nearly half the participants on enterprise training courses (which included courses for existing businesses) in London during 1988–9 came from unemployment (Blythe *et al.*, 1989). Since 1981, an average of 10 per cent of the self-employed have left self-employment each year, of whom nearly half (45 per cent) return to being paid employees, but the drop-out rate is much higher for start-ups who have previously been unemployed (Campbell and Daly, 1992). This effect is reflected in the failure rate of enterprise trainees, although, in fact, they represent only a small proportion of new self-employed who generally share with existing small firm owners a deep suspicion of the benefits of training. For these and other reasons already discussed, the failure rate of new start-ups is very high (Ganguly, 1985) and there is little evidence, in either the USA or Britain, that enterprise training for start-ups has produced many dynamic new businesses or truly innovative business ideas (Vespers, 1982; Gray and Stanworth, 1986).

One major methodological problem seems to be that there are conflicting criteria for evaluating the success of most enterprise training courses. Generally, enterprise training outcome criteria are phrased in terms of new businesses started or new jobs created. There is a lively debate about the job-generating capacity of the small business sector but, as Table 4.3 revealed, job generation is clearly not an objective of growth-oriented entrepreneurial firms (though the creation of extra jobs may flow from their growth in sales or capacity).

The evaluation studies mentioned in this section show no significant performance or survival differences between all small firm owners and those who have received short-course enterprise training, though those who attended enterprise training courses lasting longer than six months did appear to benefit (Johnson and Thomas, 1983). However, it is costly to monitor the economic effects of enterprise training and neither the absolute formation rate nor the quality of start-ups is monitored systematically, and attitudinal shifts or skills improvement are mentioned rarely if at all. The administrators of enterprise policies seemed more interested in monitoring the number of enterprise trainees recruited by course providers. This is an easy criterion to monitor but not obviously related to the stated objectives of the training courses or of enterprise culture policies themselves but clearly related to a different policy objective, the reduction in unemployment figures.

There are also severe problems in identifying appropriate training course content. As we saw in Chapter 1, the main management needs of small businesses were identified by Bolton (1971) (listed on p. 10) and have not changed substantially since then. Basically, the educational needs of dynamic small enterprises fall into two broad categories. The first relates to expanding awareness of opportunities in the external environment, including new applications of technology, new markets, new methods for reaching markets and new ways of working with other firms, the better to overcome commercial challenges. The second category relates to the skills required for the efficient operation of the business: these must be mastered before the first category of more general business educational development can be tackled. It is the second strand that dominates enterprise training design. Almost all enterprise training courses cover the same core curriculum – basic marketing, basic financial accounts and how to obtain finance, personnel issues (usually connected with hiring and firing but also often including encouragement to employ others and to delegate some responsibilities to employees) and basic planning (usually the production of cashflow projections or even a fuller business plan). The more specific programmes generally cover these topics in more depth and add other topics of particular interest to the target group.

However, it has been suggested that this type of enterprise training, in concentrating on technical matters such as accounting, market analysis, planning and so on, actually stifles the creativity which could lead to genuine innovation (Binks and Jennings, 1986). Certainly, course response studies conducted by providers and development research studies frequently reveal other priorities among small firm owners themselves. In particular, conversations with course providers and trainees, as well as direct experience with enterprise training courses, suggest that there is a need for training in the interpersonal skills of organisation, control and negotiation. As this fits in with the capitalist's role and the social skills required of successful entrepreneurs, the inclusion of this type of training appears to have strong face validity but is rarely if ever included in enterprise training programmes.

The implication is that enterprise training programmes risk being over-focused on the management needs of small businesses as identified by 'experts', and do not pay sufficient attention to the needs as perceived by the entrepreneurs themselves (Carswell, 1987; Gray, 1988).

Finally, there are problems of course design and learning methodology. There are real problems in producing generic courses in response to the different particular needs of various individuals at different stages of their own career search processes and at different levels of business awareness. Indeed, even when a training structure is appropriate, the skills must be capable of being taught and must be relevant to business success. In terms of the stages of growth models discussed in Chapter 2 (pp. 22–6), there has to be a clearly definable outcome as a learning target. The trouble with enterprise training is that many of the entrepreneurial skills – such as the ability to unearth new sources of finance, to concoct new ideas, to smell a good deal, or to manage difficult customers or employees – are imprecise and often situation-specific while the basic skills needed to manage finance, marketing and personnel issues are easier to define and are being taught successfully every day.

However, addressing small business management needs is not sufficient. Enterprise training or other small business development support measures are only effective if small business owners and managers consciously want to acquire the skills. Therefore, enterprise support measures, including management training, have to meet both the needs and the wants of the target small enterprise owners and managers. In many ways, the training and support needs have been much easier for policy makers to target than the many different training wants expressed by small business owners. The training wants of entrepreneurs have been even harder to identify. Although there are evident differences in emphasis between industries and different-sized firms, small enterprise problems seem fairly consistent over time. A study conducted by Mary Carswell (1987), which compared the training needs of textile and engineering firms as subjectively perceived by the owner-managers themselves and as observed by consultants, found wide differences in perceptions. There were significant differences in the perceived need for financial and human resource management.

This mismatch between actual and perceived training needs – which certainly poses problems for people who design, deliver and market small business courses – may be due to relative inexperience or to low awareness of the importance of each management function. Significantly, expanding firms in SBRT surveys reveal stronger interest in training – in other words, a clearer perception of the factors limiting their growth which were also under their control – than static or contracting firms. The European Community study conducted by David Storey and Steve Johnson (1987) of small firms and job creation identified premises, finance, recruitment and training as the main problems of growing firms and noted several differences between EC regions. Many of these regional differences may reflect industry differences because of different concentrations of industries in different localities.

For instance, operations management and labour relations are problems for the hotel, catering and leisure industries while poor marketing and sales management hit small retailers (LBS, 1987).

Apart from the actual physical and organisational problems of expansion, growth-oriented entrepreneurial firms do not encounter substantially different problems from those of other small businesses but, to repeat the point made elsewhere in this book, their approach to these problems is likely to be different. The challenge to enterprise policy makers and small business management trainers increasingly becomes the need to convince reluctant or busy small business managers that training will help them. The question of the inconvenience and cost of most training programmes – if not in fees, then in lost time and production – has to be faced because small business managers are concerned more with issues of immediate survival than with the strategic overview (Gibb, 1983).

It may seem a commonplace but, to have any chance of success, enterprise training must be seen to fulfil needs that are perceived to be important by the owners themselves. There is little sign that this has happened. Despite the manifest need for effective small business managerial training, it is clear that the impact of training on the overall performance of the total small business sector has been fairly marginal. Training courses reach only a tiny fraction of new businesses or expanding existing businesses. Indeed, the actual response of small business owners and founders to government-supported enterprise training courses during the height of the enterprise culture 'crusade' confirms the irrelevance of such training to most of the targeted market sector. What may be an objective small business need is clearly not a subjectively held small business want. Yet, even though the survival rates of enterprise trainees who accept enterprise agency advice (just personal counselling usually) were double the norm for new businesses (Business in the Community, 1986), only a tiny fraction of Britain's small firms benefited from enterprise training. The vast majority of new start-ups do not use available small business assistance and only a minority – roughly one-quarter to one-third – of start-ups would like more specific advice or training if they could afford the time (Gray and Stanworth, 1986). However, there are now signs that this may be changing for existing small enterprises as a result of the introduction of Business Links, a one-stop source of development and training advice. Table 4.6 summarises responses to an SBRT survey of the final quarter of 1995 which probed small business recruitment and internal staff development practices.

The first point to note is that the firms with fewer than five employees are significantly different in their management and staff development attitudes and practice from larger SMEs. Even if they are excluded from a sample, however, the expected size effects remain clearly present. Firm size bears a direct relation with the provision of internal and external training courses, as also with allowing employees time off to pursue their own development. The 'other' category in Table 4.6 included consultancy and

Table 4.6 Sources of staff development by firm size, 1995 (column percentages)

	<5	5–9	10–14	15–24	25–49	50+	All
No response	24	7	6	3	7	9	(15)
No formal training	43	36	29	28	16	14	(36)
Internal training	9	20	36	29	48	51	(19)
External training	18	34	45	59	65	63	(32)
Time off	13	26	31	32	37	43	(22)
Other	5	5	2	4	3	6	(5)
Sample number	502	245	94	94	75	35	1,049
Sample (%)	(48)	(23)	(9)	(9)	(7)	(3)	(100)

Source: SBRT 11(4) (1995).

business advisers. A second point is that the survey also revealed strong industry differences, with business services being the most likely to provide some form of training, and transport and catering least likely to provide formal courses. Manufacturers and personal services were most likely to pay for externally provided training.

It is certainly not clear that all the firms reached by government-sponsored training courses actually benefited positively rather than merely attended. Most of the start-up programmes and courses for existing businesses are quite short, from a few hours to about one week, suggesting that mere attendance would not lead to many training benefits. It is clear from the above discussion that enterprise training has not delivered the attitudinal and behavioural changes that enterprise culture policy makers expected. Yet, before other enterprise culture initiatives are examined, it is worth pointing out that this entire initiative has been bedevilled by mixed, and not always compatible, objectives and by inappropriate performance criteria. Buried among the negative outcomes are more positive signals that well-designed and appropriate training initiatives which pay attention to considerations of quality rather than quantity may improve the management of small businesses, provided learning targets are appropriate and properly specified. Available evidence suggests that small business owners who wish to improve their performance are drawn to training (CBI, 1986). Only a tiny proportion of existing firms approach enterprise agencies, yet in the survey of assistance provided by enterprise agencies to small firms a high 31 per cent of surviving firms had received some form of training, although only 8 per cent had accepted training from an enterprise agency (Business in the Community, 1986). An evaluation of London Enterprise Programme (LEP) courses in 1979–84 revealed that as many as one in five (19 per cent) participants had previous business training, yet more than half (56 per cent) would be keen to attend specific follow-up training courses if run at convenient times (Gray and Stanworth, 1985). Indeed, there is strong evidence that successful training breeds interest in further training:

this suggests that there is scope for designing more suitable enterprise training, perhaps incorporating some of the ideas of McClelland's achievement motivation training (Gray and Stanworth, 1985; CBI, 1986). In an assessment of particular enterprise training courses which paid more attention to the cultural processes at work, Sally Caird (1990: 77) concluded that 'participants on enterprise courses perceive themselves to be more entrepreneurial following enterprise training. This is an interesting result because these training courses do not explicitly aim to develop the psychological characteristics of entrepreneurs.'

It is a doubly interesting conclusion because it exposes the shallowness of current enterprise training at a number of significant levels and perhaps reveals an important clue to the development of more effective enterprise training. A tremendous amount of time and money have been spent, in recent years, on publicising small business training and support measures. Despite that publicity and evidence that enterprise training can improve business performance, the response from small firms remains low and the inescapable conclusion is that small businesses either do not believe that training will satisfy their skills needs or that courses on offer do not merit their trust. Most importantly from the viewpoint of this book, there is virtually no evidence that enterprise training has increased significantly either the creation rate of new businesses or the stock of entrepreneurs in Britain. Even ambitious small businesses do not appear to be convinced that training offers them substantial benefits, especially if they are expanding (when their time is at a premium and disruption costs at their highest). It seems that unless training is seen to be of instrumental use, it is not valued. This may go some way towards explaining why enterprise training has achieved such a poor penetration of the small business sector. From the evidence presented here, the fundamental problem seems to lie with the attitudes of small business owners towards the present provision of enterprise training. This strongly suggests that this element of enterprise culture policies has missed its mark.

Pam Denicolo and Maureen Pope (1989: 2) outlined what appropriate enterprise training ought to be from a constructivist perspective:

Enterprise requires an approach to the curriculum which recognises how learners learn as opposed to how teachers teach in order to produce a work population which is able, *inter alia*, to

- be self directed
- develop personal learning plans and establish criteria for feasible learning objectives
- define and analyse problems with which they are not already familiar and show imagination and initiative in posing a range of solutions
- work in teams and exhibit a range of interpersonal skills appropriate to the world of work
- demonstrate skills of organisation and time management

 – show initiative and skills in obtaining information which is not normally available.

The implication for curricula appropriate to the above abilities is that emphasis is moved from product, or accumulation of knowledge, to **process** skills, learners being encouraged to move from a position of dependence on the teacher to one in which they take increasing responsibility for their own learning.

Whether or not this is a comprehensive or generally agreed outline of what training designed to encourage and develop enterprising behaviour should be about, its emphasis on self-organisation is clearly a major step towards the development of a key entrepreneurial skill. This model is, however, not that of most enterprise training provided through enterprise culture policies where the emphasis, as noted above, is on management skills. As early as 1968 Cole was suggesting that successful entrepreneurial development involved fitting the actions of small firm owners 'more closely to the requirements of the economy' – which does not exactly represent a people-centred approach. By the start of the enterprise culture period, Watkins (1983) could still justifiably complain that owner-managers were too close to their day-to-day problems, suffered from too narrow an educational and experience base and 'were inward looking and information oriented and lacked a clear business strategy'.

At the height of enterprise culture policies, Allan Gibb (1987: 2) was able to summarise the key differences in learning focus between the trainers and the entrepreneurs as:

Education focus on:	*Entrepreneurial focus on:*
The past	The future
Critical analysis	Creativity
Knowledge	Insight
Passive understanding	Active understanding
Absolute detachment	Emotional involvement
Manipulation of symbols	Manipulation of events
Written communication/neutrality	Personal communication/influence
Concept	Problem or opportunity

Towards the end of the enterprise culture decade, James Curran and John Stanworth (1989) first cited Gibb (1987) in pointing out that enterprise training courses 'stress order, rationality, predictability, tried and tested methods and the general depersonalisation of economic endeavour', but that these 'emphases appear difficult to integrate into the more charismatic approach of genuine entrepreneurs without damaging their special potential'. They then go on to point out that there is no real consensus on what management skills should be emphasised in enterprise training, that most enterprise training programmes are of too short a duration to have lasting educational effects and that they are very simplistic when confronted with the complexity involved in successfully managing a small firm. Curran and Stanworth conclude by stating that enterprise training in Britain during the 1980s has been under-resourced and under-researched in terms of identifying appropriate teaching objectives. In relation to one of the central enterprise culture policies, the Enterprise Allowance Scheme, it seems that no real attempt to identify the training needs of the unemployed was made as they faced, in many cases, the daunting prospect of starting their own businesses.

ENTERPRISE ALLOWANCE SCHEME

During the enterprise culture years, the flagship operation was the Enterprise Allowance Scheme (EAS), until responsibility for enterprise initiatives was devolved to the eighty or so Training and Enterprise Councils in England and Wales and some twenty-four Local Enterprise Companies in Scotland. Introduced on the supposition that unemployment benefits act as a disincentive to the unemployed to seek work, the EAS was designed as the main enterprise culture policy instrument for encouraging the unemployed to give up their 'dependency' on unemployment and related social benefits in exchange for limited support in setting up their own businesses. When the EAS was introduced in August 1983, unemployment benefits across all types of claimants averaged roughly £40 per week. To qualify for the scheme, applicants had to be between 16 and 64 years of age, to be unemployed or under notice of redundancy, to be actually receiving benefits, to have been unemployed for thirteen weeks (later reduced to eight weeks) and to have £1,000 to invest in their business. Originally, small business management training – as distinct from half-day 'awareness' sessions – was not part of the package and failure rates of firms started through the EAS were higher than national self-employment failure rates. In part, this may have been because most EAS firms were in 'low barrier-to-entry' industries and the EAS was initially introduced in regions of high unemployment (and, therefore, poor business prospects) but its adverse economic impact was not confined to the poor quality of businesses started under the scheme.

There is strong evidence that EAS firms (competing on price due to the EAS allowance) displaced existing small businesses and that those with the highest growth and survival rates would have started anyway, whether or not the EAS existed (Gray and Stanworth, 1986; Gray, 1990). Irrespective of the success or failure of the EAS, however, the justification for the scheme is questionable. Econometric analyses of historic fluctuations in unemployment rates and benefit levels provide little evidence to support the contention that significant numbers of unemployed avoid work because of fear of losing benefits (Ormerod and Worswick, 1982). It is true that two-thirds of the EAS participants had been receiving less in benefits than the EAS allowance but only one-third reported that this financial improvement was their principal motive for joining the scheme. Another third of participants stated that their main motivation was to avoid unemployment. Most significantly from the perspective of this book, only 18 per cent stated positively that their main motivation was to seek a career in self-employment: hardly a huge endorsement for enterprise culture policies (Gray and Stanworth, 1986; RBL, 1987).

A wide range of respected studies revealing the loss of both motivation and a sense of identity connected with non-temporary unemployment (Jahoda, 1979; Stokes and Cochrane, 1984) further undermines the rationale for the EAS. Even when they do seek informal self-employment in the black economy (which is dominated, in any case, by people in employment with second jobs), the unemployed are pushed into marginal, limited jobs and their lack of drive and initiative is apparent (Jahoda M, 1988). Fewer than half the EAS participants whose businesses have survived for three years or more had been unemployed longer than six months before entering the scheme, compared with 55 per cent of the non-survivors (RBL, 1987). The EAS does not now exist although schemes derived from it are operated by many of the eighty-two local TECs in England and Wales and the twenty-two LECs in Scotland, which were set up during 1990/1 to allow local business leaders to take over the training functions of the Department of Employment. During its phase as a unified policy instrument its record was mixed and its subsequent fragmentation is unlikely to have improved its success rate as a pathway into entrepreneurship for Britain's millions of unemployed.

Initially, it seemed that the EAS had been fairly successful not only in steering many unemployed into new self-employed careers but also in generating new jobs. By 1988/9, more than 100,000 applicants were being accepted each year and 350,000 unemployed had used the EAS to try their hand at self-employment. According to the Department of Employment, 65 per cent of those who completed their full EAS year by 1988/9 were still in business three years after starting their enterprise and for every 100 of these survivors, 114 additional jobs were created (Department of Employment, Written Reply, House of Commons, July 1988). On closer inspection, this central plank of enterprise culture policy is not so firm. During the period of the pilot scheme in 1982/3, 12.5 per cent did not complete the full year and in 1986 it was confirmed that 11.5 per cent of participants on the national scheme failed to complete the full EAS year. In 1989, the all-party House of Commons Public Accounts Committee expressed concern that half the businesses started under the half-billion pound Enterprise Allowance Scheme had failed within three years – considerably worse than the failure rates of VAT registered firms (see Table 3.2).

Consequently, the role of the EAS in reducing unemployment by boosting self-employment is not impressive. In any case, as already mentioned above, the unemployed account for less than 20 per cent of the new entrants to self-employment compared with more than 50 per cent from paid employment.

About one-third of the new self-employed – the proportions vary slightly from year to year – were previously economically inactive (Hakim, 1988). An analysis of EAS job generation is even more revealing. Three-quarters (74 per cent) of the additional jobs after three years were part-time. Furthermore, all the jobs were provided by less than one-quarter of the original EAS participants – approximately one-third (34 per cent) of the survivors after three years – and most of these only employed one extra person, part-time or full-time. Significantly, the people who took the EAS allowance but who intended to start anyway, even without support from the EAS (termed 'deadweights'), had higher survival rates, employed more people and earned more than other EAS participants. Many deadweights were unemployed for the bare minimum qualifying period and were more likely to have a history of previous (often recent) employment as opposed to longer-term unemployment or first-time entry into the labour market. Certainly, few, if any, of the deadweights were non-temporary (more than six months) unemployed, yet they accounted for around 50 per cent of the EAS intake and more than 70 per cent of three-year survivors. The deadweights are the true successes of the EAS but not of enterprise culture policies. By their own admission, they had not been constrained by any 'welfare benefits barrier' and the EAS was seen as just a source of cheap capital and not the reason for starting a business (Gray and Stanworth, 1986; RBL, 1987; Gray, 1990).

In fact, more than half the survivors (53 per cent) had been unemployed for less than six months before joining the EAS compared with 42 per cent of the non-survivors. Previous experience was also a significant factor in survival. Although roughly 70 per cent of EAS participants started a business in an area where they had previous experience, survivors were more likely to have worked in the same job. Survivors (28 per cent) were more likely to have previously held a managerial or professional position than non-survivors (19 per cent) and were significantly older. Educational and work experience profiles of the self-employed and small business owners are quite different from those of the unemployed, suggesting that there are significant differences between the two populations. Nearly three-quarters of people who have been unemployed for more than six months previously held unskilled or semi-skilled lower-level industrial occupations while fewer than 10 per cent were formerly in managerial or administrative posts (LMQR, July 1988). Virtually all EAS businesses were in the lower-growth sectors of the economy.

The psychological implications are also significant. The actual outcome of the EAS reveals not only the folly of relying on the encouraging of unrealistic expectations as a means of overcoming difficult socio-economic structural realities but also the power of cultural factors in determining occupational choices and subsequent work behaviour. Certainly, the removal of an alleged 'welfare benefits barrier' has not led to a rekindling of the spark of economic motivation or capital accumulation among the least experienced and most vulnerable members of society. Osipow (1983) and Furnham (1992) both point to cultural factors in vocational choice and it seems likely that the social representation of work and employment in general and of various occupational concepts in particular will differ markedly between regions of long-term decline and high unemployment and those of relatively stable prosperity. Personal interviews with EAS participants (Gray and Stanworth, 1986) indicate that they perceive their range of business opportunities to be limited and, given the precarious nature of their circumstances, it is not surprising that they seek to minimise their exposure to risk and failure in a rational though non-entrepreneurial fashion. Indeed, many report that they were cajoled into opting for the EAS by employment exchange officials and it may not have represented their own personal career choice. It is among those who intentionally sought their careers as small business owners that we need to look in order to see whether enterprise culture policies are capable of achieving their objectives.

These considerations, and those raised by critics concerned about the quality of small enterprises encouraged by enterprise culture policies, were not addressed adequately, if at all, during the enterprise culture period. However, they emerged in the period that followed as enterprise policies gave way to those that reflected a more managerial approach. This period can be said to have started with John Major's governments and seemed to reflect the ideas of Michael Heseltine (first as President of the Board of Trade, then as Deputy Prime Minister). With the spread of TECs and LECs, larger and more professionally managed Chambers of Commerce (and, more lately, mergers between the two) and finally the emergence of Business Links, supposedly as 'one-stop shops' to provide a single point for services to small enterprises, the issues of quality and responsiveness to the needs of local economies and communities were once again on the agenda. In the sense that this new structure had to be created, the original enterprise culture model could be seen as having failed. In the sense that the more managerial approach addressed issues raised by enterprise culture policies and continued to address similar objectives, the enterprise culture model can be seen as an interesting experiment and an earlier stage of a broader approach. Whatever our views on the actual outcome of the enterprise culture model, the failure of the particular policies does not necessarily invalidate the objective of encouraging more enterprising and effective management in Britain's small businesses or in the wider economy. However, the question of cultural change is clearly more complex and challenging than the original proponents of the enterprise culture model appear to have realised.

5 Alternative development models

Basically, the concept of *development* from an economic viewpoint means the growth of all goods and services in an economy, usually measured as rates of growth in Gross Domestic Product (GDP) or in Gross National Product (GNP, when nationally owned overseas goods and services are included). In advanced capitalist market economies such as Britain, policy objectives tend to be targeted not on development *per se* but on improved economic performance, usually through direct interventions in one or more of the three principal factor markets – capital, labour and land. Although the enterprise culture model also relies on policies in these areas, it is worth repeating that its distinguishing purpose – certainly in relation to the central concerns of this book – seems to be socio-political, and to a large extent psychological, rather than mainly economic.

ACHIEVEMENT MOTIVATION MODEL

Some of the conceptual difficulties of the enterprise culture model applied in Britain during the 1980s can be seen by comparing it with another widely known psychologically based economic development model. David McClelland (1961, 1968), who developed his achievement motivation model through analysing growth patterns of past societies, holds that societies favouring a spirit of independence produce citizens with strong desires to achieve success, and that economic growth is the result of the accumulation of many individual business successes. Structural factors are understated and the psychological determinants of economic behaviour are more strongly emphasised (1968: 74):

> Some wealth or leisure may be essential to development in other fields –
> the arts, politics, science, or war – but we need not insist on it. However,
> the question why some countries develop rapidly in the economic sphere
> at certain times and not at others is in itself of great interest, whatever its
> relation to other types of cultural growth. Usually, rapid economic
> growth has been explained in terms of 'external' factors – favourable
> opportunities for trade, unusual natural resources, or conquests that

have opened up new markets or produced internal political stability. But I am interested in the *internal* factors – in the values and motives men have that lead them to exploit opportunities, to take advantage of favourable trade conditions; in short, to shape their own destiny.

McClelland's preferred entrepreneurial motivator, the *need for achievement* (or nAch, as it is usually abbreviated) – 'a desire to do well, not so much for the sake of social recognition or prestige, but to attain an inner feeling of personal accomplishment' (1968: 76) – clearly indicates a psychologically based theory. McClelland himself summarised an alternative economic development theory: 'a society with a generally high level of n Achievement will produce more energetic entrepreneurs who, in turn, produce more rapid economic development' (1961: 205). However, the achievement motivation model springs from a more socially liberal base than the enterprise culture's rather narrow economic base. Referring to early capitalism when entrepreneurial activities were seen in perhaps their most dramatic form, McClelland is quite disparaging about the profit motive as the mainspring of entrepreneurial activity (1961: 233):

> Since businessmen had obviously shifted their concern from intrinsic worth to money worth, Marx and other economists endowed man with a psychological characteristic known as the 'profit motive'. The capitalist, at any rate, was pictured as being driven by greed, by the necessity of making money or keeping up his rate of profit.
>
> That such an assumption is a typical oversimplification of rational or armchair psychology has recently begun to be realised by historians in particular who have studied the lives of actual business entrepreneurs in the nineteenth century. Oddly enough, many of these men did not seem to be motivated by a desire for money as such or by what it would buy.

Clearly, the 'oversimplification' of the profit motive as a determinant of economic development has survived longer than McClelland believed and is a central pillar to enterprise culture ideology. Our research supports McClelland's views about the profit motive in relation to the behaviour of small firm owners in general, and undermines one of the central supports of the enterprise culture model, but also provides little support for the achievement motivation model. McClelland's attack on the profit motive as the determining factor of entrepreneurial behaviour, however, also suggests that a purely psychological explanation of a primarily economic phenomenon has obvious limitations, some of which McClelland was not entirely unaware of (1961: 63):

> a high level of n Achievement might predispose any society to vigorous activity. On the other hand, it may only do so in the West or under certain conditions such as free-enterprise capitalism, a certain type of open social structure or a relatively advanced level of technology.

McClelland correctly pointed out the need for economists to include psychological factors in their explanations and models of development and he also exposed their inadequate treatment of the psychological determinants of economic behaviour. For instance, he easily demonstrated the psychologically inadequate list of 'human motives' and 'human propensities' proposed by Rostow (to develop science; accept innovations; consume; have children; and, more closely aligned to the enterprise culture philosophy, to seek material advantage). McClelland was right to question most of these as psychological factors but failed to look more closely at many more interesting economic development theories for their psychological implications.

BEHAVIOURAL THEORIES OF THE FIRM

Most critics of the neo-classical model, especially those from within mainstream economics, tend to attack one or more of the basic assumptions such as perfect knowledge, rational choice and marginal-cost decision making without jettisoning the entire model. For instance, the key profit-maximisation assumption came under fire from the influential critic Herbert Simon (1957), who attacked the fundamental concept of *optimisation* itself. Accepting that human rationality is bounded, he suggested that individuals do not require full information to attain their levels of aspiration. Instead of applying marginal analysis in their decision making as maximisers, they are *satisficers* and are usually content with limited but sufficient information. Basically, this means that business owners may seek satisfactory profits based on average costs and revenues rather than theoretically maximum profits calculated on marginal costs. As well as challenging cherished neo-classical beliefs, Simon's views also place individual motivations, perceptions and cognitions on the agenda of economic research. Another influential critic of the neo-classical model, George Stigler (1961) also attacked the assumption that information is freely available and distributed fully to buyers and sellers. Stigler drew attention to the undisputed fact that there are costs associated with the acquisition of information – the costs of researching and gathering information, plus the costs of education and experience – and that neither information nor access to it is distributed equally between buyers and sellers.

This has led to a fruitful analysis of the impact of *informational asymmetries* on business and economic behaviour and the relative importance of *transaction costs* – the initial costs of arranging exchange between parties, plus the costs of monitoring and enforcing eventual contracts – and *production costs* in making business decisions (Stigler, 1961; Williamson, 1985; March, 1988; Binks and Vale, 1990; Eggertsson, 1990). Transactions costs analysis provides an explanation for *vertical disintegration*, mentioned earlier (p. 12). Fixed internal transactions costs, often governed by rigid employment contracts, have risen while the external variable costs of the same transactions, governed by flexible services contracts, have fallen. This is a powerful structural reason for the rise in small businesses and offers a useful method for developing an economic concept of entrepreneurial opportunity. Transactions costs include information costs and are clearly important to modern capitalist competition and the efficient accumulation of capital. It can be hypothesised that entrepreneurs have a deeper comprehension of these costs than non-entrepreneurs.

Some sixty years ago, Ronald Coase (1937) had already suggested that the economic role of the entrepreneur was to handle the uncertainty of transaction costs when the costs of relying on the (neo-classical) price mechanism was high, due to expensive information costs, complex contract arrangements or government-induced distortions. Coase also saw transactions costs as the clue to understanding the entrepreneur's approach to business growth. He argued that entrepreneurial firms would grow or contract in size depending on whether or not internal transaction costs equalled external market or contracted-out transaction costs. Coase viewed the entrepreneur's role as that of a troubleshooter, lubricator or even high-pressure valve for the normal economic process. The entrepreneur's key abilities are as an organiser and coordinator. Coase's views of the entrepreneur's economic function – an addition to Schumpeter's innovative or developmental functions – add elements of both dynamism and risk to the rather stolid evolutionary approach implied in the stage models discussed earlier. Indeed, the growing enterprise, as an organisation, offers an alternative internal system of resource allocation to that provided externally by the market. This view was fairly heretical according to neo-classical thinking which held that factor market prices were determined by the independent decisions of countless small individual firms as suppliers and customers (Marshall, 1920; Knight, 1921).

In many ways, this whole area of transaction costs analysis, agency theory and the existence of informational asymmetries offers a much more flexible avenue for economic ideas to be applied to the study of entrepreneurial behaviour than the usual emphasis on factor markets. It seems clear that the transaction costs involved in personally acquiring information for effective control and strategic decision making may be too high for most small enterprise owners. This may be why they are often seen as poor business managers or averse to training initiatives. This approach fits in with some of the theoretical points raised by influential economists such as Stigler (1961) and Simon (1955, 1956, 1957), and in relation to small firms by Frey and Heggli (1989), and Binks and Vale (1984, 1990). This provides some theoretical backing to the observation that entrepreneurs have more highly developed social skills in organising, motivating and directing others, plus sounder financial judgement in assessing the costs of transactions and the value of information, than most small enterprise managers. For instance, David Storey (1990) found that, as successful enterprises which sought finance through the Unlisted Security Market (USM) grew, their entrepreneurial owner's desire to develop further their social and communications skills (already well-developed) and acquire more information also grew compared with a matched sample of non-USM firms.

Satisficing (the acceptance of sub-maximal levels of satisfaction when the marginal cost of gaining the remaining satisfaction is higher than the extra satisfaction involved) is concerned with the perceptions and informational needs of owners as decision-makers operating well within their theoretically attainable profit-maximum capacities. The transactions costs involved in obtaining full profit-maximising information are much higher than those required for 'satisfactory' profits and it is impossible to anticipate all future transactions (Simon, 1957). Even though most of the supporting empirical evidence comes from larger firms, satisficing behaviour is clearly a strong feature of small firms. Research at the SBRT and the OUBS has identified a similar concept among growth-averse small firm owners. They are more likely to view the attainment of satisfaction as a legitimate alternative to continuous striving for business growth and success. The main thrust of the behavioural approach lies in demonstrating how necessarily imperfect information must bound the concept of rational choice and, consequently, how important to business and economic performance are the identification of actual informational needs, the access to that information and the efficiency of information processing. Individual perceptions and abilities, therefore, assume a crucial importance.

INTERVENTIONIST ECONOMIC DEVELOPMENT MODELS

In its non-interventionist rhetoric, the enterprise culture model differs markedly from the more *dirigiste* models pursued by previous post-war British (especially Labour), Scandinavian and French governments and the rather less overtly formal consensus policies followed in Germany and Japan. Earlier *demand-led* and *public welfare models*, in the traditions of John Maynard Keynes (1936), usually relied on interventions in the labour market (for example, the *high-wage/high-growth model* of the 1970s, found in Scandinavia) and in the land market mainly through public building and housing programmes. Governments consciously push openly (*dirigiste*) or behind the scenes for a consensus with the private sector in pursuing particular industrial objectives. Where these industrial objectives embrace the promotion of new technologies (because of their overall modernising influence as well as their market importance), it may be more appropriate to talk of a *technology-led model* of economic development, such as that of the Wilson governments in Britain. Certain sections of the United States, the newly industrialised countries (NICs) of Hongkong, Singapore, South Korea and Taiwan, and specialised countries like Switzerland and the Netherlands have included this model as part of their development strategies.

All these models laid heavy emphasis on macro-variables and a few even touched on the processes whereby the intervening micro- and personal variables were to achieve the macro-objectives. In general, however, there has been little attempt to link policy to a broader underlying development theory. The enterprise culture model is much more explicit about these linkages. Although these interventionist models are mostly philosophically distinct from the enterprise culture approach, they share the ultimate economic aim of improving the operation of the factor markets. They are also very structuralist and far less psychological in their approach than the enterprise culture model.

Leaving aside the now discredited *capital accumulation model* of the centrally planned command economies (which is still influential in the Third World despite the political-economic upheavals in eastern Europe), there is a variant of the *dirigiste* model which may be termed the *planned development model*, often advocated by institutionalist or managerial economists. This model, long-espoused by prominent economists such as J. Kenneth Galbraith (1969) and Gunnar Myrdal (1970) and many European Social Democrats, suggests that resources and policy priorities – including planning for non-work and leisure – can be allocated rationally through debate, discussion and agreed decision. According to this model, which also embraces social engineering but is the complete antithesis to the enterprise culture model, innovation and the implementation of new technologies are now such socially complex processes that they cannot be left to the vagaries of the market and must be politically planned and directed. Advocates of the enterprise culture model claim that planned development has not been particularly successful in promoting economic development, whatever its distributive merits in social development. Indeed, criticism of the planned approach has not only come from the right but also from many liberal and left critics who feel that development is rather too evolutionary and complicated a process to be left to the decisions of small groups of people, no matter how bright or how well intentioned. However, the more liberal proponents of planned development, such as Galbraith, would argue that more democratic and open systems have to be developed to allow for more widely participative planning.

Supporters of Fritz Schumacher, the author of the influential and pre-Thatcherite pro-small business book *Small Is Beautiful* (1973), would also claim to offer an alternative model in advocating a *people's skills model*. This model denies that development starts with goods, and asserts that the crucial factors for development and the release of local resources are the education, organisation and discipline of people. It could be argued, however, that this is merely placing stronger emphasis on labour market policies and is similar to recent demands in Britain for more effective management and technological skills training. Indeed, with their emphasis on personal empowerment and self-management, currently popular *human resource management* and *total quality management* models appear to owe much to Schumacher. A stronger alternative model – the *social structuralist model* – is offered by the veteran Marxist development sociologist André Gunder Frank, who views development as a function of the social and political structures and relationship of forces present in any particular society, but also places emphasis on a planned approach that addresses local needs and empowers people through collective actions.

In the modern world, the determining structures also reflect the influences of international forces. This means that the development of small businesses in an advanced capitalist market economy will ultimately depend on the needs and requirements of the large, mainly multinational, providers and users of capital and not on the personal desires of individual 'entrepreneurs'. If a structuralist approach – not necessarily Frank's (many of the *dirigiste* or corporatist models have strong structuralist elements) – provides much of the explanation for individual entrepreneurial success, the enterprise culture model of seeking to encourage entrepreneurial behaviour through altering personal career motivation will be seriously undermined. Needless to say, the enterprise culture model – with its emphasis on individual motivation and behaviour and its reliance on government cajoling to alter attitudes – is not in the least structuralist and completely rejects the notion that social structure influences economic behaviour ('there is no such thing as society, only individuals or families!').

This is not to say that government policy from the mid-1980s ignored the socio-political structure of Britain – industrial relations legislation and monetarist policy had precisely that in view – but that the enterprise culture component of government policy is decidedly non-structuralist. The view that economic growth depends mainly on individual effort is not new. Weber's (1930) notion of the *Protestant work ethic*, often applied with suitably watered-down religious nuance to analysing the success of Japan and other economies, essentially perceives a nation's economic prosperity as the reward of the sober, hard toil of its citizens. It is significant that Frank explicitly criticises Joseph Schumpeter's emphasis on individual entrepreneurs, as well as David McClelland's achievement motivation model. Frank feels that the scope and complexities of socio-political development are too broad to be adequately explained by limited micro-theories, especially those that rely on individual motivations which have been mainly determined by previous (cultural and infantile) social realities (Cockcroft *et al.*, 1972). In Frank's view, it is mainly *present* social reality that determines economic behaviour and development (Frank, 1978) though, he would not cavil at McClelland's view that lack of personal and political autonomy stifles development. However, Frank, as a Marxist, strongly believes that development springs from power and social relations between groups of economic actors.

MARX AND THE ENTREPRENEUR

Given the inefficient and repressive command economies that developed in his name and then collapsed so spectacularly in the early 1990s, it may seem strange to link Marx to a discussion on enterprise development. Marx, however, shared with marketing theorists and advertising executives (and most modern economists) the belief that it is *consumption* driven by the needs of individuals that defines the *use* of goods and services and also 'creates the need for *new* production. . . . Consumption creates the motive for production' (Marx, 1973: 91). In a view that strikes a note with Maslow's (1954) *hierarchy of needs*, Marx felt that human beings value their own independence and that workers are motivated to give up their personal independence and sell their labour to capitalists only in order to satisfy their basic need for survival. Capitalists are in a position to pursue their own self-interests independently, although, to be successful, they will need to meet consumers' needs more effectively than their competitors.

Marx, with his aim of revealing the general determining laws and consequences of capital accumulation, had no place in his analysis for particular phenomena such as individual entrepreneurs responding to unique situations, though he occasionally used the term 'entrepreneur' in the context of situations where the relationship between the capitalist and workers was direct and personal, and occasionally in the French meaning of 'impressario' (Marx, 1969). Nevertheless, despite Marx's avoidance of individualistic explanations, his description of the skills deployed by successful capitalists in extracting *surplus value* goes straight to the heart of entrepreneurial business behaviour. Indeed, in outlining the 'counteracting influences' successful capitalists use to delay the full effects of inevitable crises of overproduction, Marx provides a brilliant model for ideal entrepreneurial behaviour. Schumpeter (1934, 1942), in his pioneering analysis of the entrepreneurial function, was particularly influenced by Marx's description of the role of 'technology advances' and the tendency for capital to seek more efficient extractors of surplus value.

Although Marx clearly stated that his prime analytic focus was *capital* and its accumulation, he was equally clear that capital has no power without human direction even though it need not attach to any particular individual. Neither capital nor labour should be idealised and Marx hinted that he did not fully agree with the old socialist adage: 'we need capital but not the capitalist'. There are three points worth considering. First, Marx felt that human actions are determined by personal circumstances and the immediate situation rather than by idealised personality characteristics. However, his recognition that individuals respond with conscious intention to the ups and downs of capitalist development and to their own economic circumstances also refutes the notion that he was a simple *social determinist*. The second point is that occupational behaviour, including the entrepreneur's, flows from the individual's role in the capital accumulation process rather than from specific individual qualities. Capital is seen not only as the material basis of production but also as the source of power and choice. The third point, which flows from the first two, is that social class is underpinned by the social relations of work and that social mobility depends greatly on an individual's relationship to capital (a notion to which Schumpeter was drawn as the prime motivator of the entrepreneur).

Marx examined the roots of success in capitalist enterprise, such as power based on *property relations* (a technical term referring to individuals' rights to make use of all their resources – not just land or premises – in any legal way), access to capital, an eye for profitable or emerging markets and an ability to organise other people. He defined growth in terms of capital accumulation and placed great emphasis on the tendency for surplus value (profits derived from surplus labour power) to accrue to capital. However, Marx also believed – a point noted by Schumpeter – that the tendency of capital to flow to new areas giving better returns on capital would continuously create crises for older firms and opportunities for new firms. At the micro level of individual capitalists, especially in smaller enterprises, this implies continual movement in and out of the capitalist classes and a great deal of social uncertainty.

The aim of the capitalist is to accumulate capital which represents not only wealth but also *power* – not a mystic concept but derived from the property rights attached to capital. As capital accumulates through the extraction of surplus value as profits (or rent, interest and dividends), Marx clearly endorsed the view that profit maximisation should be the goal of successful business owners (these can be taken to include entrepreneurs). Indeed, he defines Smith's concept of productive labour as that which augments capital (1973: 307n). It is this process of extraction of surplus value – essentially the product of surplus labour – that defines the capitalist mode of production. The key to the process – and to the social development of capitalism – lies in the property rights attached to capital giving the owner of capital the right to control and organise work patterns. Psychologically, this implies well-developed social skills on the part of successful capitalists (entrepreneurs). Although generally hostile to Marxist concepts, leading post-war entrepreneurial theorists in the United States recognised this. Norman Smith (1967) based his definition of the entrepreneur on economic historian Arthur Cole's (1949) conception of the entrepreneur as 'an individual who initiates, maintains and aggrandises a social institution which produces economic goods and has, as its manifest goal, profit making'.

Marx recognised the sense of property, independence and personal satisfaction in self-employment, or *handicraft labour* as he often called it (1964: 98), but argued strongly that self-exploitation or earning a living through selling a personal skill as an individual is quite different from capitalist exploitation or accumulation. This reflects our own distinction between the self-employed and small enterprises. His comparison of piano players with piano makers (1973: 305), a Milton labouring for love to write *Paradise Lost* with 'hacks employed to write penny-dreadfuls or popular encyclopaedias' (1969: Part I, 401), makes it clear that he would have regarded most of Britain's new self-employed as *economically non-productive* workers, exchanging their labour for revenue without reproducing capital. Productive labour is used to create capital but traders selling commodities or skilled tradespeople selling their own labour as commodities are merely receiving revenue for the use of goods or services – often at a fixed price. The basic distinctions made in this book between the self-employed and small enterprises were already of clear value to Marx last century when he contrasted the self-employed singer/song writer with the small music publishing house as a productive enterprise (Marx, 1969: 401). The distinction is crucial because the bulk of the self-employed are engaged in self-rewarding but economically non-productive labour, only a minority exploit productive labour and even fewer, the entrepreneurial self-employed, are efficient exploiters of productive labour.

Consequently, even though recession and alienation produce a constant stream of new self-employed, these new recruits to the class of artisans, non-productive individual labour and small units of family production do not provide a good breeding ground for new entrepreneurs. Those who survive will join the existing stock of pre-capitalist groupings with their own traditions of independence – artisans, skilled crafts workers, hawkers, stall traders, small farmers, itinerant labourers and so on – who are likely to be equally repelled by the threat to their property rights posed by capitalism and by proletarian collectivism. They are unlikely to be a fertile source of new entrepreneurial capitalists.

Following Marx's analysis of the workings of capitalism, it is clear that the entrepreneurs whom enterprise culture policies sought to encourage are in fact new capitalists who act as poles for new capital investment. The stated aim of the policies, and perhaps the understanding of policy administrators and many voters, is an enterprise culture with newly opened doors for *individual* opportunity but the real political-economic aim is reinvigorated capitalism – a contradiction which may be difficult to resolve despite the centrality of *individualism* to the capitalist ideology. Enterprise culture policies appear to be designed more for sustaining capitalism's 'reserve army of labour' (pre-capitalist remnants, blue-collar unemployed and the lumpen proletariat) and the distressed 'petite bourgeoisie' (the self-employed, white-collar unemployed and small business owners) than for encouraging new capitalists.

In essence, capitalism started with workers selling their labour to a capitalist as the owner of capital (premises, equipment, money) in exchange for a daily money wage sufficient to cover their daily needs. Smith, who regarded wages, profits and rent as the appropriate monetary rewards for the three factors of production (labour, capital and land), had shown that the division of labour enables capitalists to improve productivity markedly and take their return on capital as profits. Marx agreed that the division of labour would boost productivity and profits but felt that Smith's description of profit as the monetary reward for capital ignored the power of property relations. Money – the earliest form of *commercial capital* as the means of exchange and wealth storage – becomes the 'material representation of general wealth' (1973: 233) and the means for realising (*valorising*) surplus value as capital to be reinvested in accumulating further capital, a circulation of capital accumulation and deployment (investment as fixed capital or financial capital).

As capitalism develops, the process of social specialisation of labour and extraction of surplus value is intensified in existing areas (leading to increased competition between capitalists) and extended to areas previously untouched by capitalist modes of production (i.e. entrepreneurial opportunity). The process of capital accumulation, however, is neither inevitable nor continuous. As more machines are bought, the labour from which the surplus value is extracted falls as a proportion of the total labour–capital mix, so that the overall return on total (expanded) capital falls. At the same time, competition between capitalists leads to the use of increasingly efficient machines and organisational methods. Efficient capitalists attract capital away from the less efficient who nevertheless continue to produce until their costs rise above market prices or the market is flooded with unsold goods (crisis of overproduction). However, it should be stated that Marx himself saw capitalism as essentially a big business phenomenon. Apart from some discussion of pre-capitalist formations and unorganised artisanal modes of work (roughly corresponding to today's self-employed skilled tradesmen), Marx had virtually nothing to say about small businesses or entrepreneurs. He believed – incorrectly as it has turned out so far – that fierce competition and the tendency towards concentration among larger firms would eventually leave no space for small firms.

The concept of *alienation* is very powerful, the starting point for workers to develop a separate class consciousness, the basis for much of Marx's political analysis. The concept has been further developed in modern times to explain, among other things, absenteeism, poor productivity, opting out of 'the system' and the marginalisation of certain groups. It is of particular interest to us because of the link that the enterprise culture model makes between the unemployed and the self-employed, and because of the separateness and sense of autonomy that many small enterprise owners feel. Marx did not invent the concept of classes and saw them as only historical if rather long-term social formations reflecting dominant modes of production. Consequently, although collectivism may be the hallmark of working-class consciousness, individualism and anti-collectivist tendencies will always be present – especially among non-production workers or in situations where the process of proletarianisation is incomplete (new industries, first generation workers, etc.). Faced with a dominant individualistic capitalist class ideology, self-employment could provide a reasonable voluntary exit route from alienation for capable individual workers, technical and white-collar workers or those with property links not yet severed by capitalism (or, more likely in times of capitalist crises, an involuntary route).

In the main, workers reacting against alienation would be driven towards re-establishing their own property rights (*independence*) and covering their own 'costs of reproduction', but they would not necessarily be keen on using property relations to accumulate capital through the exploitation of surplus labour. In fact, alienation is more likely to produce a strong rejection of the capitalist mode of production and an avoidance of capitalist production relations. As already mentioned, this is reflected in the strength of independence as the main self-employed career motivation, their setting of mainly non-commercial business objectives and the strong tendency for self-employment to run in families. More than 80 per cent of Britain's 1,248,000 new self-employed during 1981–9 were individual crafts or labour-only subcontractors with no employees and half the new entrants came directly from employment, while only one-third who left self-employment returned to work as employees (Daly, 1991). This is persuasive if not conclusive evidence of the effects of alienation. The growth of alternative lifestyle communities, workers' co-operatives and even some advanced workers' participation schemes may be seen as products of the same forces.

If the effects of proletarianisation are unlikely to create many entrepreneurs, the intensification of capitalist competition, especially the process of concentration that we have already discussed, is a better candidate for creating entrepreneurial opportunities. As already mentioned, Marx felt that the twin effects of competition and concentration would, through economies of scale, eventually squeeze out smaller firms. However, he also felt that the same pressures would lead to periodic crises of overproduction which would result in widespread restructuring, with capital flowing from older areas of the economy towards newer areas where returns on capital would be much higher. This cyclic process inevitably creates fresh entrepreneurial opportunities for new or previously small capitalists to expand, or for failed capitalists to start afresh. Consequently, apart from technological innovation and the application of capitalist methods to new areas, entrepreneurial scope must also exist in new methods of organisation to facilitate the extraction of surplus value.

Marx rejected the argument that the capitalists' profits were their due 'wages' for accepting risk and organising labour and capital on the grounds of the unequal relations between workers and capitalists. Indeed, this inequality is compounded by the fact that a part of the workers' surplus labour appropriated by the capitalist pays for supervisors, administrators and internal support services (representing both transformed capital and another source of surplus labour). However, organisational skills are now to the fore, with technology allowing far more social specialisation of labour than in Marx's day. There has been a steady increase in the rate at which internal service relations within firms are being transformed into external contractual relations (vertical disintegration). This has led to two distinct but related phenomena. On the one hand, large, older capitalist formations have been able to sell off areas of their operations where the return on capital was below average. At one stroke, they have improved the return on capital of the parent organisation while exchanging the dead fixed capital in the sold operation for liquid investment capital (again, at higher than average rates of return). On the other hand, other capitalists see some of the sold-off operations as representing an even better opportunity for capital investment (management buy-outs were by far the largest area of investment for British venture capitalists during the heyday of enterprise culture policies).

These trends, plus the need for the capitalist class to reproduce itself as a class against the pressures of concentration, highlight the importance for the structural development of capitalism of capital investment and the entry of innovative new firms (entrepreneurs). There is a strong case for arguing that this is the position the British economy finds itself in today. In Marxist terms, therefore, there is little support for the basic tenets or the thrust of enterprise culture policies as a capitalist development strategy. From the perspective of this book, however, a useful picture of the dynamic, social and uneven nature of the process of capital accumulation, and a number of interesting points, emerge from the above thumbnail sketch of Marxist theory. Perhaps the most interesting is that the entrepreneur's power to employ productive labour and accumulate capital ultimately derives from the ownership of property: this implies that entrepreneurs are likely to come from or to have become part of the property-owning classes.

However, even armed with the power of property in their capital, successful capitalists – especially entrepreneurs starting with comparatively little capital – must have an above-average technical awareness of the product or service they intend to offer, plus strong skills to control the forces created by the process: marketing skills to introduce competitive products and methods to new markets; financial skills to recognise the new areas yielding higher returns on capital investment; and, in particular, organisational skills to combine labour and capital so as to extract surplus value with maximum efficiency. Marx's analysis of capitalism provides clear criteria for assessing the performance of entrepreneurs as successful capitalists.

The importance of the socio-economic structure at both the psychological and practical levels is apparent. Marx's dictum that 'men know society because they produce it' anticipates the *social constructivist* approach: social relations, culture, class and so on spring from agreed understandings of social realities which shape subsequent understanding and interpretation of everyday events. Fine (1975: 15) remarked that Marx believed that 'far from man's consciousness dominating his life and existence, it was man himself who determined his consciousness'. However, individual and social consciousness can only be understood 'in relation to man's historical, social and material situation'. From this position, therefore, the whole notion of attempting to graft an idealised 'enterprise culture' onto an existing material situation and economic structure becomes an absurdity.

Marx's focus on the effects of current material reality, rather than individualistic explanations, to explain economic behaviour has supplied far more useful concepts – property relations, social specialisation of labour, alienation and so on – for analysing small business and entrepreneurial behaviour than the unidimensional (but operationally loose) concept of self-interest. As for his belief that history was against small business, it is well to be reminded that Marx insisted that analysis be grounded in its appropriate historical epoch. Marx was writing during the period of developing capitalism when large-scale enterprises were beginning to dominate all sectors of the economy. His lack of enthusiasm for small business may be no more than a reflection of the dominant trends in capitalist development at that time. It is worth noting, however, that there is still little evidence to suggest that small firms have taken over as the most efficient accumulators of capital or that the rate of concentration has slowed down.

After the initial crisis of restructuring in Britain, Europe and elsewhere in the industrialised world, the 1980s saw near record numbers of mergers, acquisitions and takeovers mainly seeking to increase market share. However, it is clear that the nature and techniques of capital accumulation have evolved considerably since the last century and that the socio-economic role of the neo-capitalists which enterprise culture policies are attempting to foster need not necessarily resemble in appearance, or even in the precise content of their role, the new capitalists of Marx's day. Nevertheless, as Enzo Mingione reminds us (1991), in his comprehensive treatment of the changes and forces affecting economic and social life across a range of classes and societies at different stages of development, Marx's insights into the workings of capitalism were brilliant but stopped short at the point where he established the case for accepting the exploitative nature of the process. It is left to others to develop some of the more interesting points, such as those we have just considered, that he unearthed on the way. One of these people was Joseph Schumpeter who developed the most complete theory of entrepreneurial development, one that has great relevance to the enterprise culture debate.

SCHUMPETER'S THEORY OF THE ENTREPRENEUR

Undeterred by the demands of classical economists for neat orderly models, the Austrian economist Joseph Schumpeter (1934) placed the entrepreneur at the centre of his theory of economic development. Following the earlier concept introduced by Say, Schumpeter defined the entrepreneur simply as someone who acts as an agent of change by bringing into existence a '*new* combination of the means of production'. New combinations include process, product and organisational innovations. The means of production include capital, equipment, premises, raw materials, labour and presumably, in recent times, information. The act of combining the means of production implies both organisational skills and intentionality, as well as, by implication, the ability to spot more efficient combinations among the production possibility set.

Apart from accepting a determining role for individual motivation and behaviour in the process of economic development, Schumpeter very clearly departed from neo-classical economics in assigning the central role in economic development to the entrepreneurial function. According to his model, technological changes are transmitted into and transform the economy as a result of individual entrepreneurs perceiving new production and market opportunities, usually on the basis of some new application of technology. Overall, the pattern of economic development would follow a Kondratieff-type cycle of new technological development – jerky at first, followed by seemingly smooth growth, and finally a smaller number of mainly minor changes. Modern management theory tends to be in favour of incremental changes but Schumpeter believed that changes were bound to be discontinuous and uneven because they are based on individual entrepreneurial perceptions and implementation (Vale and Binks, 1990). The discontinuity of these changes has the effect of pushing the economy into disequilibrium, thus creating opportunities for entrepreneurs with swift and flexible reactions but making it difficult for other entrepreneurs to plan future innovations (Bellofiore, 1985). The motivation for both types of entrepreneur to overcome the barriers of economic pressure and uncertainty, according to Schumpeter, resulted from the prospects of upward social mobility into the capitalist class. However, it was not for their supposed social ambitions but for their role in introducing innovations and for improving overall economic efficiency that Schumpeter placed entrepreneurs at the centre of economic development. He felt that there were basically five types of innovation:

1 the introduction of new products or services;
2 new methods of production;
3 developing new markets;
4 identifying new sources of supply;
5 new forms of organisation.

Nowadays, new methods of gathering market information, financing and distribution would also be regarded as innovations. Obviously, Schumpeter's conception of the entrepreneur process is also social in that it involves the combining of the means of production, which include labour, but the central feature of his theory is that entrepreneurship is the vehicle for the diffusion of technology through innovation. Therefore, mere growth – which could passively reflect altered external circumstances or chance – would not be sufficient to count as entrepreneurial. An entrepreneurial growth in profits has to result from intended actions on the part of the entrepreneur in response to a new perception of the production possibility set.

Schumpeter's model provides a precise role for the entrepreneur and clear criteria for assessing entrepreneurial behaviour. Although it is sometimes difficult to decide in practice whether some production plan combinations are actually new (many firms replicate similar combinations in new environments, some adopt only minor changes, some adopt a new management style without changing the input–output combinations very radically and others grow because of external or chance factors), intentional growth is a more than reasonable proxy. Certainly, Schumpeter's approach has provided a valuable theoretical footing for subsequent entrepreneurial research. For instance, his fellow Austrian Israel Kirzner (1973) also emphasised the superior ability of the entrepreneur to perceive new possibilities for recombining the factors of production. Later, Kirzner (1982) suggested that entrepreneurs excel at identifying market opportunities and at producing new economic ideas. Baumol (1968), on the other hand, stressed the need for the entrepreneur to gain control over the productive inputs necessary to implement new production plans. The influential Science Policy Research Unit at Sussex University consciously pursued a Schumpeterian technological cycle model of innovation (Freeman, 1974). More recently, Davidsson (1989b), having conducted a review of definitions, concluded that the entrepreneur is one who takes active steps to seek change even though other people may create the ideas or bear the financial risk.

To return briefly to earlier discussions on risk, it is interesting to note that the propensity to take risks is not a necessary entrepreneurial characteristic according to Schumpeter. Instead, capitalists provide capital for the means of production and credit (including risk capital) and assume the role of primary risk-takers. Kirzner (1973) also emphasised the difference between the roles of the entrepreneur and the capitalist by asserting that entrepreneurs did not need to own capital in order to make productive use of it. This split between the entrepreneurial function and the source of capital (as investment finance seeking higher returns on capital) follows the distinction made earlier by Marx and reflects current agency theory (see Chapter 6) where managers can occupy similar positions to entrepreneurs in relation to capital.

However, there is nothing to preclude the entrepreneur from also being a venture capitalist and occupying two roles. Indeed, founders are also key or sole investors in most new small enterprises although the risk is often actually held by a bank. The crucial point is that it is the entrepreneur as innovator, constantly seeking benefits through change and therefore constantly seeking change, who is the key to economic progress. It is very important to note that Schumpeter did not consider line or even top managers who combine the means of production in a routine fashion on a regular basis to be entrepreneurs. He was prepared to accept that they may have been entrepreneurial earlier in their careers but he remarked that it was quite common for entrepreneurs to settle for a more routine life once they had attained their original goals. Some support for his view has been found in subsequent psychological and sociological research (Brockhaus, 1980; Chell, 1985), including our own studies discussed at various points in this book (Gray, 1992b). Schumpeter's approach is important because it provides clear criteria for identifying entrepreneurial behaviour, highlights the importance of personal motivation, and introduces the idea that personal motivations can change over time or as original objectives are satisfied. In particular, his linking of economic and business behaviour to the cultural and personal motives that influence entrepreneurs to enter the capitalist class from more dominated or alienated classes provides food for thought in relation to current enterprise development approaches.

6   The importance of culture

In general, the study of enterprises and business behaviour has been the province of economic theory at both the micro level within firms and the macro level within the economy. Psychology, sociology and anthropology, however, also provide valuable inputs into management theory and the study of organisational behaviour. These academic disciplines throw light on an increasingly important area – the effects of cultural influences on personal and corporate behaviour.

BUSINESS AND CULTURE

Recent years have seen an increasing awareness of the importance of cultural influences inside organisations as a determinant of individual and group behaviour within and between organisations. Corporate cultures can be characterised in a number of ways. For instance, Deal and Kennedy (1982) use the two dimensions of the degree of risk and speed of feedback to produce a four-classification model of corporate cultures: 'tough guy', longterm, 'work hard/play hard' and process cultures. Charles Handy (1985) talks about power, role, task and person cultures. In the corporate context, the concept of culture generally links behaviour, norms and performance. The Dutch social psychologist Geert Hofstede (1980) dominates the field of cultural influences in business and management in different societies, though his findings are also by no means uncontroversial (especially in any application to small firms). Following an intensive study of work behaviour and norms of organisational behaviour in large organisations in most industrialised economies, Hofstede identified a four-dimension framework for comparing business cultures. Later, following validation studies of the framework in China (Hofstede, 1991), a fifth dimension was added:

power/distance – the psychological distance between hierarchical superiors and subordinates;
uncertainty/avoidance – the need for direction and order in the face of innovation and novelty;

individualism/collectivism – the relative importance a culture places on individual effort as opposed to collectivist and group-centred endeavour;
masculinity/femininity – this really contrasts task- and performance-orientation, usually measured by money and material gain, and includes 'quality of life' issues as well as concern for others and for the environment;
short-term/long-term orientation – this contrasts an immediate concern for maintaining social traditions and status with a longer-term perspective involving deferred gratification, saving and adaptation of traditions to current and likely structural changes.

We will discuss Hofstede's concepts at the level of individual psychology later. However, it is worth noting here that the masculinity/femininity dimension reflects McClelland's observations about the early development of achievement motivation. It is an unfortunate label since the male–female divide is only evident in 'masculine' cultures, and even there only weakly. Indeed, as German sociologist Ulrich Beck (1992) has observed, there is a growing shift away from the 'masculine' model towards 'feminine' concerns; this means Hofstede's concepts may now be less applicable. Nevertheless, his cultural maps and five-dimension framework, based on an analysis of the corporate cultures of large firms in different societies, provoke interesting discussions. Theoretically, Hofstede re-emphasises the social role that national cultures play in influencing different occupational and industry subcultures as well as individual behaviour and career choice. If the concept of organisational cultural norms does hold true nationally, then it might be expected that certain management styles and conventions of commercial conduct would predominate in firms of all sizes. Where those cultural norms do not reflect the requirements of modern capitalist development, it may be that entrepreneurs will tend to be aberrant outsiders, as described by Weber (1930) and Kets de Vries (1977).

Hofstede's approach has produced some interesting findings. At the end of the 1970s, just before the inception of enterprise culture policies, Hofstede identified Britain as a central member of the 'Anglo' group which also consisted of Australia, Canada, Ireland, New Zealand and the United States. The characteristics of this group in terms of average management styles were low psychological power distance (that is, little formal distance between hierarchical levels), low uncertainty avoidance, high individualism and high masculinity. By contrast, 'Latin' groups had high power distances and high uncertainty avoidance. Japan also had high uncertainty avoidance but medium power distances and medium individualism which it shared with the 'Germanic' group. The Germanic group shared with the 'Anglo' group a low power distance. While not too much should be read into these reported cultural differences because they only represent average scores (with wide variances in some cases) concerning the behaviour of corporate executives, it is interesting that the strong individualism of enterprise culture policies was already clearly part of the culture of the dominant class in Britain. These types of national differences in business styles and attitudes and the more individualistic approach of British firms were still evident in more recent European studies (Haahti, 1993). Beck (1992) can point in Germany to a new 'societalising' tendency that is beginning to counter the effects of a pervasive 'individualisation' process of advanced capitalism (and can point to features of modern German society that are also apparent in Britain). However, observation suggests that new forms of collectivist behaviour in business are not so advanced in Britain.

Even though there are some methodological problems concerning the use of the same concept to discuss organisational behaviour in different societies or in different parts of the same society or economy (Chell and Adam, 1994), it is the behaviour of certain sections or milieux of our society that concerns us here. And it is clear that the non-economic social sciences also offer insights into what role the promotion of an enterprise culture may play in the development of entrepreneurial businesses or, conversely, what role cultural factors in modern Britain may play in limiting the business development of enterprise trainees. One of the pioneers of anthropology, Edward Tylor provides plenty of linkages with economics, sociology and psychology through a broad definition of culture as: 'that complex whole which includes knowledge, belief, art, morals, law, custom, and any other capabilities and habits acquired by man as a member of society' (1874: I, 1).

Tylor may not have been aware of Marx's analysis of class or of Weber's group identities, both of which have contributed to the study of culture and cultural influences. However, the greater emphasis placed on individual effort and the remoulding of social attitudes implicit in enterprise culture policies raises, at various different levels, a number of important issues beyond notions of personal identity, ideology, perceptions, communications and attitude change. In examining cultural issues we should never forget that, as socio-economic structures evolve, they tend to serve the needs and reflect the interests of dominant groups and classes. Consequently, although the broad class aim of dominant groups – namely, to retain pre-eminence and power – usually runs counter to the interests of subordinate groups, their values, ideologies and culture permeate most other groups in the system. It does not even require sophisticated psychoanalytic concepts such as identification, projection, transference or reaction formation to realise that 'self-interest', the favourite motivator of classical economics, becomes very confused at subordinate levels. The dominant culture at the height of its power rejects elements – including technological as well as social developments – which might threaten the structure. Entrepreneurs rarely start as members of the very top groups, so it is important, particularly if Weber's and Schumpeter's views on upward mobility are correct, that the 'objective' needs of the socio-economic structure and the entrepreneurs' perceived personal needs do not diverge too much.

It is clear that perceived needs, opportunities, constraints and abilities will help to shape the goals and expectations of individual economic actors.

However, the desirability of the outcome, the ultimate satisfaction and the choice of goals and expectations will also depend upon the values, attitudes, social position and hopes that individual entrepreneurs hold about themselves – their *self-concepts* – which reflect the broader *cultural* context – family, peer groups, social class, ethnic group, society and so on – from which they come. The cultural factors and self-concept elements are very important because they determine not only the personal goals of business managers but also, in conjunction with perceived needs and objective opportunities, why they made their occupational choice.

Social representations of occupations and economic phenomena exert a powerful influence on both career choice and business decisions. Marketing, in particular, is a business function which tests to destruction the power and validity of many social representations. Although there is plenty of empirical evidence for the power of social representations in the business world, there are two main theoretical purposes for introducing them to this model: first, to emphasise the essentially social nature of business and commerce; second, to provide conceptual underpinning for the fact that business managers, whether they are aware of it or not, actually participate in the construction of the supposedly objective commercial forces that guide their actions. It is interesting to speculate that the internal locus of control associated with entrepreneurs may reflect their clearer conception of their own power to participate in the construction of relevant social representations rather than merely accept them as representing reality.

EXISTING CULTURE OF ENTERPRISE IN BRITAIN

Despite an intense and sustained publicity campaign (not only by government departments but also by major banks and large enterprises), it seems that popular culture has remained somewhat immune to the siren call of enterprise policies. So far, there seem to be only marginal shifts in public attitudes towards the enterprise culture itself or towards the key social representations associated with it. The British Social Attitudes survey (1990) actually found that a marginally smaller proportion of employees in Britain were seriously considering opting for self-employment in 1989 (16 per cent) than in 1983 (17 per cent). While authors David Blanchflower and Andrew Oswald (1990) did not rule out an increase in entrepreneurial mood during the 1980s, they ascribed any shift in public opinion to the economic recovery at the time rather than to cultural factors. The following year with recession well under way, Curran and Blackburn, investigating the impact of enterprise culture policies on business services (a key enterprise culture policy target and major small business growth sector during the 1980s), concluded that a high proportion 'felt unable to make a link between public notions of the enterprise culture and their own lives' (1991: 28).

This point was made even more powerfully in 1992 when the Labour Force Survey revealed not only that the proportion of people seeking a self-employed career option had continued to fall but that a majority of new self-employed would prefer to be paid employees working for someone else (Campbell and Daly, 1992). Furthermore, that survey also revealed that the proportion of self-employed without employees had increased to two-thirds of all self-employed (Labour Force Surveys put that proportion at 72 per cent by the end of 1993) – hardly a sign of enterprising spirit as discussed in this book but rather one of instinct for survival. The overwhelming message is that, except where individuals already shared the policy makers' version of enterprise culture social representations, these policies have not shifted the attitudes or the behaviour of the largest groups and classes of society and must be judged a failure in terms of attitude management and cultural impact.

Given the deeply entrenched position of core cultural values, this is not surprising. And one of the cultural features of British society seems to be a stronger acceptance of traditional structures and, more dangerously from the perspective of creating a dynamic culture of enterprise, of generally lower skill levels than comparative countries. The low level of skills in areas important to the efficient managing of business and industry in Britain compared with France and Germany is clear in Table 6.1. It is not surprising that enterprise trainers failed to attract significant numbers of people to their more serious programmes and that so many self-employed start their enterprises in low barrier-to-entry industries. In 1985, only 17 per cent of young people in Britain were still enrolled in full-time education (Germany 31 per cent; France 44 per cent; Italy 50 per cent) and less than 5 per cent were in post-secondary school full-time education – universities and colleges – compared with more than 15 per cent in Italy and Germany.

Leaving aside the widespread criticisms over the quality of British vocational training, the most alarming feature of Table 6.1 is that one-third of British 17-year-olds were either unemployed or unskilled. By 1995, European Commission (1996) labour force surveys revealed that the proportion

Table 6.1 European comparisons of vocational training in the mid-1980s

Skills	*Britain*	*Germany*	*France*
Building, 1983/4	12,500	60,000	21,000
Engineering, 1986	12,000	55,000	35,000
Secretarial, 1983/4	24,000	124,000	140,000
Retail, 1986	1,700	100,000	14,500
17-year-olds in full-time education, 1988	32.5%	50%	63%
17-year-olds on training courses, 1988	35%	47%	22%

Source: National Institute of Economic and Social Research, 1987 (document not available); *Guardian*, 5 July 1989).

of 15–19-year-olds in education and training (which included many on the much criticised youth employment initiatives) had crept up to 72 per cent of the total, compared with more than 93 per cent in France and in Germany. According to Jill Rubery (1994), the acceptance of a low skills base did not happen by chance and is not due to just a few causal factors. It is now endemic to the British economy and affects all enterprises – small, medium and large (even those that do take the trouble to develop the right technical and managerial skills internally). Rubery points to a number of factors that interconnect to produce this strong cultural and economic effect:

1 an elitist educational system that tends to divide people into a minority that are expected to succeed academically and a majority that are not;
2 a poor relationship between training and career prospects;
3 limited regulation of the training system, so that enterprises are not required to provide training and, in fact, many do not use available training systems;
4 ambiguous relationships between vocational training and trade or craft unions;
5 low trust within industrial relations systems in much of British industry;
6 prevalence of a low-wage system and fear that training will increase wage demands;
7 prevalence of large-batch low value-added production.

Rubery contrasts these characteristics of Britain's 'production regime' with those of other members of the European Union which are attempting to forge a high-skill, high-value-added strategy for Europe as it faces the challenges of global competition. Although the British strategy of a low-wage, non-regulated economy (which the Major government claimed as a great post-Maastricht success) is apparently at odds with the objectives of an innovative enterprise culture, it does reflect the reality of the outcomes of the enterprise culture period. Rubery's main point is that the dominant production regime and educational/training systems reflect and interact with British business cultural values and social practice as a complex societal system. This has parallels in the OUBS use of systems theory in management development and we shall return to this model towards the end of this book (p. 180). It is important to note that other countries such as France and Germany also have their own societal systems, each of which has its strengths and weaknesses and each of which will need to change in relation to such matters as enterprise development as Europe's economies converge. It is clear that cultural values exert and reflect influences with important socio-economic consequences. It is depressingly clear also that values associated with an anti-intellectualism or 'suspicion of education' pervade large sectors of British culture. It may be that this, as much as other structural factors, accounts for the low-achievement culture that the proponents of the enterprise culture were trying to overcome and replace.

It may be that Britain is not alone in this respect. Anthropologists have long made the point that 'western' cultures are more positivist, rationalistic and individualistic than most other cultures in the world (Geertz, 1973). However, there are signs of changing attitudes along the individualism/ collectivism dimension. Pressure of global competition from Germany and Japan is producing a change in corporate culture. Within entire industries, distinctive cultures are developing which not only affect other smaller firms down the chains of production and distribution but also filter into broader cultural mainstreams as altered social representations held by managers are transmitted to other members of society (Schein, 1981; Pettigrew and Whip, 1991). Perhaps the field that is central to the process of cultural change is that of *value* concepts. Values can be seen as abstracted social cognitions that reflect and determine an individual's participation in a culture and can, therefore, be explored usefully at the levels of both the individual and society. They are similar to Kelly's (1955) personal constructs but more socially determined. An individual's set of values reflects the personal significance of different social representations, and so can relate to the range of individualist and collective needs discussed earlier (Schwartz and Bilsky, 1987). Research into value formation and value shifts provides a clear operational focus for assessing cultural influences (Hofstede and Bond, 1984) and is used increasingly by marketers in the context of lifestyle analysis in order to ensure effective communication with target customers.

A switch in emphasis towards values associated with more collectivist forms of business behaviour suggests a way forward for creating a more effective 'enterprise culture'. In terms of our business behaviour model, the focus should be on improving entrepreneurial and small business capacity for gaining competitive advantage through cooperating with other firms or with the specialist self-employed. It is now clear, however, that any mass support of or training for enterprise will have to take into account culturally accepted forms of communicating and the values systems of target enterprise trainee groups. As Figure 3.2 (p. 46) indicates, small enterprise business expectations are particularly unreliable during an economic recession when wishful thinking and pessimism seem to alternate. The values of the enterprise culture do not seem to include respect for realistic expectations in the face of the strongly adverse structural factors that are part of an economic recession.

THE ROLE OF SOCIAL REPRESENTATIONS

If cultural influences can be seen as reflecting the attempts by people to live and behave according to sets of values, it is clearly important to understand how values develop and how they affect behaviour and communications. Values and cultural influences are clearly social phenomena and represent more than just a collection of individual perceptions. The concept of *social representations*, as developed by Robert Farr, Serge Moscovici and others (Farr, 1977; Farr and Moscovici, 1984; Moscovici, 1988) in the more sociological traditions of social psychology in Europe, reflects the power that certain relations and structures – scientific, political, economic, historic, social, cultural and so on – hold in shaping our perceptions and influencing our behaviour. This concept, which springs from Emile Durkheim's (1898) contrast between *collective representations* and *individual representations*, also enables us to examine the broad role that social phenomena, cultural assumptions, expectations and habits may play in the development of entrepreneurial behaviour.

The belief that real objects, beings and phenomena actually exist in a concrete world (materialism) is widely accepted in our society and underpins most of our transactions in commerce, science, economics, psychology and everyday life. Yet, at the same time, it is also widely agreed that the perceptions of these concrete 'facts', how they are classified, the relations between them (including apparent causal relations), their significance and the values they appear to represent depend fundamentally on shared meanings as much as on individual perceptions. Certain classes of these perceived or constructed 'facts' and relations evidently transcend the perceptions of any one given individual. This is particularly true of business and trade which are highly social activities.

The power acquired by the more persistent and enduring social constructs – such as history, class, culture, ideology, ethnicity and so on – renders them into phenomena that enjoy an almost objective reality as social representations somewhere between objective facts and subjective perceptions. Basically, they can be seen as Durkheim's (1898) 'social facts' that are so important to our family, cultural and working lives. The existence of shared social representations is a necessary precondition for all commercial transactions and business behaviour. In fact, even fairly temporary social trends and fads can acquire this power of apparent independent 'existence' – a phenomenon that provides a living for a great many marketing advisers, researchers, economic forecasters and, of course, successful entrepreneurs.

In social psychology and other social sciences it is probably true to say that there is a general acceptance that reality is mediated by how individuals perceive it and communication depends on some common sharing of those perceptions. The first part of this approach is essentially the position of the constructivists and can be represented by Kelly's social corollary: to the extent that individuals construe the construction processes of another, they may play a role in a social process involving that other person. The general social cognition position is put very clearly in the introduction to O'Guigan and Shrum's (1991) economic psychology paper that 'individuals rely heavily upon perceptions of their social environment in the formation, maintenance and mediation of impressions, attitudes and behaviours. Furthermore, we know that these perceptions need not exist as reasoned, critically evaluated or even elaborated thoughts for them to impact behaviour.' The concept of social representations, however, is closer to Hampson's (1988) social constructivism in that the perceptions held by others is also part of an individual's social cognition and goes beyond the mere need to have shared meanings or common perceptions in order to communicate.

Morgan and Schwalbe feel that social cognition theory, in being generally based on information-processing models, has actually become asocial by raising 'the fence between the disciplines even higher because it seems to belie any real concern with the cognizing individual as a social being' (1990: 149). By contrast, social representations are social constructs that define groups and shape their behaviour and, as a consequence, transcend and shape the behaviour and attitudes of individual members of social groups, even those who have not fully conceptualised the shared social representations. According to Moscovici (1988), social representations

> concern the contents of everyday thinking and the stock of ideas that gives coherence to our religious beliefs, political ideas and the connections we create as spontaneously as we breathe. They make it possible for us to classify persons and objects, to compare and explain behaviours and to objectify them as parts of our social setting. While representations are often to be located in the minds of men and women, they can just as often be found 'in the world', and as such examined separately.
>
> (1988: 214)

That social representations may transcend the direct perceptions of any one individual derives from their creation as part of the 'social setting of communication'. This process is evidently very akin to that observed and reported by anthropologists as cultural transmission. Indeed the definition of *culture* by the respected social anthropologist Clifford Geertz (1973) – as a 'system of inherited conceptions expressed in symbolic form by means of which men communicate, perpetuate and develop their knowledge about and attitudes towards life' – emphasises the embracing power of social representations within cultures. Another example of the power of this process is the development of class consciousness touched on earlier in the discussion of Marx (pp. 81–7).

Indeed, Moscovici goes on to state that we 'derive only a fraction of our knowledge and information from the simple interaction between ourselves and the facts we encounter in the world. Most knowledge is supplied to us by communication which affects our way of thinking and creates new contents' (1988: 215). It is this focus on communication which broadens the concept of social representation beyond the realm of individual social cognitions into its virtually autonomous role as a group or community 'cognition' and makes it so important when investigating social phenomena and processes in general and, in particular, the possibility of the social attitude shifts and the potential for miscommunication inherent in enterprise culture policies. Morgan and Schwalbe (1990) draw a distinction between the individual social cognition or Kelly-type constructivist approach towards socialisation and that taken by the more sociological or even anthropological social representations approach. The link between social cognition and constructivism is clear when they state that, for the social cognition school, 'the key consequence of socialization (especially adult socialization) is not so much the simple acquisition of information as the organization of that information into useable knowledge'. They stress that this approach has its strengths in providing 'the tools to analyze both the content of new knowledge structures and the pace at which different individuals acquire such knowledge' (Morgan and Schwalbe, 1990: 152).

This appreciation of the strengths of constructivism (social cognition) is obviously extremely useful in evaluating the effects of enterprise culture policies on individuals (and by a process of almost economic aggregation of groups or sectors). However, citing Lave (1988), Morgan and Schwalbe emphasise that the study of social phenomena requires more than an individual information-processing approach. They suggest that a social representations approach is required, that includes the anthropological and sociological processes of role-based learning which, they feel, introduces 'the social context into studies of cognitive change . . . including factors such as the presence or absence of formal agents of socialization, whether or not a peer group was present, and the availability of positive and negative role models' (1990: 152). This has evident resonances with our own research but the process is much richer and more useful than the mere conceptualisation of different roles. Social cognition, constructivism and social representation approaches, in common with most schools of social and developmental psychological thought, accept that individuals are guided in their actions by their conceptions of themselves and what they believe they are able to do.

According to the social cognition and constructivist position, the development and validation from experience of organising elements of the self-concept, Kelly's core constructs, have more general applicability as self-schemata which allow individuals to process information very efficiently in the areas where the self-schemata are well developed (Bannister and Fransella, 1986; Morgan and Schwalbe, 1990). In effect, this is the psychological centrality that has cropped up throughout this book and provides strong theoretical grounds for asserting that a distinguishing characteristic of all genuine entrepreneurs is that their self-schema in the field of business (or at least their own business field) must be well developed. Moscovici, however, is adamant that the distinction drawn by one of the pioneers of sociology, Emile Durkheim, between individual and collective representations, between individual and society, must be rejected because it prevents social psychology 'from looking at the relationship between the individuals and the collectivity and their common ground' (1988: 218). Morgan and Schwalbe go further and point out that the social cognition view of self-schemata is unnecessarily restrictive and cite Mead's (1934) earlier work on self-imagery as offering a much more valuable conception because it 'recognises explicitly the social origins and functions of self-imagery and . . . links self-imagery to action as both cause and effect' (1990: 156). They go on to state emphatically that 'treating the self in terms of social representations can lead sociologists to appreciate more fully the importance of history, ideology, and power in creating representations of selves' (1990: 157).

Although the message of the enterprise culture can be communicated between individuals and between groups because its concepts include widely shared economic, social and political social representations, the finer distinctions and the values associated with those representations clearly vary from one group to another. This is explicitly recognised by Moscovici in a statement worthy of Marx that representations 'can be shared by all members of a highly structured group . . . without their having been produced by the group. These *hegemonic* representations prevail implicitly in all symbolic or affective practices' (1988: 221). This appears to be the determining effect of the superstructure's (presumably the government and enterprise culture's policy makers') hegemony over other groups and classes. However, Moscovici goes on to say that each sub-group 'creates its own version and shares it with the others. These are emancipating representations with a certain degree of autonomy with respect to the interacting segments of society' (1988: 221). This suggests a contrary view that each group may have its own points of reference and that a version of a more general social representation may not be valued or carry as much weight with one group as it does with another, even though members of each group may comprehend each other perfectly well.

Indeed, Moscovici makes this point absolutely explicit in pointing out that:

> there are representations generated in the course of social conflict, social controversy, and society as a whole does not share them. They are determined by the antagonistic relations between its members and intended to be mutually exclusive. These polemical representations must be viewed in the context of an opposition or struggle between groups and are often expressed in terms of a dialogue with an imaginary interlocutor. . . .
> These distinctions emphasise the transition from the concept of collective representation as a uniform view to a differentiated view of social representations, which is closer to our reality. The contrast between several kinds of social relations are more significant than the one between the social and individual element.
>
> (1988: 222)

This immediately raises a question fundamental to this book of whether the enterprise culture 'social engineers' are operating on a different agenda which has little relevance to the agendas and social representations of those they would pretend to transform into 'entrepreneurs'; it reintroduces the cultural effects of class relations into the equation. Put another way, can the social representations held by the mainly secondary sector, working-class and petit-bourgeois targets of enterprise policies – social representations concerning occupations, enterprise, careers, preferred lifestyles, business and other concepts associated with the enterprise culture, which have been discussed during the course of this book – be altered to the versions of these social representations held by the bureaucratic, policy-making elements of the dominant political-economic structure?

Moscovici states very clearly that 'representations shape what is loosely termed a social consciousness of a period, a class or a nation as a whole' (1988: 228) and it is equally clear that enterprise culture policies have failed to bridge the cultural and class gaps between policy maker and policy target. In their attempts to forge a synthesis between the social cognition and social representations approaches, Morgan and Schwalbe also believe that sociology could be used to inform social cognition 'through research that examines the effects of social structure as an independent variable upon traditional measures of social cognition as dependent variables' (1990: 160). As the discussion in Chapter 1 on the background factors and expectations that drive enterprise culture policies has already implied, the proponents of the enterprise culture have underestimated the power of class (often included as a prime example of social stratification in social psychology) and, with it, the crucial and significant differences in social representations of *collectivism* and *individualism*. This is not the same as the difference between individual and collective representations which Moscovici is right to push to one side in favour of the different versions of social representations between different classes and social groups. It is more about the relative importance of individual and collective goals as part of their social identity by members of different groups. Triandis (1989) points out that there appears to be a positive relation between affluence and individualism whereby individuals give priority to their own personal goals at the expense of the goals of their peer groups.

Triandis prefers to use the terms *idiocentric* and *allocentric* when talking about individuals, reserving the terms 'individualism' and 'collectivism' for cultures and societies, and makes the important observation that idiocentrics are 'concerned with achievement but are lonely, whereas the allocentrics report low alienation and receiving much social support' (1989: 509). Triandis points to differences in child-rearing practices and expectations as a key determining variable, suggesting that 'individualistic cultures tend to emphasise self-reliance, independence, finding yourself, and self-actualisation. . . . Conversely, in collectivist cultures, child-rearing emphasises the importance of the collective' (1989: 512) and that the main concern of parents is obedience, reliability and proper behaviour. This provides powerful theoretical support for the contention that enterprise culture policies are much less about enterprise and much more about individualism. Furthermore, Triandis indicates a strong class influence with 'upper-middle and upper-class' individuals far less collectivist than the 'lower-class' individuals who are the main enterprise culture targets. Given management guru Peter Drucker's (1985) strong case for linking innovation and business success to collective social efforts, it would appear that this clash of social expectations over the role of the individual and the collective lies at the heart of the evident failure of enterprise culture policies and the ineffectiveness of enterprise training.

THE IMPORTANCE OF CLASS AND FAMILY

Given the importance of class in the formation of cultural attitudes, it would be desirable to start by considering how useful this concept might be in predicting entrepreneurial success and in assessing the effectiveness of enterprise culture policies. Goldthorpe *et al.* (1987) and Blanchflower and Oswald (1990) suggest that mobility between classes and class-based attitudes have changed far less in recent years than is often imagined. The process of socialisation and acculturation, described by anthropologist Anthony Wallace (1970: 154) as the manipulation of an infant cohort 'at the hands of a preceding cohort that has undergone the same transformation' which he claims is 'logically comparable to models of genetic copying in biological reproduction', suggests that class influences will persist over time and be highly influential in the determination of attitudes and values (and, by implication, career expectations). Psychological studies reveal a weak to moderate positive relationship between social class and self-esteem, an important characteristic of entrepreneurs and top managers, but the relationship becomes much more significant among people for whom work is psychologically central (Gecas and Seff, 1990). Work is likely to be more psychologically central for people with power to make their own decisions – top managers and small business owners certainly, but also many artisanal firms and self-employed who exist further down the social scale.

Unfortunately, class has become a rather sociologically and politically impure concept and presents certain methodological difficulties though it does open up interesting psychological issues concerning attribution theory and the self-concept. For instance, Gecas and Seff (1990), in their study on the effects of the psychological centrality of work compared with home, found that the stronger self-esteem associated with higher social class could not be transferred to occupational status without taking into account the importance of work in self-evaluation. Using a basically occupational definition of class, they found that people for whom work is psychologically central are more influenced by class effects. They found that generally 'contexts that permit greater self-direction, personal agency and discretion are more likely to be important to one's self-definition because they give more information about oneself' (1990: 166). Conversely, Marx's concept of alienation is confirmed because 'the degree to which work is routinized and supervised [is] related negatively to self-esteem' (Gecas and Seff, 1990: 165). Higher self-esteem also has the effect of producing a tendency towards more positive self-attribution whereby the causal agency for positive and favourable outcomes is attributed to the self (in a similar way to the *internal* locus of control beliefs). These findings have obvious implications for career choice and work performance. So too does Farr's (1977) critique of Herzberg's work motivational theory on the methodological grounds that it mainly reflects attribution of cause effects and should not be used to make statements about situational or context effects (the influence of the actual environment).

However, sociological studies in this field are also influenced by the fact that a growing number of service workers often do not describe themselves as working class even though the basic power relations and mechanisms for the extraction of surplus value remain in place, and political parties deliberately obscure the boundaries in their search for national votes. This means there are few consistent empirical data and that occupational definitions or even family backgrounds, although still impure, offer the best estimate of class. The strong family inter-generational occupational patterns among the self-employed and small business owners as distinct career paths have been recognised since Bolton (1971). There does not seem to be great cross-over between the two over time, suggesting once again that they are basically different groups with distinctive cultures (Cooper and Dunkelberg, 1987; Bannock and Stanworth 1990). Further analyses by Curran and Burrows (1988) of findings from the General Household Survey (1984) clearly reflect this, as Table 6.2 shows.

Two interesting features clearly stand out: first, a significantly higher proportion of small business owners (and the female self-employed) come from families where the father held a managerial position; second, significantly fewer had fathers who were unskilled although this is not true of a sizeable proportion of the male self-employed, many of whom are in low-skilled

Table 6.2 Family occupational backgrounds (GHS, 1984): self-employed, small business owners and employees (percentages)

Father's work	Self-employed (no employees)		Small business (1–25 employees)		National workforce	
	male	female	male	female	male	female
Employer/manager	16	28	28	33	15	16
Professional	4	6	2	4	3	4
Self-employed	10	3	7	4	4	5
Clerical-supervisory	17	14	18	16	17	14
Skilled manual	24	22	19	22	30	31
Unskilled manual	18	14	9	8	20	21

Source: Curran and Burrows (1988).

Table 6.3 Family influences on career choice for self-employment

Influence: Self-employed background	Family			Spouse	Non-family		Nobody	Total Replies	(%)
	Father	Mother	Other		Employer	Outsider			
					(column % of mentions)				
Parents	38	25	29	21	12	21	36	109	(27)
Relatives	33	40	47	29	24	31	28	122	(31)
Spouse	9	15	12	25	4	5	5	39	(10)
None	20	20	12	25	60	39	39	129	(32)
(Mentions	91	20	17	48	25	75	133	399)	(100)
(Firms	59	13	13	34	22	62	108	307)	
(%)	(19)	(4)	(4)	(11)	(7)	(20)	(35)	(100)	

industries. This lends further support to the conclusion that there are several categories of self-employed and that self-employed careers may have different meanings for different socio-economic classes. This family link as a factor in the choice of self-employment as a career (Bolton, 1971; Curran and Burrows, 1988; Hakim, 1988) again suggests there is little in terms of family or educational backgrounds to suggest that the longer-term unemployed should be a fertile source of new self-employed. Our own studies based on SBRT data revealed even stronger inter-generational links when the mother's occupation is also taken into account. Table 6.3 shows the family background in self-employment (rows), with some 80% of the sample mentioning at least one strong family connection, and how this relates to the reported strong influences on the decision to seek a self-employed career. (The columns are grouped into family and non-family influences and multiple mentions mean that both columns and rows total more than 100 per cent.)

It is clear that there is a strong conscious family influence in career choice to be self-employed or to run a small business. Most (55 per cent) ascribed the decision to run their own small enterprise to non-family influences. Indeed, in keeping with their strong individualism it is not surprising that more than one-third (35 per cent) attribute their self-employed status to themselves. However, only 20 per cent of these self-employed small enterprise managers claimed to have no family connection with self-employment in their own backgrounds and many with no close family background in self-employment nevertheless reported strong family influences on their own decision to start a small enterprise. General Household Survey (GHS) data suggest that a father's occupation as a manager is also a strong influence on female self-employment. It is also clear (see Table 6.4) that there are strong cultural influences at work in the determination of future career goals. A reasonable conclusion to draw from these findings seems to be that the role of parental or cultural influence is felt most at the point of initial career choice but perhaps less so as personal experience accumulates.

Table 6.4 Career goals by family background in self-employment

Career goal	Non-family self-employed		Parents self-employed		Other family self-employed		Total	
Self-employment	13	(30%)	18	(42%)	12	(28%)	43	(37%)
Manager/MD	17	(40%)	19	(44%)	7	(16%)	43	(37%)
Employee	17	(57%)	2	(7%)	11	(37%)	30	(26%)
Total	47	(41%)	39	(34%)	30	(26%)	116	(100%)

Note: Twenty-five respondents did not state parental background and another ten did not indicate career goals.
Percentage figures in brackets are in rows.

The influence of parental background in self-employment does seem to be linked to the initial decision to seek a career in self-employment and to the tendency to persist in pursuing a self-employed career. The linkage between a background family culture of self-employment and the intention to pursue a career as the owner of an independent business, especially in self-employment but also as an owner-manager, is clearly evident. The strong influences of class and family are present but they are certainly not static. Career choice push factors were much weaker for people entering employment twenty years ago (respondents over the age of 35) and the likelihood of their having self-employed parents was also much lower. It seems reasonable to conclude that the nature and pattern of self-employment has altered significantly over the past twenty years and looks like being seen in the future as a valid career choice for an increasing number of people. Whether this necessarily implies a greater propensity to entrepreneurship or innovation in Britain will also remain a matter for debate.

CULTURAL INFLUENCES ON SMALL ENTERPRISE OWNERS

Another important factor associated with cultural influences is the level and quality of education. Small firm owners are generally more poorly educated than other sectors of the population in similar positions of responsibility (Bolton, 1971), except high-technology entrepreneurs who tend to be highly educated. As Table 6.5 reveals, Labour Force Surveys show a relative decline in the self-employed without qualifications from 1981 to 1989.

The most consistent features concern gender differences and the stronger propensity for higher educated people to employ others. It is worth repeating that the founders of high-technology small businesses and those in the financial and business services tend to be well educated, as do self-employed professionals and technical consultants. There are clear differences between the two surveys and variations within each. Apart from methodological differences, the LFS includes professional and some foreign qualifications under 'Degree' but they are included under 'Other' in the GHS. The most

Table 6.5 Educational levels, 1981–9: self-employed, small business owners and employees (percentages)

| Qualifications | All employees | | Self-employed | | Small firms | |
	Male	Female	1981	1989	1981	1989
Degree	10	5	14	15	20	19
A level	11	6	32	36	31	35
O level	18	23	9	13	10	14
Other	27	26	7	10	6	9
No qualifications	35	41	40	28	36	25

Source: Labour Force Surveys (1981, 1989).

consistent features concern gender differences and the stronger propensity for more highly educated people to employ others. There seems to be a shift away from low-skilled male self-employment towards self-employed women with relatively high educational levels compared with the relatively low level for self-employed men and also compared with female employees. Relatively few male self-employed and female small business owners have degrees or technical qualifications and many of them have no qualifications at all. The proportion of people with foreign qualifications is not large (5 per cent for self-employed and small businesses, 3 per cent for all employees) and is included in 'Other' but provides some slight support for the 'outsider' or marginal groups theory of entrepreneurial development mentioned on p. 48. It is instructive to note that strong fear of failure is associated with lack of parental (particularly maternal) support and a critical, over-structured upbringing (Atkinson and Feather, 1966). This is the same background process that is described by Kets de Vries (1980) who has focused on the 'neurotic' nature of entrepreneurs who, he feels, ultimately doom themselves to self-created business failure. The bi-polar dimensions he uses to analyse the role of their families in their psychodynamic development – acceptance vs. rejection and support vs. non-support – plus the phenomenon he describes (inability to function in large organisations and unrealistic levels of aspiration) are very similar to those described by Atkinson and Feather (1966) in relation to the development of fear of failure (which is the mirror image of the need for achievement, or nAch, discussed in the next two chapters).

Significantly, the conditions for developing high nAch include supportive parents (especially the mother), use of praise for achievements rather than blame for failures, acceptance and the encouragement of independence and self-reliance. These are very similar to the processes that produce internal locus of control – the key entrepreneurial belief in self-control over one's own behaviour and destiny (Atkinson and Feather, 1966; Rotter, 1966). This suggests that entrepreneurs differ from other small enterprise owners not only in their business behaviour but also in their family backgrounds and, probably, in their psychological maturity. Research into career development which we mention in the next chapter, such as personality and job congruence, self-concept, occupational concept, job search and so on, also highlights the importance of family and cultural background in developing exploratory behaviour, reality testing and an ability to deal with ambiguity, frustration, tension and unmet expectations (Super, 1980). Encouraging such self-reliance and exploratory behaviour in their children is characteristic of mothers who themselves have high nAch and, not surprisingly, is linked to educational level, social class and parental (especially paternal) occupation (Atkinson and Feather, 1966; Curran and Burrows, 1988).

However, it is worth repeating that the founders of high-technology small businesses and those in the financial and business services tend to be well educated, as do self-employed professionals and technical consultants. There has been a tremendous growth in these areas but these more advanced sectors are still swamped by the more numerous traditional self-employed and small businesses in retailing, distribution and, particularly, construction, many of which are low-skill occupations. Once again, the patterns revealed here are linked to class and cultural factors. Occupational and developmental psychologists have long recognised that education is the primary agent for occupational and social mobility but have also found that educational decisions among lower-level occupations are often made casually even though they affect future job prospects. The middle classes, including the petite bourgeoisie, are keen to use education for family advancement whereas working-class parents often remain outside the educational system (Osipow, 1983), which adds further weight to the view that enterprise training is extremely unlikely to be capable of transforming the industrial unemployed into self-employed, let alone into entrepreneurs. These deep differences are reflected in the many different types of enterprises and organisations set up by people who work on their own account.

The cultural influences of the family have a strong impact on career choice, confirming the findings of many sociological studies which reveal a strong inter-generational link in the career choice to be self-employed or a small business owner (Bolton, 1971; Stanworth and Bannock, 1990; Stanworth and Gray, 1991). Self-employment as a means of survival rather than growth opportunity became an involuntary stage in the personal careers of many people from other backgrounds as well, and they are often more growth-oriented than people from the milieu of self-employment.

If entrepreneurs do have a role to play in socio-economic development, it is important to analyse what features distinguish them from the bulk of self-employed and small business owners in relation to the processes of development. However, it is also important not to lose sight of the fact that owner-managers' plans for future development, and their business behaviour in furtherance of those plans, will also depend on their access to resources and on the resource base they are starting from. SBRT surveys suggest that the most ambitious group clearly comprises those who have survived their start-up in self-employment. More than half of them (55 per cent) would prefer to manage a business rather than remain as a self-employed sole-trader, as would half the mature firms more than five years old. It is worth noting that more than half the not-trading group (55 per cent) were graduates, which suggests interesting differences between the samples. The same cultural and size effects were found in an SBRT survey (see Table 6.6) that explored the business objectives which small enterprise owners set for their enterprises. Indeed, the relatively non-entrepreneurial nature of most very small firms employing fewer than five people is clearly demonstrated in the table.

There is a marked direct relation between the profit motive and size, and an almost equally strong inverse relation between size and both lifestyle and

Table 6.6 Business objectives by firm size

Number of employees	Sales growth	Profit growth	Staff growth	Status	Safe future	Assets growth	Lifestyle	Total firms	(Col. %)
				(row percentages)					
1–4	7	12	1	18	11	3	42	595	(44)
5–9	7	21	4	16	14	5	24	324	(24)
10–14	4	27	1	15	19	3	23	124	(9)
15–49	8	37	3	11	11	4	19	233	(17)
50–99	8	54	0	8	6	4	16	50	(4)
100+	6	38	0	6	19	0	19	16	(1)
Total	88	289	30	209	164	50	409	1,349	(100)
(%)	(7)	(21)	(2)	(16)	(12)	(4)	(30)	(100)	

Source: Further analysis of SBRT survey data.

Table 6.7 Personal motives by firm size

Number of employees	No choice	Family tradition	Indepen- dence	Secure future	Make money	Total firms	(Col. %)
			(row percentages)				
1–4	9	2	54	8	16	595	(44)
5–9	5	6	52	8	15	324	(24)
10–14	4	7	51	9	20	124	(9)
15–49	3	11	40	10	25	233	(17)
50–99	0	14	44	4	34	50	(4)
100+	0	13	31	6	37	16	(1)
Total	80	71	678	111	251	1,349	(100)
(%)	(6)	(5)	(50)	(8)	(19)	(100)	

Source: Further analysis of SBRT survey data.

status. The self-employed and mini-firms in the 1–4 employee band, where lifestyle (42 per cent) is the dominant business objective, are clearly less entrepreneurial than the more dynamic firms in the 15–49 employee band, where 37 per cent have growth in profits as their main business objective. Certainly, this view is further supported by the results in Table 6.7 which show that *making money* as a personal motive for being in business increases with the size of the firm, coupled with an equally distinct decline in *independence* as a personal motive.

Obviously, making money as a personal motive is strongly linked to having increased profits as a business objective, but it is interesting to note that money is often seen as a badge of success by entrepreneurs (Timmons *et al.*, 1977). It is also important to note the increase with firm size of family tradition as a motive. It may be that these respondents represent a stable, non-entrepreneurial sub-group of the generally more active 15–25-employee businesses. On the other hand, active later generations can put an established business to new uses. The 9 per cent of the smallest firms that reported they had no alternative are likely to be recent start-ups who chose self-employment as the only alternative to unemployment. Table 6.8 shows the relationships between personal motives and business objectives, and provides some interesting clues to the existence of distinct types of small business – entrepreneurial, traditional, avoiders, etc.

Most of these results have an intuitive face validity. For instance, it is not surprising that 40 per cent of respondents motivated to make money – twice the average 21 per cent – have the growth of profits as their business objective or that 38 per cent of those concerned to create security – three times the average – should aim at building protection for the future. Nor is it strange that respondents motivated by family tradition are five times more likely than most other respondents to aim for an accumulation of assets (for their successors). However, the non-entrepreneurial nature of many of those pushed into self-employment by, among other things, fear of unemployment

Table 6.8 Personal motivation by business objectives (percentages)

Objective	No choice	Family tradition	Indepen- dence	Secure future	Make money	Total firms	(Col. %)
Sales growth	6	4	7	5	8	88	(7)
Profit growth	15	24	19	11	40	289	(21)
Staff growth	0	0	1	5	1	30	(2)
Status	35	16	16	15	14	209	(16)
Protect future	10	18	10	38	11	164	(12)
Assets growth	8	16	3	4	4	50	(4)
Lifestyle	18	17	40	19	19	409	(30)
Total	80	71	678	111	251	1,349	(100)

Source: Further analysis of SBRT survey data.

(see Gray, 1989), is reflected in the relatively low importance they place on growth of profits and the strong importance that achieving a reasonable standard of living (status) holds for them. The responses from those who felt they had no choice other than to turn to self-employment not only indicates high *external* locus of control but also reflects the importance of basic needs – such as achieving a certain minimum standard of living – among small businesses and the self-employed. Having as a business goal the preservation of a certain lifestyle could reflect a variety of needs, though not necessarily any likely to lead to business success. This lends added interest to the replies from the half of the total sample who reported that attaining *independence* was their main motivation for running their own business. The 40 per cent whose main business objective is to support a preferred lifestyle is the largest sub-group, followed by the profit maximisers (19 per cent) as a smaller but, presumably, more dynamic sub-group exhibiting high *internal* locus of control. These differences are highlighted in Table 6.9 where the business objectives of the entrepreneurial growers (those who reported increases in both sales turnover and employment over the past year) are contrasted with those respondents whose businesses actually declined over the past year.

The importance of profits and, to a lesser extent, sales turnover to their business success is clearly understood by the growers, who represented one in five of the total sample. The relative unimportance of supporting a lifestyle was also a feature of the growers. The declining firms were also aware of the need to boost profits (though less so than the growers) and were comparatively more interested in setting business objectives aimed at attaining a certain standard of living (status) and supporting a lifestyle. Indeed, more than half the declining businesses (51 per cent) had these rather non-business goals as their objectives compared with only 42 per cent of the growers. These differences suggest that the more active firms may have a different outlook on business and a different set of priorities from the less active or more reactive firms.

Table 6.9 Business objectives by actual growth, 1991

Performance	Sales growth	Profit growth	Staff growth	Status	Safe future	Assets growth	Life-style	Total
			(*row percentages*)					
Growers	9	28	4	16	10	3	26	313
Decliners	4	24	0	19	10	4	32	115
Neutral	6	19	2	15	13	4	32	921
Total	88	289	30	209	164	50	409	1,349
(%)	(7)	(21)	(2)	(16)	(12)	(4)	(30)	(100)

Source: Further analysis of SBRT survey data.

SMALL ENTERPRISE CULTURE

These cultural differences in attitudes towards growth and even in the social representations of the role of an enterprise became particularly apparent in the SBRT survey on small enterprise growth orientation, which was conducted during the severe recession of the early 1990s. A 1991 SBRT survey on growth orientation attracted 1,719 replies from small enterprise managers. Once again, the cultural and size effects were very clear: there is no difference between the growth-oriented and growth-averse firms in relation to personal independence, and the slight drop among the 'others' is no doubt due to the inclusion of respondents who want to sell or merge their businesses. The dominance of 'independence' as the most commonly cited career-choice motivator is a widely reported finding in small enterprise research. The ideology of individualism that pervades enterprise policy and the constraints on growth imposed by fear of loss of personal control by owner-managers have been discussed extensively at Institute of Small Business Affairs conferences and elsewhere (Stanworth and Gray, 1991; Gray, 1992a, 1992b; Storey, 1994). However, an important point made earlier, that 'independence' is an ambiguous concept, needs to be examined further. The respondents to the survey were asked to define what independence means to them, with choices ranging from to 'be left alone', through 'be responsible for own decisions' to ' be responsible for autonomous operations (as part of a larger system)'. Table 6.10 reveals a strong preference for an individualistic 'Take own decisions', with the less individualistic run 'Autonomous operations' a distant second.

In terms of power relations or personal control, the first category ('Take own decisions') can be seen as a form of personal empowerment but the 'Autonomous operations' category also recognises the social and inter-dependent nature of business. There are some very slight size effects, with the sole-traders and micro-firms clearly less able to define independence in terms that also accept social or work obligations. Virtually all the sixty-three respondents who wanted to be 'left alone' were sole-traders or 2–3 people family firms. Respondents from all size bands are clearly concerned

Table 6.10 Definitions of independence by firm size (full-time employees, 1995)

Staff size	Take own decisions	Not told what to do	Decide for others	Be left alone	Auton-omous operations	Other	Total	(Col. %)
				(row percentages)				
Sole-trader	52	5	2	5	22	14	686	(27)
2–9	54	6	1	2	28	10	1,262	(50)
10–14	48	6	2	–	34	11	191	(8)
15–24	50	5	2	1	34	9	175	(7)
25 +	50	4	2	–	33	9	203	(8)
Total	1,319	132	38	63	695	270	2,517	(100)
(%)	(52)	(5)	(2)	(3)	(28)	(11)	(100)	

Source: Further analysis of SBRT survey data.

about their own personal control and empowerment but those who manage small enterprises are also noticeably more prepared to define their independence in a less individualistic manner. Given the strong social desirability effects, it is not surprising that few small enterprise owners admitted that they like to impose their will on others or that they fear being told what to do by others. It is to be expected that these types of small enterprise owners are less likely to complete questionnaires and are almost certainly underrepresented in this sample. However, even with capable and successful small enterprise managers, the desire for independence can impede further growth if owners set themselves unrealistic or unattainable goals.

Notwithstanding its ambiguity as a concept, concern over independence is obviously a central feature of small business culture. There is a real risk, however, that many small business owners and self-employed rate their independence above the success of their business. There is a strong reluctance to cede, or even share, control of the business either internally or externally. Yet, for the active minority of business owners who do wish to grow successfully, the internal organisation of their firms must move away from one of concentrated personal control to a more devolved system. There are grounds for believing that it is problems to do with span of control, the reluctance to delegate authority, which create many of the strong internal barriers to growth. The above results reflect this confusion and point to the need for more research into management styles and systems within small firms with growth potential. Table 6.11 shows a stronger relationship between the setting of clear business objectives and growth orientation.

The dominance of maximisation of profits or sales (a reasonable objective for firms keen to increase market share and operating within fairly fixed profit margins) as a business objective among growth-oriented firms reflects their more professional approach towards business. Nearly half the growth-oriented firms (47 per cent) have these objectives compared with only 15 per

Table 6.11 Business objectives and growth orientation (percentages)

Objectives	Growth-oriented	Growth-averse	Other	Total
Sales growth	11	4	4	7
Profit growth	36	11	16	21
Status	12	18	20	16
Future assets	12	18	20	16
Lifestyle	23	45	34	34
Total	232	240	167	639
(%)	(100)	(100)	(100)	(100)

Source: Further analysis of SBRT survey data.

cent of firms with non-growth targets. The dominance of *lifestyle* – itself another ambiguous concept, ranging from distinctly anti-business behaviours to those of conspicuous consumption – as a business objective among the non-growth firms also supports the general observation about their non-professional approach. The stronger business culture of growth-oriented firms is also evident among the 1,068 respondents who replied to the 1989 quarterly survey on inter-generational links and number of previous businesses owned. A large proportion of members of the SBRT database have close relatives who are also self-employed (44 per cent have self-employed parents and/or siblings) but non-growth firms are slightly lower (40 per cent). Almost half (48 per cent) the growth-oriented firms have close relatives who are also self-employed. In terms of previous businesses owned, again almost half the growth-oriented respondents (45 per cent) have previously owned another business, compared with just one-third (33 per cent) of non-growth firms.

The growth-oriented owners of more than one business (27 per cent) were more likely than the non-growth owners (24 per cent) to have sold the previous business to a third party or to be still running the other business as well. However, the ultimate test of growth orientation is whether those owners actually manage to achieve higher growth than owners with non-growth targets. After all, growth is not merely a function of intentions but also of ability and economic conditions. In fact, growth-oriented firms represented 58 per cent of all growing firms. The other feature of these results is the high 'Others' category for declining firms (those registering decreases in sales and either employment or investment). To an extent, this is an artefact of the classification procedure because the vast majority of these 529 declining respondents want either to sell (46 per cent) or to merge their firm with another (20 per cent). The one-quarter of the whole sample, mainly owners of the smallest firms and the self-employed, who are personally seeking independence and set 'lifestyle' as a business objective do not hold their business as psychologically central and are unlikely to want to grow. In fact, declining businesses are more concerned (51 per

cent) about securing a certain standard of living and lifestyle than are growing businesses (42 per cent). The opposite holds true for the 12 per cent who
are motivated to make money and set profit growth as their business objective, and for the other 12 per cent seeking independence with the same profit
growth business objective. However, not all firms seeking to expand profits
are necessarily growth-minded – owners with a family tradition in business
may only seek to maintain their business at its present size but recognise that
maintained profits are the best defence against business failure.

However, this raises another issue concerning small business growth and
growth orientation. Business growth, particularly for people who are reluctant to give up personal control, may take the form of founding several businesses rather than expanding one business to a larger size. The SBRT
quarterly survey in the third quarter of 1989 explored the effects of certain
aspects of business culture on the behaviour of small business owners. The
first question asked about the extent of self-employment among members of
the respondent's immediate family. The results confirmed the strong influences of family tradition on small firm ownership from previous research
studies (Bolton, 1971; Stanworth and Gray, 1991). The findings here in relation to enterprise trainees show three-quarters of respondents having other
family members also self-employed. The second question explored the
phenomenon of multiple ownership of firms. Some 40 per cent of the
2,236 respondents had managed one or more enterprises previously. Many
were still operating the other business.

Roughly one-quarter (479) of the 1990 SBRT quarterly survey had also
responded to the 1989 survey, so it was possible to explore the business culture effects further. In general, the importance of the independence motive
was stronger when the wider family was also engaged in self-employment
and slightly weaker if there was no family involvement or if only the
mother had been self-employed. However, having a self-employed mother
or no family involved was also linked to the setting of profit growth as a
business objective. There was not such a clear pattern among the previous
business owners. This may be because the previous business was a family
concern and the second the respondent's own venture, because the respondent feels the lessons have been learned from a previous business failure,
because the original investment is the main source of income or because
the main motivation may have been the starting of a business as opposed
to the continued managing of a business. The findings in Table 6.12 on
number of businesses owned and personal motivation suggest that there
are two sub-groups in the cross-sample.

There is a clear difference between those who have owned more than one
business and those who have owned fewer. In fact, those who have only
owned one other business previously – perhaps its dissolution gave birth
to the present business, more of a continuum than two separate businesses
– have virtually the same personal motivations as respondents who have
only ever owned their present business. The more experienced small business

Table 6.12 Personal motivations by number of businesses owned

Businesses	No choice	Family tradition	Indepen- dence	Secure future	Make money	Total
			(row percentages)			
One only	9	3	59	6	17	290
One before	10	2	59	6	15	94
Two before	14	4	44	9	23	57
Three and more	7	7	45	3	28	29
Total	45	14	270	30	86	479
(%)	(9)	(3)	(56)	(6)	(18)	(100)

Source: Further analysis of SBRT survey data.

owners are markedly less concerned about independence – though it does remain their main motivation – and are more interested in making money. However, the ambiguity of the independence motive weakens its value as a tool for analysing small business behaviour even though it is clearly important in cultural, political and marketing terms. Members of the SBRT database – the common respondents to the two surveys were recruited from the database – unambiguously identify themselves as small business owners and display strong independence motivation. These surveys suggest that the more active firms have a different set of priorities and outlook on business and lifestyle than the more reactive enterprises.

On the whole, however, we can sum up small enterprise culture as one of aversion to control and to growth, but favouring a strong sense of personal independence. These anti-development attitudes, even in firms employing up to, say, 5–6 people, are reflected in a strong reluctance to increase their employment of others: it is clear that the government's removal of employment and strike protection 'barriers' in the labour markets has had little or no influence on most small firms (which, in any case, recruit from a less qualified and less formal labour market than larger firms (Stanworth and Curran, 1973; *NatWest/SBRT Quarterly Survey of Small Business in Britain* 4, 1989; Goss, 1991). A number of plausible reasons for this growth-aversion have been suggested, including the need to maintain personal control, problems with the span of control, a rational decision to avoid the increased transactions costs involved in managing larger organisations (the 'hassle' factor), low levels of aspiration and satisfaction, and the lack of personal management and planning ability on the part of many small firm owners. To these reasons may be added the existence of a subculture where the social representation of legitimate work includes a hostility towards large organisations and the public sector, coupled with an attraction towards working alone or in small intimate groups. Certain personal abilities, occupations, expectations and outcomes will be valued more highly than others and these do not appear to include those associated with the formal organisation of other people.

7 The small enterprise owners

We have established that there is a strong family and inter-generational influence present in the career choice of a large proportion of the self-employed and of the owners of very small (often family) firms. Many come from particular social milieux. Although individualism and informality are strong elements in the culture of this milieu, the behaviour and expectations associated with business growth appear to run counter to the culture. Indeed, we have found that only around one-third of respondents to our surveys do not have a self-employed family background but these 'newcomers' are more growth-oriented and own bigger firms. It is the non-entrepreneurial micro-firms and the self-employed, often family firms, which report the strongest attachment to personal independence and the individualism that underpins enterprise culture policies. It is becoming clear that the individualism fostered by enterprise culture policies rarely leads to the creation of the dynamic, growth-oriented enterprises needed for the development of a successful modern, capitalist economy. To devise successful enterprise development policies we need to know a great deal more about the people who start and manage successful enterprises.

SMALL BUSINESS TYPOLOGIES

An early two-way classification of small manufacturing firms, which reflects the distinction made by Henri Pirenne (1937) about medieval 'entrepreneurs', divided them into *jobbers* – those with technical production skills, producing on specific demand from customers – and *marketeers* – competitive, entrepreneurial firms. A later two-way classification emphasised the distinction identified by Schumpeter by contrasting *entrepreneurs* with paid managers in organisations, termed *hierarchs* (Collins *et al.*, 1964). Using the same data source of mainly manufacturing owner-managers, a similar dual classification was adopted by Norman Smith (1967) who contrasted the *craftsman-entrepreneur* (technically inclined, product-driven, low education, socially isolated) with the *opportunistic-entrepreneur* (better educated, socially adept), and suggested that only the latter had true growth potential. All these dual typologies highlight the essentially active, acquisitive nature of the 'true' entrepreneur though it is interesting that Smith links this to social class with the *craftsman* seen as 'blue-collar' (it is not clear whether this means working class or petit-bourgeois) and the *opportunist* as middle class. Smith also made it clear that industry, sector and management-style differences made it inconceivable that there could be one entrepreneurial 'type'.

It may be tempting to recast these distinctions, with the self-employed and small businesses operating in pre-capitalist sectors as one group, petty or nascent capitalist and mercantile enterprises as another group, and career managers as an important element in the bourgeoisie as a third group. Empirical studies have suggested that dual classifications are too simple and, as is clear from the examples mentioned above, were mainly developed with manufacturing firms in mind. A psychological model based on a factor analysis of careers split some 1,800 small firm owners into the *growth/ change*-oriented, *independence*-oriented and the *craftsman*-oriented (Dunkelberg and Cooper, 1982). A more sociological approach divided small firm managers into *artisans* possessing technical skills and strongly involved in their products, *classic entrepreneurs* with well-developed marketing skills and *managers* relying on administrative skills (Stanworth and Curran, 1973). This model was later extended to include *survivors* – people with survival skills who have turned to working on their own account as a result of redundancy, career blockage or lack of alternative opportunities (Gray and Stanworth, 1986). The self-employed tend to be non-entrepreneurial artisans or survivors, mainly operating in the pre-capitalist sector. Most entrepreneurs are small business owners but even those who begin as entrepreneurs through founding their own firm frequently lose their entrepreneurial qualities when they achieve relative stability through accumulating sufficient capital (Schumpeter, 1934; Davidsson, 1989a).

One interesting finding from the SBRT surveys reported here was the identification of two distinct types of dynamic small business – one characterised by marketing and selling skills, the other interested in improving the skills of finance and control as part of a process of evolving a professional management structure. These two 'types' correspond to existing, widely used typologies of dynamic businesses – the *classic entrepreneur* and the *manager* (Stanworth and Curran, 1973) – and contrast with the majority of small firms with high product orientation but low growth orientation. This was reflected not only in the differences between the total sample and the target 5–50 employee firms, especially those actually expanding where the organisational and social skills were particularly valued. Organisational and social issues may be more likely to be identified and taken seriously in larger firms but the increase in interest with firm size in attaining and assuring quality suggests that awareness of organisational matters may be a mark of more proactive firms. US entrepreneurial researcher Karl Vespers (1980) linked small business types to their behavioural response to underlying socio-economic conditions and produced an eleven-category typology, some of which should be familiar:

1 self-employed;
2 team builders;
3 independent innovators;
4 pattern multipliers;
5 economy-of-scale exploiters;
6 capital aggregators;
7 acquirers;
8 buy–sell artists;
9 conglomerators;
10 speculators;
11 apparent value manipulators.

Whatever the merits of these distinctions, one strong point should be clear: it is impossible to imagine that one personality trait or collection of common traits could account for the business behaviour of these different types of entrepreneurs. Skills-based typologies were not the only basis for classification. For instance, the social development model proposed by Gibb and Ritchie (1981) uses life stages to provide a useful typology of small businesses: *improvisers* in the early stages, *revisionists* going through their mid-career switch, *superseders* in a second career, and *reverters* attempting a retired post-career business. On closer inspection, however, this scheme seems to be as much about organisational differences as about the different motivations of the founders as the different types of business. Finally, there is a widely used *de facto* distinction between entrepreneurs and other small enterprise owners. Carland *et al.* (1984: 354–9) used the following definition which strongly reflects the findings and approach of this book:

> An entrepreneur is an individual who establishes and manages a business for the principal purpose of profit and growth. The entrepreneur is characterised by innovative behaviour and will employ strategic management practices in the business.
>
> A small business owner is an individual who establishes and manages a business for the principal purpose of furthering personal goals. The business must be the primary source of income and will consume the . . . majority of time and resources.

This implies that such owners or managers have a conscious intention of using their abilities to start and expand their businesses, further implying that they consciously set appropriate commercial and strategic business objectives. To distinguish them from the vast majority of owners and managers who do not actively have such an intention, these growth-oriented owners and managers are termed 'entrepreneurs'. Small firms with employees are fewer but apparently more active on the whole than the self-employed working alone. Having employees implies different attitudes towards business growth and the control of others. However, the strong tendency of small firm owners to remain in the same industries and the reluctance to employ more than a couple of other people, plus the strong family links to career choice, imply that financial motivation beyond survival is not as strong as other more personal goals. Most small firms appear to have well-defined financial peaks of satisfaction.

Uncertainties in the socio-economic environment appear to have pushed issues of financial security and survival to the fore but have not resulted in large numbers of small firms seeking financial gain. This also suggests – a finding supported by the rich patterns of change revealed in this chapter – that structural factors rather than personality determine a great part of business behaviour. It seems more likely that certain cultural sub-groups enter fairly low-skilled self-employment or switch from one form of self-employment to another as a function of the prevailing economic climate while another type of more qualified professional or manager ejected from larger organisations will start on their own in the absence of alternative work.

WORK PSYCHOLOGY OF THE SELF-EMPLOYED

It has been determined that entrepreneurs, like non-entrepreneurs, draw on a mix of motivations to spur their efforts but that the characteristics of intentionality and proactivity seem to be a feature of entrepreneurial behaviour. The most obvious places to investigate these issues are during the career-choice phase, as the decision to start or develop a business dominates, and during the growth phase. Starting with the first, it is clear that, although occupational and organisational psychology has grown in recent years, career theory ignores the entrepreneur almost completely. Business and work have been legitimate areas of psychological interest for most of this century but the self-employed have been tucked away in a forgotten corner even though many of the issues addressed by different approaches to career theory clearly have a bearing on the work behaviour of the more active self-employed. It should be noted, however, that the vast majority of self-employed are reactive, in the sense that there is little self-direction in their career choice which is mainly determined by external economic and social events or through cultural (family, class and locality) tradition (Hakim, 1988). Given the proactive nature of entrepreneurs, however, it is likely that they will not be reactive about their decision to seek a successful career working on their own account and that a more proactive and considered approach to their work lives will distinguish them from most self-employed and other small firm owners. The question mark hanging over enterprise training and all enterprise culture policies is whether such proactivity and clear goal setting can be induced in mature people where it was previously absent.

Basically, there are three approaches to career development theory: trait and factor, developmental, and humanist/self-awareness. Trait and factor theories are based on two underlying assumptions: first, that every occupation has an ideal personality profile and, second, that every individual's personality profile is predisposed towards one particular occupational area. Trait and factor theories seek to identify the distinguishing characteristics and features of both occupations and people, so that they can arrive at an optimum match. In pursuing these aims, they have generated a large number of scales and questionnaires to test personal differences, so that individuals can decide which jobs they want. According to trait and factor theory, successful small business career attainment would depend on a person (or people in the case of partnerships, cooperatives and team starts) exhibiting a reasonably wide range of the relevant traits and the enterprise offering a suitable outlet for that particular set of skills, attributes and qualities. Occupational psychological studies have identified two broadly contrasted approaches to work – *task-orientation* and *people-orientation*. Basic or modal people-orientation and task-orientation have been clearly demonstrated to have an influence on vocational choice (Osipow, 1983). It is a feature of small manufacturers, and certain other small business owners in the services (particularly high-technology), that they are often extremely deeply involved in their products (product-driven). Their work behaviour, consequently, tends to be task-oriented (Smith, 1967; Bolton, 1971; Dunkelberg and Cooper, 1982). Task-orientation or people-orientation appears to help explain the attraction of particular jobs and some industries but not necessarily why someone would prefer self-employment over work in a large organisation.

Where career changes represent a conscious and intentional choice, it seems likely that the failure to attain an expected level or type of job may provoke a career switch to self-employment, as Stanworth and Curran (1973) found in certain textile and printing firms. However, successful entrepreneurs clearly require some degree of both people- and task-orientation skills. They may be very focused on the task of making money or producing a new product but, as successful capitalists, they invariably need strong people skills to realise their objectives. Indeed, as businesses grow, it is the interpersonal skills that assume a greater significance. This suggests a process of development with changing occupational and self-concepts, rather than a static people-only or task-only orientation. Although trait and factor theories have produced a large volume of interesting research, they rest on the fundamentally flawed assumption that individual choice is the most important element in finding employment.

Structural factors, not the least the actual supply and demand for different jobs in the local economy, will usually have far more pronounced effects on employment behaviour. Even confining comment to areas of psychological interest, it is important not to overlook the basic distinctions between occupational preference, selection and actual attainment when discussing career choice (Vroom, 1964). Occupational satisfaction raises more issues which can add to the confusion. In general, it seems reasonable to accept that occupational preference is a function of individual development but that the processes of job search – occupational selection and attainment – and to some extent job satisfaction, are clearly constrained by socio-economic realities. By contrast, the *developmental* career choice approach is more flexible, viewing individual personalities as the outcome of personal development processes and experiences since infancy. It includes both psychodynamic and social developmental theories. The humanist approach holds some similar views to those of the social development school but places greater stress on the notion of self-concept, self-awareness, development and context, plus the belief that most people are striving for Maslow's fifth-level need of self-actualisation. Developmental theories move away from the search for the right personality mix and take the development of the self-concept as their starting point. As the self-concept forms, the young begin adopting work role models (social representations of work itself and of particular jobs) mainly through identification with their parents but later, as the self-concept develops, with other people. However, instead of seeking a compatible work environment, Super sees individuals as trying to develop their self-concepts by entering occupations likely to further self-expression.

According to Super (1957, 1980), people who can tolerate the ambiguity, uncertainty, tension and frustration which can result when job-search feedback clashes with their expectations deal with this cognitive dissonance by adjusting their concepts appropriately. This is more likely to happen if they actively explore real, external options rather than mentally speculate about outcomes. The development of both the self-concept and occupational knowledge relies on exploratory behaviour and evaluating the resultant feedback, though problems may arise if feedback clashes with expectations. Individuals who can tolerate ambiguity, uncertainty, tension and frustration can deal with this cognitive dissonance by adjusting their concepts appropriately. Social psychologist Henri Tajfel claims that 'even when facts do turn against us and destroy the useful and comfortable distinctions, we still find ways to preserve the general content of our categories' (1981: 132). This ability to be positive about reality-testing has been used consistently to describe entrepreneurs. It contrasts with the behaviour of defensive, unrealistic people who find it hard to handle cognitive dissonance, seek to rationalise the contradictory experience and do not gain from exploratory behaviour (in other words, exhibit high fear of failure and resistance to learning). Such individuals are likely to be drawn to self-employment in low barrier-to-entry industries or into areas reflecting family and cultural traditions. Many people drawn to enterprise training courses fall into this category. Consequently, self-employment may also be seen as the line of least resistance for many people rather than the challenge it is portrayed as in enterprise culture promotions. This helps to explain why many self-employed are reactive rather than proactive (Osipow, 1983).

Developmental theories recognise some limitations on individual decision making but these are also of an individualistic nature. To a large extent, the main weaknesses of most developmental theories spring from their overly tight focus on educational variables. Development is almost defined as moving from one educational situation to another, which is not particularly relevant for the 85 per cent of 18-year-olds in Britain who have left school. It is less relevant for the 20 per cent of under-25-year-olds who are long-term unemployed. The situational and social-learning approaches to career choice develop some of the processes of developmental career-choice theory and take into account some of the actual external constraints of the labour market. Lofquist and Dawis's (1969) work adjustment theory takes the basic personal needs fulfilment model but, instead of seeking ideal personality–job matches, they analyse work behaviour and career choice in terms of job satisfaction. Also building on the concept of congruence, they see vocational choice as a process whereby the individual seeks maximum satisfaction through congruence between occupational reinforcers and individual needs. Work adjustment is a constant process – not a stage process – and incongruency between work and personal environments leads to four interesting outcomes.

Flexible people will be able to tolerate this lack of congruence while *reactive* people will adjust their personal life to suit work. On the other hand, *active* people will adjust the work environment to enhance their personal lifestyle. The fourth concept is that of *celerity* which is the speed at which individuals will try to attain congruence between the work and personal environments. The active and reactive concepts have already been mentioned in the discussion of a self-employed typology. Indeed, people who are active tend to display leadership, organisational skills, achievements, innovative procedures, initiative and so on. In short, they are entrepreneurial and the opposite of reactives who tend to be conformist and normative. Again, the self-employed have not been addressed directly. For the majority of self-employed, the situational approach which is heavily influenced by sociology and admits the importance of social class, economic opportunities and even chance factors – especially for lower-level occupations – seems more applicable. For instance, Osipow (1983) recognises that education is the primary agent for occupational mobility but admits that educational decisions are often made casually and can affect future job prospects and behaviour enormously. It is mainly the petite bourgeoisie who are keen to use education for family advancement while the working class often remain outside the educational system. It is clearly the case that many self-employed and most unemployed also remain outside the reaches of the educational system.

However, inheritance of occupation can also play a role, especially where the parents work in a state of isolation from other people. This can be either physical or psychological isolation but the mechanism of identification and self-concept formation remains the same. Osipow mentions farming, fishing, medicine and the military as isolated occupations, but isolation is one of the biggest complaints of the self-employed and very small businesses (Gray and Stanworth, 1986). Unfortunately, isolation is also one of the big problems for the unemployed, raising the spectre of learned unemployment if the core of long-term unemployed cannot be reduced. The most important point to note is that the self-employed are almost completely neglected in career-choice theory. Indeed, the very concept of 'career' is itself questionable in this context. The mass of workers in the secondary sector do not have careers, they have jobs. If they are unemployed they lack jobs, not careers.

In analysing career-choice motivators, it is useful to distinguish the personal pull factors (intrinsic satisfaction, potential extrinsic financial reward, higher status and so on) from the external push factors (unemployment, famine, family pressures and so on). Push factors are much stronger for self-employed sole-traders than for the owners of small businesses. Although attribution theory would suggest some social-desirability risk of attributing the career change to oneself and a tendency to downplay the effects of push factors (except in the case of failure), it is reassuring to note that the findings show little difference between existing and lapsed self-employed. Of course, this does not rule out social desirability effects on causal attribution but it is interesting that the former self-employed admit to having been motivated more strongly by extrinsic financial pull factors than the survivors. Push factors (mainly labour market) and expectations concerning profits or revenue pose few problems for economists. In fact, a drift in and out of self-employment would conform with economic job search theory. However, even though there is little difference generally in causal attribution between people who actually are self-employed, who have left self-employment or who are thinking about entering self-employment, closer scrutiny reveals significant differences in emphasis, suggesting different conceptions of 'independence'.

The dominant concept of independence among people considering a career switch to self-employment is clearly of an 'avoidance of control by others' type, with two-thirds mentioning 'to be my own boss' or 'not to be told what to do' responses and one-third mentioning these feelings as their main reason. By contrast, just 20 per cent of the surviving self-employed mentioned these reasons and 10 per cent mentioned reasons connected with organising their own work (only 5 per cent of potential self-employed mentioned these reasons).

Tables 6.8 and 6.10 provide strong grounds for believing that the 'leave me alone' type of independence – which, in any case, has very limited economic appeal – is a feature of self-employment rather than small business management. Independence appears to remain a short-term objective as well as a longer-term goal for many self-employed whereas business concerns take over as short-term objectives for most small business owners, especially those who are interested in attaining any form of growth. This conclusion is supported by the large cultural, educational, social and demographic differences between the self-employed who work alone (69 per cent of all businesses in Britain) and the owners of small businesses – almost one-third of all businesses – that employ up to twenty-five people (Curran and Burrows, 1988; Department of Employment, 1989; Daly, 1991). Certainly, in terms of hours worked, small business owners seem much more work-oriented than the majority of the self-employed. This may be due to greater financial risk in a bigger enterprise or the fact that small business owners tend, on average, to be older than the self-employed with different concepts of work, self and freedom from control.

Social environmental theories which take into account the economic climate and the effects of socio-economic class offer the best framework for including non-conventional occupations such as self-employment, casual and part-time work and the workless occupation of unemployment. The concept of work and personal environment congruence is also helpful, especially in the context of a constant need to maintain work adjustment. Presumably, a failure to maintain congruence is a major reason why so many ex-employees seek an alternative career through self-employment, where they have greater control over their own work environment. Once again, however, it is not apparent how enterprise training can intervene effectively in this process, especially as its methodology in terms of learning theory and expected outcomes looks extremely weak. Indeed, it appears that career-choice theory has had little impact on enterprise culture ideology or practice.

CAREER MOTIVATION AMONG SELF-EMPLOYED AND SMALL ENTERPRISES

Early debates in psychology over whether motivation springs from an internal driving force (termed variously *drives* or *needs*) or from conscious striving towards external *goals* have been replaced by a more dynamic synthesis which, developing earlier work by Kurt Lewin (1938) on social learning and the positive or negative attraction of goals (*valence*), takes into account not only the valence but also the relative importance of goals (*value*) and the power of needs but also the degree of expectation (*expectancy*) that certain behaviours or outcomes will actually lead to attainment of a desired goal and the satisfaction of a need (Vroom, 1964; Atkinson and Feather, 1966; Schein, 1981) or the earlier and less challenging *statisficing* of a need (Simon, 1957). This model starts from a similar provenance to the constructivists' in that the individual is central and assumed to have a fairly complex set of preferences and goals. Faced with and making many choices (even if only by default), the individual is assumed to be an active participant. Earlier models (which include Freud's pioneering psychoanalytic model) were very deterministic, generally emphasising a *push* process, with the drives or needs providing the impetus. By the 1960s, following an analogous path to the constructivist psychologists', the notion of active individual choice in goal seeking challenged the earlier deterministic model, so that Rokeach in commenting on changes over the previous twenty years could state that an individual was 'seen to be not only a *rationalizing* but also a *rational* creature – curious, exploratory, and receptive to new ideas' (1968: 168).

The contrast between the two approaches can be seen through a comparison of Murray's (1938) list of psychogenic needs and Maslow's attempts to classify needs according to different levels of satisfaction or urgency without specifying any particular universal needs or goals. After a number of studies, Murray identified twenty separate needs which he believed impelled action on the part of individuals as a means of reducing tension caused by the unsatisfied need. Murray drew a distinction between physiological needs, which he termed *viscerogenic*, and affective or cognitive needs, termed *psychogenic*. As the following list in alphabetical order of Murray's psychogenic needs reveals, however, not all the needs (signified by the prefix *n*) are evidently independent of each other:

nAbasement	submit passively to external force;
nAchievement	accomplish something difficult, surpass others;
nAffiliation	enjoy cooperating, win affection;
nAggression	beat foes forcefully, fight, revenge;
nAutonomy	free from commitment and restraint, independence;
nCounteraction	overcome, persist, make up for failure by striving again;
nDefendance	resist assault, criticism, blame, vindicate the ego;
nDeference	admire superiors, praise, conform, be subordinate;
nDominance	control and command others, persuade;
nExhibition	create an impression, be seen and heard;
nHarm avoidance	avoid pain, take precautions;
nInfavoidance	avoid humiliation and act through fear of failure;
nNurturance	console and support others, give comfort;
nOrder	organise, achieve order, neatness, cleanliness;
nPlay	laugh, make jokes, fun for its own sake;
nRejection	expel, exclude, snub, dislike others;
nSentience	enjoy sensual pleasure;
nSex	enjoy sexual pleasure;
nSuccourance	be nursed, supported, protected, consoled;
nUnderstanding	interest in theory, seek answers, analyse events, logic.

Furnham (1992) points out that, although these twenty needs are actually descriptive labels and not very helpful in understanding the dynamics of how and when a need is activated, a number of other researchers have been influenced by Murray's treatment and taxonomy of needs. The most obvious example is David McClelland's interest in the achievement motive (nAch). McClelland was also interested in nAffiliation (nAff) and nDominance (which he slightly redefined and retitled nPower). Hofstede's cultural concepts also find an echo here. For instance, behaviour associated with Murray's nDeference and nDominance is likely to be a feature of the power/distance dimension; perhaps nAchievement, nInfavoidance and nUnderstanding are associated with uncertainty/avoidance; and, a central finding of this book, nAutonomy and nAffiliation are associated with the individualism/collectivism dimension that is so important in analysing the work behaviour of the self-employed and small enterprises. Murray's work on motivation has clearly provided a useful springboard, though, in many cases, needs in the list appear to be just the opposite poles of other needs (for instance, nAggression – nAbasement; nDominance – nDeference). This bi-polar approach is dealt with more effectively by Kelly's personal construct theory. Indeed, McClelland's colleagues John Atkinson and Norman Feather (1966) branched off in a very interesting direction by considering *fear of failure* as the mirror image of nAch but producing behaviour that much more closely describes the business behaviour of most self-employed and growth-averse small enterprise owners.

Almost twenty years after Murray published his lists of psychogenic needs, Abraham Maslow (1954) published his 'hierarchy of motives' theory which introduced the notion of individual choice and preference into Murray's essentially deterministic framework. Maslow also elaborated Murray's *viscerogenic–psychogenic* dichotomy into a five-stage model reflecting different levels and types of psychological needs, which has become widely used in management and business literature. Essentially, Maslow describes a process whereby people move from needing to satisfy primary drives through increasingly complex secondary needs until they reach a stage of needing to arrive at full self-awareness or self-actualisation. Maslow viewed the process as a hierarchy or pyramid consisting of the following five stages of needs:

physiological needs from primary or viscerogenic drives such as hunger, thirst, sex, physical activity, etc.;
safety needs including physical security, shelter, clothing, as well as protection from emotional and psychological deprivation;
social and *emotional* needs including belongingness, love, affection, company, etc.;
esteem needs including respect, self-esteem, appreciation, etc.;
self-actualisation needs which draw together all the other needs in an integrated desire for self-realisation and fulfilment of the individual's total capacities.

Maslow saw these different types of needs as being arranged in an upward progression with lower-level stages always dominating and requiring satisfaction before the next level becomes a strong motivator. Although there is little empirical evidence that people actually do pass sequentially from one level to another, the notion that there are different levels or broad types of motives and needs seems reasonable and, in business schools, has stood the test of time as an instructional model. For purposes of analysis, however, it has not been found too difficult to reduce Maslow's five categories to three broad types – basic primary needs (hunger, thirst, sex, safety, physical security, shelter), social transactional needs (love, affection, appreciation, company, esteem, respect, power, etc.) and personal development needs (self-actualisation, creativity, altruism and, possibly, need for achievement) – and actually improve their explanatory power (Gray, 1989). Furnham (1992) refers to the first three stages as deficiency needs and the last two stages as growth needs; this has a resonance with Herzberg's (1966) two-factor 'hygiene theory' which introduces the very useful idea that there can also be negative effects from occupational demotivators and that the absence of an expected level of work conditions or 'hygiene factors' can be as powerful a spur to action as need satisfaction.

The Herzberg two-factor work motivation theory is interesting from the viewpoint of career choice because it fits in with (and may partly explain) the line developed by Stanworth and Curran (1973) from Weber's (1930) concept of the 'outsider', that many people turn to self-employment because they find working in large organisations too onerous. However, both Antonides (1991) and Furnham (1992) emphasise the lack of convincing empirical support for these models, the low correlation between satisfaction and work performance, and lack of precision about what actually triggers behaviour in response to the motivators or demotivators. Even more devastating is Farr's (1977) methodological critique on the strong attributional effects present in Herzberg's studies. In effect, Herzberg's subjects were ascribing positive outcomes to their own actions but the negative outcomes were externalised as being 'caused' by their firms or working conditions. Herzberg conducted interesting studies into his subjects' attitudes towards their work and workplaces but was not entitled to draw his strong conclusions about the actual effects on performance or behaviour of his supposed 'hygiene factors'. This highlights a profound methodological challenge for all researchers attempting to investigate work motivation and any effects such motivation may have on actual performance.

Despite their limitations, Maslow's and Herzberg's models raise interesting questions in relation to small business behaviour. It is not too difficult to see how different career choices could result from different Maslow-level 'triggers'. For instance, it is clear that a large proportion of the self-employed, pushed into self-employment by the fear of unemployment, are mainly satisfying their more basic, lower-level needs for psychological and material security. Their principal business objective is usually survival rather than growth. People keen and able to network or work in organisations may well be motivated primarily by the second-level needs which most self-employed would find hard to satisfy through their work. At the top end of Maslow's pyramid, it could be argued that, while self-actualisation is a worthy human goal, the higher-level needs may actually represent a shift away from entrepreneurial goals except in the case of the entrepreneurs who feel a need to start new firms continuously one after the other.

The basic *expectancy* model of motivation mentioned earlier in this section (p. 127) can be seen to be an advance on the rather static models just described. Incorporating Herzberg's (1966) insights if not his methodology, the expectancy model also allows for goals having negative valency and the motivation relating not to need satisfaction but to anxiety reduction. Yet, although there is plenty of debate – certainly in management literature – on the links between motivation, satisfaction and performance, there is little on how these elements of the basic motivational model actually apply to entrepreneurial behaviour. As there has never been a serious suggestion that business or entrepreneurial success is due to an innate 'business drive', however, studies and theories of motivation in the present context are usually more concerned with socially learned needs. Before moving on to consider how these concepts of motivation apply to business behaviour, it is worth noting one important distinction between socially learned needs which reflect inner, psychological desires such as status or social esteem (the satisfaction of which is said to be *intrinsic*) and the attainment of external goals such as money (*extrinsic* satisfaction). This basic psychological debate over whether motivation reflects inner drives and needs or the conscious striving towards external goals is very important when business motivation, including the effects of incentives, is considered.

MOTIVATION IN BUSINESS

We have already examined the economists' notions of main business motivations and seen that the rationally economic profit motive may be dominant but not unique. Even in the classical tradition there are others such as Adam Smith's (1776) emphasis on self-interest (wealth maximisation) as well as a 'human propensity to barter and trade', the Benthamites' pursuit of happiness (utility maximisation) and John Stuart Mill's (1848) tendency of firms to concentrate (the maximisation of power or control). In the non-classical tradition of political economy, Marx (1867) stressed accumulation of capital as the prime business motivation, Schumpeter (1934) linked economic motivation and growth to the need to innovate and the desire to improve social status while Keynes (1936) – not completely outside the neo-classical framework – identified the fear of lost opportunities (e.g. liquidity trap, investment preferences, etc.) which induces business owners to keep their options open. Other issues connected with business motivation are also important, such as the differences in self-interest between owners and their managers or the differences in market power between big and small firms.

The distinction made by Carland *et al.* (1984) between entrepreneurs in particular and small business owners in general highlights another important distinction between personal motivation and the target objectives set for the business. This distinction does not discount the possibility that entrepreneurs may treat their businesses instrumentally as the means to enable them to achieve non-business goals (such as status, lifestyle, etc.) but modern management experts are agreed in linking business success – the ultimate goal of the entrepreneur – to the setting of clear, measurable and appropriate business objectives. Indeed, there is evidence to suggest that entrepreneurs actually enjoy business and that their firms are central to their lives (Timmons *et al.*, 1977; Stanworth and Curran, 1973; Brockhaus and Horwitz, 1986). It is also clear that many self-employed and the owners of smaller businesses, especially those seeking to avoid unemployment or failure in larger organisations, do not view their business as central to their lives, and their eventual lack of success may be due to this lack of focus. This also highlights the importance of accurately framing the subjects' situation when conducting research of this type because, as Kahneman and Tversky (1982) found when analysing risk perception, subjects will have quite different sets of expectations and preferences depending on their objective situation.

Indeed, despite the importance of setting appropriate goals to business success, it is the entrepreneurs' needs and expectations which is of most interest psychologically. Although there is still plenty of scope for more focused psychological studies of the entrepreneur, a number of key elements in the entrepreneurial profile have been identified on pp. 51–2 – internal locus of control, need for achievement, controlled risk taking, setting attainable goals, money as a measure of success, persistence, keen problem solvers, etc. (Timmons *et al.*, 1977; Chell, 1985; Brockhaus and Horwitz, 1986). At first sight, most of these features are more descriptive of attitudes and behaviour than of psychological needs but, especially in the context of work, psychological needs reflect a variety of situations. Despite the overwhelming evidence confirming the importance of such a non-economic motive as independence, economists still seem to rely on theories of the firm and research models based on neo-classical profit-maximising assumptions (albeit with some or all of the more rigorous assumptions considerably relaxed). There seem to be three main reasons for this rather widespread economic myopia. First, despite the size of the small firm sector, economists tend to be interested mainly in larger firms where interest in their findings and supporting evidence for their models is stronger. Second, it is difficult to model non-economic behaviour econometrically (except, in certain cases, as constraints). The third reason, which is a concern of this book, is that many economists quite rightly feel that non-economic motivators – such as independence – are too imprecise to allow for accurate modelling and rigorous testing. Morris Silver (1984) explains the economists' reluctance to include behavioural variables in their analysis on the grounds that it is hard to fit non-quantifiable elements into factor-market models.

It would be difficult not to feel some sympathy for these objections were it not for the fact that management literature is riddled with references to the importance of intrinsic motivators – those that satisfy inner, personal needs, such as the desire for independence – over the more obvious extrinsic, economic and financial motivators (those satisfying external, material needs). Indeed, some prominent economists have recognised the economic importance of intrinsic motivators such as status, income relativities and social recognition (Duesenberry, 1949; Hirsch, 1977). However, the purpose of this book is not to provide an econometric, or even psychometric, model of the small firm but rather to analyse the concept of work motivation from a small business perspective with the aim of distinguishing the areas amenable to economic analysis and policy from those where more creative work needs to be done to incorporate essentially non-economic behaviour into an economic framework. Studies of small business owner-managers from many different industrial sectors have found consistently that their reasons for starting their businesses are more likely to be a desire for independence, autonomy, self-awareness, self-actualisation and a sense of achievement rather than any of the more traditional economic business motivations (Bolton, 1971; Stanworth and Curran, 1973; Curran and Stanworth, 1981; Gray and Stanworth, 1986). Furthermore, it is equally clear that the traditional ideas of business motivation – such as growth, wealth, accumulation of capital or the maximisation of profits – have very little influence, even in a peripheral sense, on many small businesses (especially the self-employed).

Timmons and his co-workers (1977) suggested that entrepreneurs are interested in money not so much for its own sake but more as a measure of their success over business competitors. This is in keeping with the treatment by certain economists of intrinsic motivators – in particular Dusenberry's (1949) 'keeping up with the neighbours' effects on consumer behaviour and Hirsch's (1977) 'positional goods' argument that economic growth can never produce total satisfaction. This introduces another element to consider when interpreting the true significance of responses to questions about business objectives such as 'lifestyle', 'continued growth', 'make money' and so on. However, the fact that many small businesses do not appear to be economically rational does not mean that profit maximisation is irrelevant as a business motive. In fact, if entrepreneurs, as owners of relatively new small businesses, have continued to grow successfully (in turnover, profits and/or employment), it is likely that they measure their success in terms of increased profits because, as Timmons *et al.* (1977) suggested, profits are the best measure of business efficiency and personal success. Accepting the motivational significance of profits to small business owners and the use of business performance measures as evidence of entrepreneurial motivation enables the concept of entrepreneurship to be operationalised. It also provides a yardstick for measuring business achievement though other measures such as growth in market share, perceived quality image and positioning in the market could also provide valid measures. For the present purposes, a stated preference for profit growth as the main business objective will be taken to imply an entrepreneurial approach. The attainment of sales without increase in labour costs is a reasonable proxy for successful achievement. Psychologically, it is important to establish that this type of achievement is the hallmark of the entrepreneur and a valid target for enterprise training.

NEED FOR ACHIEVEMENT

It is difficult to mention the psychology of the entrepreneur or entrepreneurial motivation without some reference to need for achievement (nAch), as developed by David McClelland and other researchers. As already mentioned, nAch was considered with two other of Murray's (1938) psychogenic needs – the need for social contact or affiliation (nAff, a third-level need in Maslow's terms) and the need for dominance or power (nPow, third or fourth level). Entrepreneurs and top managers are distinguished – in big firms as well as small – by their strong nAch and comparatively higher nPow and lower nAff (Murray, 1938; Atkinson and Feather, 1966; McClelland, 1961; McClelland and Winter, 1971; Davidsson, 1989a). It is interesting that nPow constructs predominate not only among both top- and bottom-level managers but also among many small firm owners while nAff constructs characterise non-entrepreneurial mid-level managers (Stewart and Stewart, 1981). Earlier work by McClelland (1961) on achievement motivation produced some interesting results which had an impact on course selection and skill training, especially in India. Indeed, one of the strengths of the nAch concept has been its apparent applicability across cultural boundaries (Wainer and Rubin, 1969).

Critics, however, have cast doubt on the validity of the work and have suggested that achievement training only touches surface behaviour and that the effects are usually temporary (Fineman, 1979; Brockhaus, 1982; Gasse, 1982). Also, achievement is usually measured by Thermatic Apperception Tests (TAT) which are often criticised on the grounds of subjectivity and lack of consistency. Furthermore, a number of studies have suggested that nAch is not one single need but is, in fact, multidimensional with as many as seven different factors (Cassidy and Lynn, 1989). Although there are grounds for doubting that the seven factors – work ethic (pleasure from hard work), pursuit of excellence (performing to the best of one's ability), status aspiration (social status and respect), dominance (need to be dominant), competitiveness (desire to compete with others), acquisitiveness (low Maslow-level material rewards) and mastery (overcoming difficult problems) – are independent, there is little doubt that nAch is a fairly complex construct, likely to reflect different processes of development in different individuals. Research at OUBS suggests that there are at least two different aspects of nAch, the first of which does relate to continued striving for success but the second to the fall-off in motivation with the satisfaction or satisficing of goals. It seems reasonable to assume that individual or even aggregated levels of satisfaction will be affected by many different factors. Therefore, even though it may be meaningful to use nAch as a broad construct to examine entrepreneurial behaviour, its complexity poses the operational problem of completely separating the small business owner's extrinsic goals (business objectives) from the intrinsic goals. Furthermore, the identification of an opposite but separate concept to nAch, fear of failure, suggests that the other psychogenic needs may also be multi- or bi-dimensional (see pp. 128–9).

Before any discussion of the applicability of these theory to small business development in Britain, it is instructive to examine McClelland's social learning theory that underpins it for the light that it casts on the process of acquiring strong achievement motivation. McClelland's methodology is fascinating and he managed to tap an incredibly rich vein of social data mainly through a structured content analysis of children's stories, myths and legends, as well as by employing a more direct clinical approach through thematic apperception tests. He was mainly concerned to elaborate a psychologically rooted theory which basically holds that economic development is a function of the entrepreneurial spirit in a society as revealed through the average or aggregate nAch among its citizens. This he established to his own satisfaction even though others may remain not quite so convinced. At the same time he discovered interesting phenomena such as the pattern of high nPow and low nAff in the children's stories of countries where dictatorial regimes were to come to power (which he called a psychological index of ruthlessness). At the individual level he demonstrated that the profit motive accounted for comparatively little small business behaviour and reaffirmed the Timmons *et al.* (1977) finding that 'money served as a ready quantitative index of how well [entrepreneurs] were doing' (McClelland, 1968: 85). This, plus the knowledge, judgement and skill which inform decision making, are explicitly linked to nAch in that a justified decision can give the entrepreneur 'a sense of personal achievement from having made a successful move' (McClelland, 1968: 86).

It is easy to see how McClelland's work provided the platform for a lot of subsequent entrepreneurial research and nowhere is this clearer than in his discussion on how high nAch is acquired. According to McClelland, high nAch is acquired fairly early in life 'say, by the age of eight or ten, as a result of the way his parents brought him up'. He manifestly links this to class and cultural influences. Drawing on Weber's marginal man theory, McClelland states that, by contrast with underdeveloped countries where the educated elite secure privileged jobs in the professions, in successful developed economies business has a higher status with a 'constant "natural" flow of entrepreneurial talent from the middle classes [providing] economic leadership of the highest talent' (1968: 90). He demolishes the argument that entrepreneurial talent could be hereditary (on the grounds that changes in nAch are too rapid) and points to the fact that parents of high nAch children set higher levels of aspiration for a variety of tasks for their off-spring than the parents of low nAch children. The high nAch parents also provided much more positive feedback to their children on their performance though high nAch mothers tended to be rather domineering (and the fathers far less domineering). Although this contrasts with the pattern described by Kets de Vries (1977, 1980), the psychodynamic development process is very similar though different parental behavioural inputs are used. McClelland is extremely clear that 'the family is the key formative influence' in developing high nAch but that because of this the general levels of nAch 'are very hard to change on a really large scale' (1968: 93). This reaffirms the real challenge facing policies of the enterprise culture type.

The importance of nAch for this book rests on two pillars: the fact that it does seem to distinguish between growth-oriented entrepreneurs and other growth-averse small enterprise owners, and the claim that it may be possible to encourage it through appropriate training. However, enterprise training does not generally include achievement motivation training. Also, OUBS surveys confirm other studies, findings that the strength of achievement motivation wanes with age. There are strong signs that this actually reflects Kahneman and Tversky framing effects (or what economists refer to as an endowment effect) related to the stage of personal life-cycle development of the respondents and a higher perception of risk among those who have something to lose. A factor analysis of OUBS data yielded two factors – 'achievement' and 'satisfaction' – of which *satisfaction* had the greatest discriminatory power between more and less enterprising subjects. This also fits Schumpeter's predictions and undermines the economic case for enterprise culture policies.

However, the real clue to small business behaviour may not lie with achievement motivation but with its opposite, *fear of failure*. Individuals with high nAch also have a low fear of failure and tend to take calculated risks rather than gamble (though they are not risk-averse). People with high fear of failure set themselves tasks with either too high or too low levels of aspiration, contrasting strongly with successful entrepreneurs who tend to set themselves high but attainable goals (Atkinson, 1957; Brockhaus, 1980). Atkinson and Feather (1966) summarised the sort of upbringing that people strongly motivated to avoid failure are likely to have experienced. They are more likely to have been punished for failures (and more heavily for failing easier tasks) than rewarded for achievements, and their mothers, who are likely to be 'anxious and avoidant', are likely to encourage them to play safe or fantasise, but not to encourage realistic expectations. This pattern of behaviour is similar to that described by Kets de Vries and fits current patterns of small business behaviour in Britain. With few exceptions, low levels of growth and high failure rates characterise Britain's small business sector.

Very few small business failures admit that they set their sights too high or too low and virtually none – apart from certain self-employed who had previously been unemployed – state that they are motivated by a fear of failure. However, analyses of small business failure point to unrealistic targets and a failure to match their finances to their expectations (LBS, 1987). The patterns of occupational choice among the self-employed in low barrier-to-entry industries reflect the findings reported by Atkinson and Feather that people afraid of failure tend to 'choose occupations only remotely related to the kinds of gratifications that they desire and expect to find in their vocations often because the fearful person may be expected to lack information concerning his own ability and that required for his choice of occupation' (1996: 170). This will be reflected in avoidance of realistic and mildly challenging choices in favour of easy tasks or absurdly hard ones, a pattern not only reflected in many self-employed career choices and also in their business objectives. Indeed, even the well-known small business goal of independence – which is another apparently simple yet multidimensional construct – is likely to be an unreal aspiration in most cases, reflecting more a desire to be left alone than any real prospect of growth to a size where independent action is a genuine possibility (Bolton, 1971; Curran, 1986; Gray 1990). Whether the type of enterprise training offered in Britain can change such deep-rooted and habituated behaviour is doubtful.

NEED FOR AUTONOMY AND INDEPENDENCE

One of the most noted psychological features of small business owners and the self-employed is their strong desire for independence, or nAutonomy in Murray's (1938) terms. The Bolton Report (Bolton, 1971) found the expressed need to attain and preserve independence to be a stronger motivator than the desire to make money. These findings have been confirmed in one research report after another – Stanworth and Curran (1973), a national Gallup poll for Legal and General (1985), an Infoline telephone survey for the Department of Employment (Hakim, 1989), a NatWest/SBRT *Quarterly Survey of Small Business in Britain* (SBRT, 1990) and a 1991 tracking exercise conducted by NatWest Bank among 2,000 newly started small business clients. Some 37 per cent of the Gallup poll's 2,500 self-employed respondents reported the 'need for independence' as their main reason for setting up on their own; 42 per cent of the NatWest clients and half (50 per cent) of the 1,300 respondents to the SBRT quarterly survey stated that 'independence' was their main reason for being in business. Furthermore, the allure of independence is felt by the self-employed and founders of small businesses not only in Britain but also in such other industrialised economies as the USA, the Netherlands, Belgium, Ireland, Italy and so on (Sexton and Smilor, 1986; Donckels and Dupont, 1987). In the SBRT study, just 19 per cent of the respondents reported that 'making money' was their prime motivation for being in business for themselves while according to the NatWest

Table 7.1 Motivation for self-employment (percentages)

Main motives	New self-employed	Former self-employed	Potential self-employed	Enterprise trainees	SBRT small firms (1990)
Independence	31	32	42	29	50
Financial	18	26	23	14	19
Unemployment	15	13	14	44	–
Other push	3	1	1	–	25
Family	4	6	2	3	5
Total	243	90	139	206	1,349
(%)	(100)	(100)	(100)	(100)	(100)

Source: Hakim (1989); Blythe *et al.* (1989); SBRT (1990, 1996).

study 32 per cent of the clients were motivated by the prospect of greater financial reward and 14 per cent mentioned the avoidance of unemployment. In Table 7.1, which summarises the findings of a Department of Employment report (Hakim, 1989), a study of enterprise trainees in the Greater London area (Blythe *et al.*, 1989) and two SBRT surveys, a clear majority of existing, failed and potential self-employed reported being driven by independence-related motives, with financial motivators (20 per cent) a distant second place and unemployment third.

The importance of independence as a central element of the small firm owners' self-concepts at even the earliest stages of small business development is clear and consistent. Furthermore, the responses from the SBRT samples of existing small enterprise owners reveal how resilient these different motives are, consistent through the recession of 1990 and the recovery of 1996. It appears that enterprise training programmes attract only certain types of potential self-employed and small enterprise owners. The potential founders of small businesses are clearly the most concerned about independence but their concerns are not so strongly felt by the participants on enterprise training courses. These differences may reflect the higher educational levels of enterprise trainees (more than half – 51 per cent – have higher education qualifications compared with 15 per cent of the self-employed nationally), which may also partly explain the extreme difficulty enterprise trainers have in reaching the self-employed (Gray and Stanworth, 1986; Blythe *et al.*, 1989; Daly, 1991). Even though high failure rates suggest that independently minded small business owners need to improve their management skills, enterprise training does not seem to feature in their plans for independence, which may reflect some of the negative features of the need for achievement.

The desire for independence has been linked to resentment at the power of larger organisations or at not attaining the expected status within larger organisations, and is clearly an important factor in the career choice of many self-employed (Bolton, 1971; Stanworth and Curran, 1973; Gray,

1988). However, as we have seen, there are suggestions that the desire for independence or autonomy is a function of more deeply rooted socio-cultural factors associated with unequal class power relations resulting from present and past political-economic developments. In the search to escape from these unequal power relations at the individual level, the stated objective of independence is an assertion of control over one's own destiny and can be seen as an expression of nPow. By analogy with fear of failure, it could be termed fear of dominance. The essentially anti-social or isolated nature of a great deal of self-employment has also been well documented and expressions of desire for independence of this type – to be left alone or fear of social exposure – can be seen as the opposite pole of a nAff dimension (Gray and Stanworth, 1986; Curran, 1986; Curran and Burrows, 1988).

On a more positive note, however, independence can also refer to an ultimate state of self-control and defeat of alienation which, as a personal development goal beyond business objectives, would be an appropriate target for someone with high nAch who had succeeded in satisfying basic and social transactional needs. Indeed, this may explain why many early entrepreneurial careers reach a plateau and, as Schumpeter observed, cease being entrepreneurial. As mentioned earlier (p. 79), on achieving a certain level of wealth or security, this type of entrepreneur could seek new challenges of a non-business kind. Therefore, there are at least three different types of independence as a motivational goal which may be linked to McClelland's treatment of psychogenic needs. Actual patterns of business behaviour suggest that the fear of dominance (nPow) and fear of social exposure (nAff) types of independence are dominant among the self-employed with fear of dominance and, to a lesser extent, nAch present among many small firm owners.

Psychologically, it is not too difficult to see how different independence needs could lead to different patterns of small business behaviour. Needs that are closest to an individual's central areas of concern – those that are psychologically central – will obviously produce stronger motivation, provided there is a realistic and attainable way of satisfying those needs. Therefore, if work is more psychologically central than home or leisure, then the need to engage in work that provides positive self-validation will be stronger – in general, work that is seen to be challenging, creative, self-directed and more autonomous (Gecas and Seff, 1990). The self-employed and small business owners for whom work is psychologically central may need to maintain their own positive self-esteem by viewing their jobs as autonomous and self-directed even when, in reality, they are actually dependent on a few large customers or suppliers. Positive attitudes towards growth may also be part of their self-concept from which they derive their self-esteem. The importance of business cultural values in influencing how independence may be defined by firms with growth potential was highlighted in a 1993 OUBS management development study which followed up a sub-sample

Table 7.2 Business objectives and centrality of 'business' to owner

Business centrality	Business/ economic		Security		Lifestyle		Other		Total (%)	
Non-business	14		27		39		4		84	(28)
Business	77		66		65		9		217	(71)
Total (%)	91	(30)	93	(31)	104	(35)	13	(4)	301	(100)

of SBRT respondents. Table 7.2 outlines differences between owners who are business-centred and those who are more concerned about the non-business sides of their lives.

These differences were statistically significant ($p < 0.027$) and suggest that those who define their interests and independence in business terms are more likely to want to pass through the various stages of entrepreneurial growth. These are likely to provide the bulk of small firms that grow to a size where delegation, division of labour and formal systems are features of survival and success. When leisure or home is more psychologically central than work, the self-employed and small business owners will mainly treat their business as a source of funding for their other activities. They will not be strongly motivated towards business growth, and independence could well mean little more than freedom to have the time and money to support their non-business activities.

In addition, there will be a large number of self-employed who, recognising the routine and dependent nature of their work (conditions associated with low self-esteem), defensively seek to minimise work-related social contacts; for them the independence motive will be a desire to be left alone. Indeed, this type of 'leave me alone' independence may either reflect or even cause much of the essentially anti-social or isolated nature of a great deal of self-employment (Gray and Stanworth, 1986; Curran, 1986; Gray, 1988). There is little doubt that the psychological meaning of independence, when reported by the self-employed and the owners of smaller businesses as a motive for being in business on their own account, is cloaked in ambiguity. Because of severe limitations in their resources and market share, functional independence for most small businesses is likely to be an unreal aspiration. In most cases, the question is not over actual functional independence (which is also an illusion for most large firms) but whether the behaviour of small business owners reflects a desire to take personal responsibility for decision making or a desire to be left alone. The first implies a learning curve and the prospect of growth as the owner seeks to address new and more complex problems while the second implies dogged seclusion and no real prospect of growth to a sufficient size where independent action is a genuine possibility (Bolton, 1971; Curran, 1986). Certainly, the self-employed who are mainly motivated by various push factors or by 'leave me alone' independence needs are extremely unlikely to be strong growth prospects.

Most aspects of business involve social transactions and, therefore, growth implies not only the possession of a reasonably high degree of social skills but also a positive desire to take charge of one's own destiny. It seems intuitively likely that growers feel they can control their own lives and that they opted for business growth intentionally if not always in a planned fashion. Although the survival rates of the 'pushed' self-employed do not always differ significantly from other small business founders (Storey, 1986a), they are not likely to be so keen to view independence as an extension of personal control and responsibility because genuine autonomy usually involves an element of choice and intention (Deci and Ryan, 1985). Official Labour Force Surveys indicate that overall 19 per cent of the self-employed have moved straight into self-employment from unemployment, with another 18 per cent – excluding the 5 per cent of students – entering self-employment from previous economic inactivity (Daly, 1991). Because it is unlikely that many of the 'leave me alone' independence seekers actually reply to surveys, the role of push factors may very well be underestimated.

Consequently, the number of small business owners who genuinely and actively opted for self-employment as an extension of their self-control are likely to be fewer than suggested by surveys based on self-report. This reference to self-reports is not intended to be pejorative because, although self-reports are open to methodological criticism if their purpose is to reveal unconscious or socially sensitive data, the self-concept must – by definition – represent the opinions that one holds about oneself. Whatever proportion of the total small business population the more active small business owners represent, they are likely to hold a strong conception of themselves and the type of work, the social status, the level of responsibility and the remuneration they consider appropriate. In other words, they should have strong and well-defined self-concepts and, if they have taken the step of seeking personal responsibility in achieving their aims, they must believe that they have the skills and capacity to attain those aims in spite of existing external barriers. Of course, these are the features of people with high internal nAch and locus of control which leaves open the possibility that certain entrepreneurs may exhibit similar psychological features and, possibly, some similarities in personal or business development background factors.

RISK PROPENSITY

Schumpeter (1934) felt that entrepreneurs would use their skills to minimise the risk they have to bear – correctly, in the light of modern banking practice and assessment of risk – and assigns the risk bearing in a new venture to the capitalist (provider of investment capital). However, earlier definitions and popular current conceptions of the entrepreneur usually view risk taking as an essential element. If a softer definition of *risk* as tolerance of uncertainty is used, this does not pose a conceptual problem and is inherent in such expressions as 'taking a chance', 'prepared to have a go', 'dare to win' and so on. Certainly, popular notions of the entrepreneur and Schumpeter's more technical conception agree that entrepreneurs cannot be risk-averse, yet equally entrepreneurial success is not seen as mainly due to luck or chance. In this sense, risk is clearly linked to uncertainty, and risk taking seems associated with proactivity and intentionality. However, as Kahneman and Tversky (1979, 1982) have demonstrated over a wide range of situations, perceptions of risk, reward and uncertainty not only differ from one economic actor to the next but also, to a very large extent, depend on the framing of the situation and the perspective of the risk assessor. At the small business end of the market, however, perceptions of risk vary enormously (borrower, lender, foresight, hindsight and so on) and the concept of risk is not, therefore, particularly helpful in entrepreneurial research in spite of its theoretical value.

For practical and research purposes, therefore, risk as uncertainty is a psychologically imprecise term even though economists can model uncertainty as an informational constraint. However, a harder definition of *risk* – the probability of a negative outcome from any action or decision – has taken on an almost purely financial character in the eyes of modern bankers. Both this financial risk approach and a similar economist's definition by Knight (1921) – a future variability, predictable according to the laws of chance, hence insurable – demand an intellectual approach which is at variance with the observed financial decision-making behaviour of actual small firm owners (Binks, 1991). In psychological terms, these tougher definitions, which imply an active assessment of realistic risk as opposed to a vaguer acceptance of uncertainty, also require a well-developed ability in probabilistic calculations – which may or may not be a cognitive feature of successful entrepreneurs. Thus risk is clearly also an issue that cannot be ignored but is too complex to operationalise for current research purposes or to investigate thoroughly in the present context. The propensity for risk taking and risk aversion in business people has been studied extensively but it is only possible to say that potential benefits must be seen to outweigh the potential risk and, where the doubt is high, people who already enjoy substantial benefits tend to risk aversion while those who are without tend to risk taking (Kahneman and Tversky, 1979).

Brockhaus (1980) compared managers who had taken a risk in leaving their jobs to start their own businesses with managers who had avoided such a risk and stayed. He found no significant differences in risk-taking propensity. Despite these theoretical, practical and empirical objections, entrepreneurs are still often thought to be risk takers even though actual responses to risk by managers in general – entrepreneurial and otherwise – 'are not easily fitted into classical conceptions of risk' (March and Shapira, 1987). Psychological studies have distinguished entrepreneurs from most other small firm owners – though not from successful big firm managers – in their efforts to calculate and control risks (Timmons *et al.*, 1977;

Brockhaus, 1980). However, for present purposes it is accepted that the full weight of empirical evidence and theory indicates that entrepreneurs are neither risk-averse (unlike mid-management in larger organisations and traditional small business owners) nor reckless (unlike gamblers and certain failed small business owners). Certainly, this fits McClelland's (1968) and Timmons *et al.*'s (1977) findings. Risk perception is not a central issue in this book except in so far as it relates to the original decision to switch careers and embark on a new life of self-management.

8 The entrepreneur: nature or nurture?

The targets of enterprise culture policies were particularly psychological – in general, the transformation of attitudes, behaviour and values – and, more precisely, the creation of new entrepreneurs. We have already examined extensively the wider and more ambitious targets they sought to achieve as well as the cultural issues inherent in the policies. The more precise target of creating new entrepreneurs goes right to the heart of the age-old psychological debate: are entrepreneurs born or are they created through their life experiences? Given the central themes of this book and the empirical evidence considered so far, it is difficult to sustain the 'entrepreneurs are just born that way' argument. I recall one Minister for Small Firms devoting an entire speech to the notion that entrepreneurship was 'in the blood'. And a central tenet of early enterprise culture policy was that the removal of barriers and disincentives would allow thousands of previously blocked entrepreneurs to take their rightful place in the British economy. However, as we have seen, that has not happened. Instead, there has been a shift from large-scale fairly fixed employment into various forms of more temporary and precarious occupations, including self-employment. Small, innovative and growing enterprises have sprung up in areas and industries where new opportunities and skills have appeared, mainly due to external structural changes.

At a more philosophical level, it is hard to hold that entrepreneurs are born and, at the same time, promote policies designed to help people to become entrepreneurs. Economic and social development policies imply a belief that our behaviour and future prospects can be improved as a result of appropriate interventions and new experiences. The question then becomes one of how to nurture the cultural and behavioural changes we have been discussing. Basically, the arguments and issues presented here reflect a *constructivist* position which presupposes the existence of a material world populated with material objects and beings but perceived, described and interpreted uniquely by each and every individual. At the individual level, this is the approach of George Kelly's (1955) *personal construct psychology* which implies a continuing learning process as individuals construe and reconstrue the external material and social world, and their own roles in it, according to their past perceptions, present realities and anticipations. Each individual behaves like a scientist, categorising his or her own experience into a system of constructs, then continually testing and adapting this construct system in the light of subsequent experience. This provides a powerful and useful model of self-development and learning, not necessarily at odds with enterprise culture objectives.

In keeping with the generally individualist traditions of social psychology in the USA, Kelly proposes that when individuals share similar 'construings' of events or phenomena there is scope for a type of 'social construction'. However, the historic and actual power of certain social relations (such as socio-political structures, ideology, institutions, culture, class, etc.) is too strong and persistent to be adequately explained by Kelly's social corollary. However, even though these pervasive social constructs are crucially important for communication and influential in determining individual behaviour and attitudes (including the concept of personal identity), they are also subject to the same effects of individual perception that filter concrete reality.

In occupational psychology terms, it is reasonable to argue that entrepreneurs display sharper judgement and closer congruence between perceptions and reality than other less successful or less entrepreneurial business managers. Business judgement then becomes a matter of how closely individuals' perceived needs, abilities and opportunities correspond to their objective possibilities and their objective ability (*competence*) to act upon that information. The question of competence is extremely important. Just as levels of individual capability and levels of work effectiveness have been seen as key determinants of the structure and career-path opportunities of bureaucratic hierarchies (Jaques, 1976), similar factors determine career choice and relative performance within the small business sector. This suggests that one obvious yet important distinguishing feature of entrepreneurs is that they must be capable and competent as enterprise managers – certainly much more so than most small business owners or managers.

In essence, this is the rationale behind the strong emphasis on 'enterprise' training as a crucial element of enterprise culture policies. There may be strong doubts about the possibility of teaching 'entrepreneurial behaviour' but there is little doubt that basic business techniques can be taught. The important questions remain of whether the basic business techniques taught on most enterprise training programmes are sufficient to produce a skilled approach to business and whether their new skills and awareness are sufficient to transform naive business owners or non-business people into effective innovating entrepreneurs. Gary Becker's (1964) *human capital theory* provides an economic rationale for explaining why individuals might consider investing in training to effect a career shift of this type but there is little empirical evidence, as we have seen, that these economically rational considerations explain much recent small business or entrepreneurial development without taking into account cultural and social psychological influences. Before examining these issues, however, we need to be clearer about what exactly an entrepreneur is.

CHANGING REPRESENTATION OF THE 'ENTREPRENEUR'

Strictly speaking, the term *entrepreneur*, which derives from the French words *entre* (between) and *prendre* (to take), refers to someone who acts as an intermediary in undertaking to do something. The term was apparently originally used to describe the activities of what today we might call an *impresario*. The entrepreneur first made an appearance as a distinct economic concept in France, twenty years before Smith published his *Wealth of Nations*. Richard Cantillon (1756), an Irishman living in France, suggested that the entrepreneur was someone prepared to bear uncertainty in engaging in risky arbitrage – buying goods and services at *certain* (fixed) prices to be sold elsewhere or at another time for *uncertain* future prices. This concept is clearly influenced by the dominance of trade as the chief means for accumulating new wealth and capital.

This earlier notion of the risk-taking trader, however, began to be challenged by the view of the entrepreneur as an adventurous self-employed manager capable of combining, to personal advantage, capital and labour. It is interesting to note that in France today the entrepreneur is a more generic term, mainly referring to small property developers and owners of small construction firms. It would be wrong to state that the element of risk bearing has completely disappeared from the modern concept of the entrepreneur but it does seem that a swift perception of opportunities and the ability to coordinate the activities of others emerge as the more central skills of the modern entrepreneur. This shift was clearly demonstrated in the virtual absence of risk taking as an important element in the concept of the entrepreneur among enterprise owners.

Yet, although the entrepreneur has long been recognised as an interesting character in the economic landscape, economic theory has virtually ignored the importance of the attitudes, values, abilities and personality of owners and managers to a firm's economic behaviour. Economic 'agents' or 'actors' are treated in neo-classical economics as abstractions rather than individuals. Nevertheless, speculation on the motivation of business owners in general was quite common in the earlier tradition of political economy. For instance, Adam Smith (1776), widely regarded as the father of economics, wrote about the greedy nature of business owners and their tendency to conspire, with the aim of increasing their own accumulation of wealth, against consumers whenever they grouped together. However, one century later a more abstract analysis of markets came to the fore, and economics was dominated by the mathematical equilibrium analyses of Alfred Marshall (1920) which, according to Silver (1984), have no place for such an awkward concept as the entrepreneur.

Smith's central thesis was that the pursuit of individual self-interest, bound by the imperatives of commercial competition, produced the greater specialisation and diversity of products and services which ultimately led to the betterment of society. Smith believed that humans had an inherent 'propensity to truck, barter and exchange one thing for another' and that it was this *propensity to exchange* (in the labour market as well as the goods market) that gave rise to the division of labour. He also claimed socially beneficial impersonal effects for competition and the pursuit of personal self-interest (hence his famous throwaway phrase, 'the invisible hand of competition'). Although Smith drew no distinction between entrepreneurial and non-entrepreneurial business owners, or between small and big (perhaps they were all smallish and entrepreneurial in the eighteenth century), he saw the accumulation of wealth as the sign of success and the attainment of high rates of profit as the sure path to that success. For him, it appears that all capitalists, as a newly emerging class, were entrepreneurs.

Smith implicitly recognised that motivations change with circumstance and that circumstances change as people become more wealthy. Indeed, he regarded rich successful merchants as the best defenders of society against the worst 'anti-environmental' effects of unbridled competition because of their altered priorities due to their recently improved station in life. It is important to note, however, that Smith was writing when capitalism was only just emerging from its infancy and the role of managers and entrepreneurs was quite different from today. As capitalism grew and developed, the central issues which concerned political economists – Smith, Ricardo, Say, Bentham, Mill and so on – were the 'laws of human nature'. In this, they tried to parallel the methods of natural science, which was also developing rapidly, in describing how their 'laws of human nature' were manifest in everyday commercial life and in society at large.

In the early nineteenth century, the French political economist Jean-Baptiste Say (1817), an early theoriser on the economic function of the entrepreneur, conceptualised the three factors of production – land, labour and capital. Say conceived the much debated nostrum that 'supply creates its own demand' which was described and attacked from different perspectives by both Karl Marx (1867) and John Maynard Keynes (1936) in their respective criticisms of the classical political economists. Ironically, Say's 'law' is a direct repudiation of Smith, the 'father' of classical political economy, who believed that the economic focus of a well-run business should be on satisfying its consumers, not on its own production as an end in itself:

> Consumption is the sole end and purpose of all production; and the interest of the producer ought to be attended to, only so far as it may be necessary for promoting that of the consumer. The maxim is so self-evident that it would be absurd to attempt to prove it. But in the mercantile system, the interest of the consumer is almost constantly sacrificed to

that of the producer; and it seems to consider production, and not consumption, as the ultimate end and object of all industry and commerce.

(Smith, 1776)

This difference in emphasis between the relative importance of *supply* (the producers' interests) and *demand* (the consumers' interests) reflects fundamental differences in approach towards political and economic issues which persist to the present day. The stress that modern marketing and quality theory place on satisfying customer needs as the key to business success suggests that, although most self-employed and small business owners do appear to be 'product-driven', entrepreneurs may be more alert to 'demand-side' issues. Indeed, the debate over Say's Law goes right to the political and psychological centre of enterprise culture policies in that, despite the introduction of 'citizens' charters' and 'internal markets' within public services, the unambiguous aim of the policies is to increase the absolute number of small-scale producers. Whether or not this is likely to produce more entrepreneurial business behaviour is the key issue addressed in this book.

Basically, Say's Law holds that it is the increased tempo of production and exchange which creates wealth, increases demand and leads to growth. This belief in a widespread and undifferentiated increase in the 'supply side' as the motor of economic development is, as discussed earlier (p. 51), an important part of the philosophical underpinning of the enterprise culture but sits uncomfortably with concepts like social specialisation and modern marketing and quality practice. The apparent belief of 'supply-siders' that it is mainly constraints and imperfections in the land, labour and capital markets that prevent economic growth flies in the face of empirical evidence (periodic cycles of overproduction, Britain exporting capital during times of labour and land glut, etc.) but does explain why proponents of the enterprise culture policies pay so much attention to psychological variables such as attitudes and 'confidence'. By contrast, structuralists and Keynesian demand-management economists argue that business people are aware of the current economic structure and that their perceptions and expectations are psychological responses to actual business and economic conditions. Generally, 'demand-siders' believe in direct intervention in the various factor markets. Typical demand-side interventions include stimulating demand for goods and services through public works programmes and, as a direct comparison with enterprise training, improving the quality and flexibility of the labour market through targeted skills development training initiatives and, sometimes, subsidised employment support schemes.

Despite the fact that his 'Law' reflects decidedly non-entrepreneurial business practice, in a definition that has resonance today Say described the entrepreneur as a sort of problem solver, an agent whose function was to coordinate and combine the factors of production. Say's definition influenced John Stuart Mill (1848) and Joseph Schumpeter (1934), although

Mill was also drawn to the concept of risk as the defining characteristic which distinguished entrepreneurs from managers: entrepreneurs show willingness to accept risk.

However, it is important to note that the early political economists were writing during the transition of *mercantilism* (trade-based economy) into early capitalism. Many new entrepreneurial opportunities were connected with trade where physical risks were rarely absent. Apart from commerce in items of clothing and staple foods, the enormous profits of the mercantile age came from trade in high-value luxury goods where the risk of theft or natural damage was always high. Founders of new businesses had to battle and shoulder certain risks to break into an economy dominated by a relatively small number of wealthy landowners and large merchants: in other words, the socio-economic structure was such that virtually all newcomers to business had to be risk-taking entrepreneurs in order to survive and prosper. Even during the previous economic era of *feudalism*, as Europe struggled to escape the 'dark ages' (and, in so doing, sowed the seeds of mercantilism), the Belgian economic historian Henri Pirenne (1937) has identified two types of contrasting entrepreneur drawn from the rootless class of people who took the risk of escaping from their feudal bonds to seek freedom in the newly emerging towns. The first type of entrepreneur to emerge he termed *craftsmen-entrepreneurs*, who sold their artisanal products direct to their local consumers and cherished their independence. The second type to emerge were the *trader-entrepreneurs* who were prepared to accept the risks of foreign travel to exchange their local goods for rare goods from abroad.

The individualism of the first type, whom Pirenne describes as 'non-capitalist' early petit-bourgeois, eventually led them to establish non-entrepreneurial, risk-averse guilds as a protection against newcomers, the aristocracy and the growing power of the merchants. In China, the pervasive influence of the ancestor-related clan system diverted otherwise enterprising merchants away from forming wider entrepreneurial networks (Weber, 1984). This essentially non-entrepreneurial behaviour of many people in business was remarked on by Adam Smith (1776) in his well-known observation that, when business people meet together, they generally 'conspire' against the interests of consumers and competitors. The same theme was picked up by Schumpeter (1934) who observed that early, seemingly entrepreneurial behaviour can quickly give way to non-entrepreneurial behaviour once a certain level of satisfaction has been reached. Basically, the evidence presented in this book suggests that the average level of satisfaction among new firms of the enterprise culture years is very low, not much above personal or family survival levels. The essentially non-entrepreneurial expectations of most present-day small firm owners in Britain was highlighted in the 1991 SBRT quarterly survey which asked 1,718 small business owners about their growth intentions (marked as 91:q3S2 on the base axis of Figure 3.2 on p. 46). Of the 38 per cent who expressed any intention to expand their firms (a key enterprise culture policy target), only a few were able to quantify their projected growth.

This means that, after a decade of enterprise culture policies, only 5 per cent of small firm owners planned to continue to expand their enterprises significantly. Most of today's small firm owners are more strongly motivated to seek their own individual independence, as their medieval forerunners were. It was the activities of the much smaller group of active *trader-entrepreneurs*, and their financiers, which led Europe out of the Middle Ages into the era of mercantilism and, eventually, to capitalism. We shall meet these types again. The important point to note here is that the concept of the entrepreneur and what constitutes entrepreneurial behaviour is very much bound up in the socio-economic cultures and developments of the time. In analysing medieval Chinese society Weber (1984) makes the point that, although the Chinese were very enterprising and motivated to accumulate wealth, neither capitalism nor a sturdy, independent merchant venturer class took root there. Another important point to note is that brave and risky behaviour cannot be reduced simply to a psychological propensity to take risks. Pirenne provides convincing evidence that most of the early trader-entrepreneurs, though undoubtedly energetic and motivated by the prospects of good profits, did not risk losing much because disease, war and family pressures had uprooted them from their homes, leaving them few options other than those of artisanal worker or bonded peasant. In their case, a more rugged, self-sufficient individualism appears to characterise their behaviour though it seems clear that they were not risk-averse. The important conclusion to draw from this summary is that the entrepreneur as a concept is very much a product of its times and the current state of economic development which shifts as the economic structure evolves. That said, we are still left with the question of whether entrepreneurial skills can be developed later in life.

THE ENTREPRENEURIAL PERSONALITY?

The first point to emphasise is that none of the various economic models suggest that entrepreneurs should have special personalities although there is a strong implication that entrepreneurs are not risk-averse in the sense that they need to be competitive (achievement-oriented), and that they are reasonably able at calculating the relative costs and success probabilities of various options. If risk taking was a key feature of entrepreneurial activities during the early stages of capitalism, it is quite clear from the economic and management literature that successful innovative capitalists (entrepreneurs) need to be skilled at offsetting risk rather than allowing it to settle on their shoulders. Also, there is a hint in most economic theories of the judgemental ability, persistence, self-confidence and social control generally found in many psychological studies of entrepreneurial characteristics. These qualities are, for the most part, implicit and not central to the concerns of political-economic theory. The most evident issue of psychological importance raised by this review of economic and development models concerns entrepreneurial motivation. The basically financial motivations advanced by proponents of the enterprise culture and others – *make money, maximise profits, become wealthy* and other similar motivations (including enterprise culture critics' *greed* and, ironically, Marx's *accumulation of capital*) – are challenged by other less obvious business motives such as Smith's *propensity to trade*, Bentham's *maximisation of personal happiness*, Schumpeter's *social mobility* and an implied managerial *desire to control*. It is difficult to see how one 'personality' could encompass all these motives.

Indeed, if the problem of definition with respect to the 'entrepreneur' is problematic, uncertainty over a clear definition of 'personality' is almost overwhelming. In outlining the fundamentals of personal construct psychology, Don Bannister and Fay Fransella (1986) admit that George Kelly, who seems never to have been at a loss for words, did not have a precise definition but point out that Allport (1937) had already identified fifty different meanings more than fifty years ago. There still appears to be no generally accepted definition. Bannister and Fransella inferred that Kelly's definition of personality would be 'our way of construing and experimenting with our personal world' (1986: 44). Adrian Furnham (1992) in his overview of the place of psychology at work managed to avoid making a definition while still giving a thorough account of relevant personality theories and a review of research findings relating to personality at work (including small firms). Similarly, Elizabeth Chell and her colleagues (1991) in their analysis of the entrepreneurial personality also manage to discuss the main personality theories relevant to their inquiry without providing an overall definition.

However, in the context of entrepreneurial research, Elizabeth Chell (1985, 1986) has identified a number of broad approaches to personality theory (*trait* or typological, *psychodynamic* and *social developmental*). Chell, with Jean Howarth and Sally Brearley, later broadened the focus of discussion to consider the *interactionist* approach, which explicitly accepts the 'influence of social contexts on behaviour' (1991: 30), before turning to Susan Hampson's (1988) constructivist approach which is in the same tradition as Kelly's personal construct theory and concedes a role for individual intentionality and the self-concept. Furnham (1990, 1992) agrees with Chell that personality theory (especially in entrepreneurial research) has been mainly driven by the trait approach, which has sought relatively durable and predictive characteristics or features of an individual's 'normal' behaviour. They agree that this approach is fundamentally flawed.

There is little empirical evidence to support the notion that a single trait or collection of traits can explain the business behaviour of many widely different entrepreneurs. However, psychologists interested in entrepreneurial research have often seized on particular psychological characteristics and traits as being likely to be distributed more widely or to a stronger degree among entrepreneurs. Also, researchers into entrepreneurship who tend to use the trait approach, such as Timmons (1989; Timmons *et al.*, 1977), generally point out that they do not expect entrepreneurs to exhibit all the supposedly defining traits, just a fair proportion of them. Whether even this looser approach is valid or aids understanding of phenomena such as entrepreneurship or enterprise training is part of a broader debate of concern to the discipline of psychology (which should have a major role to play in understanding the dynamics of the enterprise culture and in evaluating the learning effectiveness of enterprise training). After considering the trait approach in general in this section and the specific locus of control trait in the next section, following sections examine in some detail other key psychological approaches and contributions to the understanding of the small business mentality.

Psychologists have long displayed an interest in the entrepreneur though significant studies have been sparse. Indeed, much of enterprise culture has its roots, perhaps unconsciously, in the early attitude and personality studies conducted in the United States. For example, the Allport–Vernon–Lindzey scale (1951) specifically includes a business/practical value as one of its six fundamental values to be used in distinguishing between groups. Early factor analytic research by Thurstone (1931), which was used to help identify people with an interest in business, led to later studies in attitude change; McClelland's (1961) influential studies on achievement motivation may be said to belong to this tradition albeit using a completely different methodology. Yet, even though business and work have been legitimate areas of psychological interest for most of this century, small business owners and the self-employed, who are not perceived to be as interesting as the entrepreneur (though they are treated as synonymous by many psychological researchers), have been tucked away in a forgotten corner. Indeed, psychological studies of the entrepreneur have tended to fall into the broader categories of work or occupational psychology.

The typological approach – which includes many who use factor analysis but can be split between the biological inheritance and psycho-development schools – attempts to classify entrepreneurial attitudes and behaviour into traits, factors and types. Jung, Cattell, Eysenck, McClelland, Rotter, Atkinson and many others fall into this camp. *Types* are broad descriptive patterns used to identify sub-groups in a given population so that they can be meaningfully compared with each other. The basis for classifying the different types can be physical, sociological, economic, psychological or some combination of these. Usually the specific psychological elements of behaviour used in classifying types are called *traits* which can be used individually to describe aspects of human behaviour. A good example of a type theory founded on factor analysis is that of Hans Eysenck with his two basic modal types – extrovert/introvert and neurotic. Eysenck draws a distinction between behavioural extroversion, an impulsive preference for doing rather than thinking about action, and social extroversion, a preference for social situations and social contact. In a study of 1,500 business-men, he found a stronger than expected incidence of general extroversion, which increased as the business function became more entrepreneurial (Eysenck, 1967). It is interesting to note that extroversion, both social and behavioural, has been used to describe entrepreneurs, often without much hard evidence in the case of behavioural extroversion, by a number of small business researchers.

Although typologies based on empirical observations can be useful for descriptive and theoretical purposes because they facilitate the analysis and interpretation of complex processes and data, they can also be danger-ous – like most stereotypes – if they are misconceived or are based on false distinctions. Indeed, type theory is open to the criticism that it is relatively easy to find specific instances of any given type but virtually impossible to classify most people precisely into one type or another. Some type theorists attempt to overcome this problem by employing a number of different types in flexible combinations but then there is a danger that the types can become indistinguishable from descriptive traits. For example, the type system of Carl Jung (1953) proposes four functions (thinker, feeler, senser, intuiter) plus two attitudes (extrovert, introvert); and Myers-Briggs scales to measure Jung's types in a personality inventory produced sixteen different type pro-files. The types are described as distinct collections of traits but they actually each just describe a few central traits so the distinction between traits and type profiles is considerably weakened. For instance, a widely quoted empirical and desk research study of new enterprises conducted through the Massachusetts Institute of Technology by Jeffry Timmons and col-leagues (1977) identified as many as fourteen important entrepreneurial characteristics which resemble traits:

1 drive and energy;
2 self-confidence;
3 long-term involvement;
4 money as a measure, not merely an end;
5 continuous pragmatic problem solving;
6 clear goal setting;
7 moderate risk taking;
8 low fear of failure;
9 use of feedback;
10 high initiative and personal responsibility;
11 use of resources;
12 self-imposed standards;
13 internal locus of control;
14 tolerance of ambiguity.

Timmons admitted that few entrepreneurs would possess all traits but felt that strengths in one might compensate for weaknesses in others. This obvious lack of priority, order or centrality conceptually weakens claims that these are defining traits of the entrepreneur rather than a list of characteristics of successful small business owners. Many of these characteristics are self-explanatory (such as high personal drive and energy, self-confidence and setting clear goals) and some appear to be linked (which would mean that Timmons's compensation principle would break down if there were weaknesses in linked traits). Despite their obvious softness as defining variables, these traits, including the less evident such as successful small firm owners' use of money as a measure of personal success rather than as an end in itself, appear consistently in entrepreneurial research studies. For example, in a study of Irish entrepreneurs, Cromie and Johns (1983) identified achievement, persistence and self-confidence as general successful business characteristics, and internal locus of control and commitment to the business as the characteristics peculiar to entrepreneurs. Timmons also recognised that successful small firm owners give almost everything to their businesses, especially in the early years, and that this commitment may be at the expense of family.

Research has, however, not been able to identify any set of traits as central and it seems reasonable to assume, therefore, that more than one factor or trait accounts for or is descriptive of entrepreneurial behaviour. Trait models tend to focus on the descriptive elements of an individual's behaviour and address issues of predictability and success. Perhaps the best-known specific trait associated with entrepreneurial research is that of *locus of control* (LoC) – the extent to which people believe they control their own destinies – which was originally conceived as a learned behavioural response, not a genetically determined trait (Rotter, 1966), and is discussed on pp. 155–9. Another widely used concept in entrepreneurial research, which is often treated as a single trait but is perhaps more correctly linked to motivation, is the need for achievement (nAch), described by McClelland (1961) as 'a desire to do well for the sake of inner feeling of personal accomplishment'. It is worth noting here that there is plenty of empirical evidence that entrepreneurs and small business managers in general do tend to score highly on various tests designed to measure both nAch and LoC when compared with many other groups of employees or non-business populations. However, there has been far less success in distinguishing successful entrepreneurs from unsuccessful small business owners. Certainly, their value as predictors of behaviour – the key operational function of traits – is questionable.

The main interest in both nAch and LoC as concepts in this book is less for their supposed power as predictive traits and more for their conceptual value within the development theories from which they spring. There are strong grounds for suggesting that they represent states of mind or sets of attitudes linked to current or anticipated situations rather than immutable traits. This should offer scope for their alteration through training or other means. Indeed, Caird (1990) has tried to push the question of individual traits to one side and refer not so much to entrepreneurs but to 'enterprising behaviour' as being the appropriate focus of enterprise training. However, as regards the central issue of this section, there appear to be strong theoretical grounds for doubting the value of traits as concepts that can help us to understand, as opposed to describe, human behaviour. Any attempt to differentiate entrepreneurs on the basis of traits must not only face the problem of identifying appropriate characteristics but also meet the general criticisms usually levelled at personality trait theory, including low correlations between trait-assessed and actual behaviour, imprecise physiological definition of traits, failure of trait theory to account for human behavioural inconsistencies and an inadequate account of situational effects on behaviour (Chell, 1985). Also Chell *et al.* (1991), following Mischel's earlier criticism (1968), point out that trait theory often rests on the unlikely assumption that human behaviour is consistent across time and circumstance. By contrast, they are drawn to the constructivist approach, a position which fits more neatly with the shift in the concept of the entrepreneur over time which we have already discussed.

Even at the individual level, this key assumption of trait theory seems to be particularly inappropriate when discussing entrepreneurial behaviour which is often characterised by a non-conventional and unpredictable approach to business. Certainly, there is no one single, dominating characteristic which reflects stable underlying traits that distinguish successful small firm owners from the unsuccessful or the growth-oriented from the growth-averse (though, as we shall see, there are some 'tendencies' in support of LoC and nAch). To complicate the issue further, it seems clear that certain traits are determined by or reflect cultural differences (McClelland, 1961; Osipow, 1983; Lynn 1969, 1991). It is reasonable to speculate that, say, a Japanese entrepreneur may exhibit different traits from an English or Scottish entrepreneur, or an entrepreneur of working-class origins from one of a more privileged background. As a result of these and other criticisms, modern occupational and personality psychology theory now explicitly recognises an interaction between personality and situational variables, an approach which is more rooted in the humanist tradition.

LOCUS OF CONTROL

Locus of control (LoC) – the extent to which people believe they control their own behaviour and influence their own destinies – features fairly prominently in most lists of the defining psychological characteristics of entrepreneurs. As Timmons *et al.* (1977) identified in the list on p. 153, successful small business owners are said to have high *internal* locus of control, meaning that they believe that their behaviour determines what happens to them and that they can control their own behaviour. It is not surprising that LoC has featured fairly consistently in studies on the psychological characteristics of entrepreneurs and other business populations though the concept has always had a broader frame of reference than just work-related behaviour.

Indeed, it is clear that Julian Rotter (1966) believed that individuals tended to exhibit similar LoC beliefs and behaviour across a range of circumstances. Essentially, the concept implies three separate beliefs on the part of individuals:

1 that the outcome of events and situations is susceptible to intervention;
2 that individuals can intervene and influence the outcome of situations positively from their perspective;
3 that they themselves have the skills and capacity to intervene effectively in certain situations or to influence certain events.

The self-confidence, energy, flexibility and opportunism associated with entrepreneurial behaviour suggests that entrepreneurs are individuals who are accustomed to getting involved and that they expect positive results from their involvement. In other words, they are prepared to expend energy and mental effort because they expect and often receive appropriate or, in their terms, valuable rewards. Also, they are flexible and opportunistic because they believe they have the capacity to become involved across a broad range of situations. It is clear that internal LoC beliefs are likely to form a central core of the entrepreneur's self-concept. Bandura, in demonstrating the link between the related concept of perceived self-efficacy and higher performance attainments, states that there are no beliefs more central or pervasive in relation to successful self-generated behaviour than those 'about their capabilities to exercise control over events that affect their lives' (1991: 411).

However, it is equally clear that entrepreneurs will not be the only people sharing internal LoC beliefs. Most reasonably successful students at all levels realise that their own efforts in studying have a lot to do with passing exams (even though 'rogue' questions can throw them off the track). Most people for whom sport is more than just an occasional leisure activity know the value of expending their own efforts on training and the importance of self-confidence. And in business, more significantly for current purposes, most reasonably able mid-level to senior managers will be accustomed to obtaining positive responses from their personal interventions. It becomes evident that internal LoC can be exhibited across a range of situations and that, in many cases, it is likely to be a function of success itself. Rotter recognised that, in certain situations, individuals would recognise that they actually had very little control over events but he maintained that people who believed that outcomes basically depended on their own behaviour and that they could control their own behaviour would generally, in most circumstances, believe that the control of events of importance to them ultimately rested internally in themselves. Heavily influenced by the behaviourist concepts of B. F. Skinner (1957) though with a more motivational and goal-directed approach, Rotter's definition of internal and external LoC emphasised the origins of the concept as a learned response. External LoC, according to Rotter, was learned when:

a reinforcement is perceived by the subject as following some action of his own but not being entirely contingent on his action . . . it is typically perceived as the result of luck, chance, fate, as under the control of powerful others, or as unpredictable because of great complexity of the forces surrounding him . . . we have labelled this a belief in *external control*. If the person perceives that the event is contingent upon his own behavior or his own relatively permanent characteristics, we have termed this a belief in *internal control*.

(Rotter, 1966: 1)

In other words, events are largely unpredictable because their occurrence is due to luck, fate or the decisions of other powerful people. By contrast, internal LoC is exhibited by people who believe events are contingent upon their own behaviour. However, their effective interventions may spring mainly from their confidence in manipulating their own systems and, depending on how risk-averse they are, they may be reluctant to transfer themselves to other equally challenging situations. In general, if the situation lies within their control and is open to their manipulation, internals exert more effort on skill-demanding tasks than on those depending on chance, while externals do not differentiate between the two types of task. Also, internals tend to be more open to information, take more initiatives, assume more responsibility and be more creative (Antonides, 1991). Given Rotter's mainly behaviourist approach, the implication seems to be that the internality or externality of LoC is capable of being manipulated by appropriate external stimuli though not by internal self-awareness. Whether or not this is so is of fundamental significance to the validity of enterprise training as a policy instrument.

The most widely used instrument for measuring LoC beliefs is Rotter's twenty-nine-item Internal-External (IE) scale which includes a six-item 'lie-scale'. In introducing his IE scale in 1966, Rotter reported several validation studies, including one involving 400 US college students, which found strong evidence for a general LoC factor. He interpreted this as strong evidence supporting a unidimensional construct. However, its claims for universality as a single behavioural trait have attracted strong criticism (Wolk and Ducette, 1973; Phares, 1976). Critics would have to acknowledge, however, that the LoC concept has stood the test of time; this suggests that, together with similar concepts such as self-efficacy (Deci and Ryan, 1985; Bandura, 1991) and locus of causality (Deci and Ryan, 1985), it is a useful and valid tool in social and economic psychological research.

The classification of entrepreneurs as internals is not in doubt but the central developmental question is whether entrepreneurial behaviour primarily depends on an early and fairly fundamental acquisition of internal LoC beliefs and associated behaviour or whether later circumstances or training can develop a more widely transferable set of LoC beliefs and behavioural patterns. Proponents of the enterprise culture would clearly like to think that later development is feasible but it seems likely that LoC beliefs (sometimes also termed self-efficacy) are influenced by situational variables. This poses a methodological problem for enterprise trainers who may well induce increased self-confidence and internal LoC behaviour during their courses but discover that the latter does not transfer to the tougher environment of real business. Rotter's IE has been used frequently in studies involving entrepreneurs (Rotter, 1966; Lefcourt, 1966; Phares, 1976; Jennings and Zeithanl, 1983) but it is often criticised because, as mentioned above, although LoC does predict success well, it does not distinguish clearly between entrepreneurs and non-entrepreneurs. Successful corporate managers, who apparently display administrative rather than entrepreneurial skills, also exhibit high internal LoC (Brockhaus, 1982). However, this criticism itself may be misplaced because there are no logical grounds for excluding entrepreneurial activity from big corporations. Also, these results may be an artefact of the sampling procedures. Indeed, current management practice often aims at encouraging entrepreneurial behaviour inside big organisations in the form of 'intrapreneurship' or management buy-outs. In any case, it is to be expected that senior managers and chief executives with considerable responsibility and discretionary powers over their own budgets should exhibit high internal LoC.

A more fundamental problem stemming directly from attribution theory, however, can arise in relation to the measurement of LoC when self-report or questionnaire scales are used. As already mentioned on p. 130, Farr's (1977) critique of Herzberg's two-factor work motivation theory shows clearly how attributional effects (positive outcomes being self-ascribed and negative outcomes ascribed to others) can distort the findings. Rotter tried to evade this problem through using paired forced-choice questions but other scales may measure notions of self-efficacy rather than real underlying LoC. Entrepreneurial researchers need to go deeper and inquire whether internal LoC beliefs about personal business effectiveness that rest mainly on a structured, controlled and methodical approach are essentially different from a more fundamental and general belief that individuals create their own 'luck', in the sense of having the power to produce their own opportunities and the capacity to turn most events towards a desired outcome. It is clear that Rotter himself tended towards the second description. The fundamental internal LoC beliefs and behavioural patterns were said to have been learned in early childhood as a result of psycho-dynamic processes similar to those that McClelland believed, for different reasons, led to high nAch. Rotter recognised that learning can be a continuous process, with the possibility of internal LoC beliefs being acquired through later experiences. Indeed, Robert Brockhaus (1977) has reported that successful business careers appear to encourage stronger internal LoC beliefs in corporate executives.

In fact, Rotter's development of the LoC concept was part of a wider learning theory which seems at times to represent a fusion of behaviourist language and a more constructivist approach (such as that underpinning the work of Kelly, McClelland and Hampson, discussed on pp. 160–2). As mentioned previously, Rotter's is a goal-directed motivational theory of learning. Behaviour is seen as dependent on the expectancy that it will lead to a particular outcome (the attainment of which provides reinforcement) and that the outcome is desirable (cf Vroom's *valency* concept). Drawing on their experience across a variety of situations, people develop *generalised* expectancies and norms concerning behaviour and its outcomes. This is similar to Kelly's (1955) description of the 'scientific man' or Heider's (1958) 'naive scientist', and is grounded in similar assumptions about human behaviour reflecting an interaction between people and relevant environments. According to this view, learning is a continuing process, with aspects of personality capable of being learned or modified at any stage of development. Personality is rooted in an interaction between a real world and the environment as constructed by the learner. Consequently, the lack of reinforcement will not necessarily extinguish an internal LoC set of beliefs because internals will have learned the ability to estimate the connection (or will have attributed causal links) between their own behaviour and the occurrence of the desired outcome.

Rotter related the development of internal LoC to stable and supportive early development and verbalisation of the origins of causality as well as the linkages between certain behaviour and certain outcomes (in other words, explaining things to the growing child). Training in personal causation may support the later development of internal LoC beliefs but peer pressure and socio-economic realities may cause other general expectancies to be learned (Lefcourt, 1976). It is worth noting that the development of internal LoC has been linked to upbringing, education, economic status and social class (Antonides, 1991). Ethnic group differences have also been reported (Wright, 1975; Lefcourt, 1966, 1976). To some extent, the tendency to attribute unpleasant situations or circumstances to external causes is a feature of those who suffer them, and it may be speculated that internals may prefer to define themselves out of situations over which they actually have little control (and possibly for externals to have not learned stable patterns of causal attribution). Thus, even if LoC beliefs reflect generalised tendencies there is plenty of scope in any given situation to mask the internality or externality of any individual's behaviour in response to particular socio-economic conditions.

Weiner's (1985) finding that there is a general tendency among business people to attribute successful transactions to internal causes but unsuccessful transactions or outcomes to external causes represents an extension of attribution theory (see also Farr, 1977) familiar to many small business researchers but does not invalidate Rotter's more general approach. Weiner found that business outcomes were basically ascribed by business people to four key causes – their own skills, their efforts, the difficulty of the task and luck. Clearly, the first two are internal and the second two external. Weiner added another bi-polar dimension – the stability or instability of the cause – and demonstrated that business people are more likely to alter their strategy if they attribute certain outcomes to perceived stable causes rather than simply if their prior expectations have not been met. It seems reasonable to hypothesise that entrepreneurs are also more likely to seek stable causes as explanations rather than unstable, non-predictive causes and respond accordingly. Indeed, an early recognition in the shifts in stability in the socio-economic structure and a belief in having the capacity to respond (internal LoC) seem ideal entrepreneurial psychological attributes. Whether these attributes are amenable to encouragement by training, and whether enterprise training is the most appropriate means for achieving these ends, must, for the moment, remain open questions although the indications in relation to enterprise training are not particularly encouraging.

PSYCHO-SOCIAL DEVELOPMENTAL APPROACHES

One key distinction between the trait and typology approaches and the more humanist, social developmental approaches is that the former basically represent an attempt to identify external descriptors, which – like commercial labels or brands – can be used as a convenient shorthand when making decisions involving some degree of psychological information. The latter represent more of an attempt to describe the processes that produce the relevant behaviour, attitudes and values. Clearly, the accurate identification of certain traits relevant to personnel and marketing problems can have immense commercial value. However, for a proper understanding of economic and organisational processes and outcomes, the latter approaches are more likely to yield genuinely useful information in the longer term.

Individual personalities, including those of entrepreneurs, are often explained as the outcome of personal development processes and experiences since infancy, with differences between psychodynamic and social developmental theories broadly reflecting the basic nature–nurture split in personality theory. Psycho-developmental approaches in the Freudian tradition would also expect little change to basic personality after a fairly young age while social developmental approaches would usually accept that learning from experience continues beyond infancy and adolescence. A psychodynamic model of the entrepreneur is that of Manfred Kets de Vries (1977, 1980) which states that the entrepreneurial personality is shaped by parental behaviour along two dimensions: high–low control and acceptance–rejection. The father exhibits low control plus rejection while the mother displays high control plus rejection, producing a somewhat deviant personality. Incapable of functioning effectively inside large organisations, entrepreneurs feel compelled to start their own businesses. To an extent, our repertory grid experiments provide some support in showing a low identification with parental views among some enterprise trainers (though others were the opposite). Also, sociological studies have identified certain entrepreneurs who lack formal qualifications and have started their own businesses out of frustration at not achieving promotion or due status (Curran and Stanworth, 1981).

According to the General Household Survey data, most self-employed and most small firm managers are married males, work longer hours than employees and tend to devote much of their time to their business (Curran, 1986; Curran and Burrows, 1988). As fathers, the self-employed are likely to have relatively little time for their families or to exert much control at home. This appears to lend some support to Kets de Vries's theory which provides an explanation additional to the role-model theory for the high tendency for the self-employed to have parents who were also self-employed or managers (Gray and Stanworth, 1985; Curran and Burrows, 1988). There is also some anthropological support for the view that cultural attitudes most resistant to change are 'learned early in life (such as kinship terminology and certain basic values). Change in the areas of culture that are learned early in life . . . required the presence of a different parental model in the child's early experience' (Wallace, 1970: 160–1). However, the Kets de Vries type of psychodynamic model is open to the criticism that it is not valid for all types of small business and fails to explain why only some of the people who share similar formative experiences eventually become entrepreneurs. It seems reasonable to assume that entrepreneurial behaviour is not unidimensional and that there is more than one entrepreneurial personality, just as there are many different types of small enterprises and many types of small enterprise owner.

Social developmental theories move away from the search for the right personality mix and take the development of the self-concept as their starting point. For instance, Super (1980) sees individuals as developing their self-concept by trying to enter an occupation which is likely to further self-expression instead of seeking a compatible work environment. Super believes that childhood experiences are important in developing a self-concept and offers a stage model of occupational behaviour. As the self-concept forms, the young begin adopting work role models mainly through identification with their parents but later, as the self-concept develops, with other people. It is interesting to note that this process runs counter to that of Kets de Vries where future entrepreneurs are said to be rejected by their fathers and form their businesses almost as a refuge from authority figures ('to be independent'). However, it is difficult to research Kets de Vries's assumptions empirically and most research on the economic *search theory* of employment lends support to Super. Similar to Becker's (1964) human capital theory, in that the prospects of economic gain from acquiring necessary qualifications have to exceed the search costs, search theory and the more psychological career-choice theory have very little application to the secondary sector where most small firms are located and where employment shifts are often involuntary. Indeed, for many people during the search stage, feedback produced as a result of exploratory behaviour can often clash with expectations.

It has been found that people who can tolerate ambiguity, uncertainty, tension and frustration – common entrepreneurial characteristics according to the list identified by Timmons *et al.* (1977) – can deal with this cognitive dissonance by adjusting their concepts appropriately. This is more likely to happen if they actively explore real, external options rather than mentally speculate about outcomes (Lofquist and Dawis, 1969). This active, exploratory behaviour – and, incidentally, high nAch and low fear of failure – has been linked to the presence of a supportive family structure (Atkinson, 1957). This contrasts with the behaviour of defensive, unrealistic people who find it hard to handle cognitive dissonance, seek to rationalise contradictory experience and do not gain from exploratory behaviour. It has been suggested that self-employment may offer the line of least resistance to these people, which may explain why so many non-entrepreneurial self-employed are reactive rather than proactive (Osipow, 1983). Also, through the process of identification, the inheritance of occupation can play a role, especially where the parents work in a state of isolation from other people – either physical or psychological isolation. Osipow mentions farmers, fishing, medicine and the military but the self-employed and very small businesses must also qualify because their own personal isolation is one of their biggest complaints (Gray and Stanworth, 1986).

The humanist approach ascribes more weight to individuals' self-awareness as a continuing influence on their behaviour throughout their adulthood. Individuals have a concept of themselves as actors in their own lives (economists often use the same term to describe the participants in economic transactions). Carl Rogers is a well-known theorist in this field and the work of Abraham Maslow – with its five categories of human need, culminating in self-actualisation – is widely used in management education. During the past twenty years, however, the personal construct theory of George Kelly and his repertory grid techniques have been expanded for use in a range of social contexts including the fields of business and work (Stewart and Stewart, 1981). Before discussing the contributions that the constructivist approach may offer in understanding entrepreneurial behaviour and the likely effects of enterprise training, it is worth summarising the main implication of this section as suggesting that early personal development appears to play a large role in later entrepreneurial behaviour which is unlikely to be replicated in skills-oriented enterprise training sessions.

CONSTRUCTIVIST APPROACHES

Essentially, constructivist approaches to personality and personal psychology place strong emphasis on the individual as an active participant.

Individuals are assumed to play an active part in interpreting and responding to the world they perceive. This implies a continuous lifelong process, though with wide differences between individuals and at various stages within any one individual's lifetime. The pioneer of this approach, George Kelly believed that individuals – as they perceive, interpret and anticipate future experience – develop hierarchical systems of constructs to make personal sense of what they perceive, which they continually arrange and rearrange in response to feedback from their external reality. He called the process of developing constructs 'construing', and developed his personal construct theory (PCT) originally in a clinical context where emphasis was placed on revealing an individual's construct system. Although Kelly is firmly rooted in the US ideological traditions of *individualism* (as discussed in the Introduction) and developed his system to explore the construct systems of individuals, he also recognised the importance of social dimensions and shared construals to human existence and communication (Fransella, 1984). Kelly's approach seems to fit the entrepreneur and offers an extremely effective technique for exploring the entrepreneur's individual attitude and value systems. Indeed, during the past twenty years, the theories of George Kelly and the techniques he designed have been expanded for use in more social contexts including many applications in the fields of business and work (Stewart and Stewart, 1981).

According to Kelly, each person interprets the world in a unique fashion based on both past experience and future anticipation. We approach an objective reality as subjective scientists, sifting past experience to anticipate the future, defining our own view of the world by a linked pattern of bipolar concepts called constructs (which are defined by an individual not only by what they are but also by what they are not). Each individual's construct system is ordered in a complex hierarchy or pyramid with the most fundamental constructs – those applicable to a broad range of situations and events – dominating the system and other more situation-specific constructs playing a less central role (Kelly, 1955). Kelly's fundamental postulate – that our processes are psychologically 'channelised' by the way we anticipate events – might almost have been written with the entrepreneur in mind. It provides theoretical support for placing strong emphasis on personal expectations as the key to understanding entrepreneurial behaviour. Experiences in dealing with small firm owners and many of the findings of this book suggest that Kelly's approach may be useful when researching entrepreneurs. David Storey's (1990) matched study of ordinary small firm owners and those who obtained finance through the Unlisted Securities Market revealed that the more entrepreneurial owners exhibited something closely approaching Kelly's 'active scientist' approach.

The emphasis on individuality, which is a strong feature of entrepreneurial behaviour, is central to Kelly's approach. Individuals differ from each other in their construction of events through evolving their own unique hierarchical (or ordinal) systems of constructs to enable themselves to anticipate events. Furthermore, the potential for change and adaptation as a result of changing perceptions or self-awareness is always present because constructs are not seen as immutable. However, there are certain core constructs, some of which could be construed as modal personality traits perhaps, which are considered to be fundamental or central to a rich, well-developed system and, consequently, are less likely to change. As Gecas and Seff (1990) have pointed out in their analysis of the psychological centrality of work or non-work, an individual is less likely to develop a strongly integrated system about situations, people or events which are of peripheral personal importance. A system without much focus, unclearly structured or not psychologically central is described in personal construct theory terms as *loose*. Systems which are well developed are generally *tight*, with clear central constructs and a well-defined hierarchy.

The tightness or looseness of a construct system, however, need not necessarily be an impediment to the communication of information or understanding. Communication is a very important enterprise management ability: Kelly saw effective communication as depending on the extent to which different people share each other's perceptions and evaluations of a given situation, event or phenomenon. And the cultural dimension he saw as the extent that an individual construes experience in a similar way to other people and construes those people as a reference group. According to Kelly, to the extent that individuals construe the construction processes of another, they may play a role in a social process involving that other person. This provides a clear psychological target for enterprise training (though whether the goal of influencing non-entrepreneurial people to adopt construction systems more akin to those of entrepreneurial people is attainable, and whether entrepreneurs even share identifiable construal systems, are matters for debate). It is important to note that the mere fact that people have experienced a situation or event together, such as an enterprise training course, is no indication that they have construed that experience in the same way. At a practical level, however, the effectiveness of training can be measured by whether any construct 'tightening' takes place in the area of training focus over the life of the course or shortly thereafter.

Kelly's attention to the process of sifting external experience, the active categorisation of that experience and interpretation by the individual, has steadily gained ground as a fruitful and valid area for research and explanation of behaviour. However, his very strong emphasis on the individual hampers the usefulness of Kelly's approach when dealing with social phenomena such as business, management and enterprise. Chell points to the work of Hampson (1988) as addressing these issues in the constructivist tradition but broadening the approach beyond Kelly's essentially individualistic approach. Recognising that people are not especially consistent in their expression or concept of personality, Hampson sees personality at three different levels: the theoretical, where categories and traits are often imposed by the researcher; the lay level, where 'commonsense' views prevail; and the level of the self, where an individual's self-concept must be taken into account. This approach is more socially constructivist than Kelly's more individualist approach, and makes it much easier to take into account the effects of situation and circumstance which are often ignored as too awkward. Certainly, any study of the enterprise culture must take into account public or lay perceptions as well as those of individual small firm owners.

Basically, Kelly's methodology relies on eliciting the language individuals use in describing the events or objects that are the focus of the research, then having the individuals rank or score elements of those events or objects on bi-polar scales based on the concepts that have emerged from the language elicitation process. The scores are presented as a matrix, or repertory grid as it is called, which can then be factor analysed to reveal the underlying constructs. We have used Kelly's grid techniques at OUBS to explore the effectiveness of a number of different types of enterprise training initiatives, including one set up near Naples to encourage young graduates to remain in southern Italy. From an analysis of their grids, the students fell into two broad camps which match almost exactly those found in organisational theory – the task-oriented and the socially oriented. They were also distinguished by whether their construct systems were tight or loose. From tutors' comments and ratings of each trainee at the time, and a subsequent follow-up three years later on the actual careers of the trainees, it was clear that the first distinction correlated strongly with job choice while the second was a good predictor of job success and performance. It was interesting, however, that the objectives of that enterprise training course were not fulfilled because none of the trainees obtained management jobs in southern Italy and none founded their own business.

Another repertory grid study was more psychological in application, the aim being to determine who influenced British enterprise trainees in their career choice and in their construal of the entrepreneur. The elements were people likely to be important influences, including parents, existing entrepreneurs, self and an idealised self. Again, the looseness–tightness distinction was reasonably predictive of subsequent business behaviour according to a follow-up interview with the course director two years later. People with tight construct systems did start or develop their enterprises (usually but not always in the directions they had originally intended). Those with loose construct systems often did not start up any sort of enterprise at all. Also, clear and significant differences in psychogenic motivators were identified between graduate start-up business and existing non-graduate small firm owners and self-employed, especially in relation to achievement motivation, the construal of power relations and the need for sociability. These differences provided an interesting psychological profile on the effects of alienation and power relations. Interesting data were provided on the effects of parental influence in career choice. Although there are clear limitations on how these types of data can be used, these studies provided new insights into what enterprise training could constitute and how it can be evaluated.

The final point to make about the constructivist approach is that it explicitly allows for the way individuals' priorities are always shifting. Kelly's notion that constructs are more or less fundamental depending on their range and focus of convenience (in other words, on what is important to the individual at any given time) and Hampson's contribution on the importance of recognising that there are several different valid perspectives to most situations tie in with Gecas and Seff's (1990) ideas that individuals generally respond to events and circumstances that are psychologically central to them. This clearly explains a lot of small enterprise behaviour. A valuable conclusion to this discussion of the constructivist approach is that the dominance of 'business' constructs appears to be a common feature of growth-oriented entrepreneurs. The extraction of surplus labour from others is very probably construed in positive terms by most capitalists, especially new start-up entrepreneurs. Put conversely, people for whom business constructs are not central or for whom the power relations of business are disturbing will find it extremely hard to behave entrepreneurially (Gecas and Seff, 1990; Gray, 1989). Whether it is possible to alter construct sets through training and other initiatives, and whether new constructs can be developed or learned, are crucial questions that go right to the heart of enterprise culture policies and, more broadly, to the role of training in management development.

LEARNING THEORY

Apart from the obvious fact that all types of training, as an educative process, must have some form of learning as the outcome, many of the concepts and characteristics associated with entrepreneurs and enterprising behaviour also have their history rooted deeply in learning theory. The most obvious examples dealt with in this chapter were Julian Rotter's locus of control and David McClelland's and John Atkinson's approach to achievement motivation. Most definitions of learning appear to include the notion of actual or potential changes to behaviour which are relatively permanent. This definition takes into account that the effects of learning may not be evident immediately and excludes temporary effects from sources such as drugs or fatigue. It should by now be clear that enterprise training has as its target permanent changes towards more enterprising behaviour on the part of large numbers of previously non-enterprising people (using *enterprising* as a softer, less demanding notion, in business and innovative behavioural terms, than *entrepreneurial*).

Rotter's concept of locus of control draws heavily, though not exclusively, on Skinner's (1957) behaviourist principles. Essentially, Skinner held that learned behaviour is not actually created, but the probability of its occurrence is increased, through the provision of an appropriate sequence of *reinforcement* (this is often defined in a circular way as something likely to increase probabilities, but it may also be viewed as a satisfier or something that engenders a positive feeling of hope or anticipation). This approach could appeal to the proponents of enterprise training because it raises the prospect that, with appropriate schedules of reinforcement, masses of people with inherent business qualities could be conditioned into exhibiting enterprising behaviour. However, the twentieth century has seen a number of unpleasant mass-conditioning programmes and history suggests that they are neither particularly effective nor politically acceptable. Moreover, learning is now often viewed as a proactive, lifelong experience rather than as a passive reaction to instruction and reinforcements.

More recent developments in education research support a more *cognitive* approach to learning theory which places more emphasis on mental reasoning and insights leading to behavioural change. Judging from the style and content of most enterprise training courses, this seems to be the underlying theoretical base of most enterprise training in Britain. This model is developed further as a social learning model, the mechanisms and implications of which will be discussed on pp. 168–70 in the discussion on the role of social representations in entrepreneurial development. This approach also provides some theoretical underpinning on the role of the family or parents in the process of occupational choice. Learning is assumed to take place not just through conditioning but also through observation and imitation, using the results of other individuals' behaviour to develop cognitive plans and strategies for learning (Bandura, 1991). Training, however, is more than its theoretical learning base. It is also a process of education which needs to be examined as a process.

According to Maureen Pope and Terence Keen (1981), educational methods in colleges and schools can be divided into three main ideological traditions: *cultural transmission, romanticism* and *progressivism*. The first tradition, cultural transmission, as implied by its very name and its emphasis on the transmission of information, rules and values gathered from the past, is basically the tradition in which most enterprise training is found.

> Much of the basis of modern educational technology and behavioural approaches to education can be seen as variants of the cultural transmission approach. Knowledge and values are seen as located in the culture and are internalised by children imitating adult behaviour models or through explicit instruction and the use of such training procedures as reward and punishment.
>
> (1981: 4)

Once again, the influences of behaviourist thought are clearly at work. The romanticist tradition is far less 'scientific' in stressing feelings and unveiling the student's 'true' gifts and aptitudes. This tradition has been influenced by psychoanalytic concepts and could be more appropriate for ideological awareness sessions than for direct training in business skills.

The third tradition, progressivism, holds that 'education should nourish the person's natural interaction with a developing society or environment' (1981: 7) and has as its goal Maslow's fifth order need, self-actualisation. In the constructivists' camp, the progessivists would see the educational system and structure as needing actively to stimulate 'development through the presentation of a milieu in which the organising and developing force in the person's experience is *the person's active thinking*. Thinking is stimulated by cognitive conflict' (Pope and Keen, 1981: 7). It is very interesting that virtually no enterprise training programmes fall into this category but it is easy to see progressivism as representing the pattern through which entrepreneurs learn from experience. Indeed, following an approach similar to that of the constructivists, progressivists 'see the acquisition of knowledge as an act of change in the pattern of thinking brought about by *experiential* problem solving situations' (1981: 7). When applied to enterprise culture policies, this approach could easily have been used to spread the enterprise culture message and encourage enterprising behaviour, but the reality of most enterprise training is far removed from this theoretical ideal.

The very consistent and strong message from the various studies and concepts discussed in this chapter is that while there is no unique entrepreneurial personality or set of defining characteristics, entrepreneurs usually do share certain common features such as strong internal locus of control, high need for achievement, persistence, proactivity and a desire for operational independence; but it is difficult to disentangle the causal links, and these features, in not being exclusive to entrepreneurs, do not have high predictive value. Instead, a consistent pattern emerged whereby the clue to entrepreneurial behaviour appears to lie in the cultural, family and class backgrounds of successful founders of small firms; it would be hard to recreate this in a formal classroom setting. Certainly, enterprise training as it is currently designed in content, methodology and intensity is unlikely to transform the crucial social representations of enterprise-related concepts and attitudes among the bulk of people who are drawn towards enterprise training programmes and other policy initiatives. While more entrepreneurs may have emerged from their social and cultural milieu during the enterprise culture years, their numbers are unlikely to have been large and their emergence is unrelated to the mass programmes of enterprise culture policies. The question is then posed: does this mean that successful small enterprises are created because of chance or favourable circumstances or because they are founded by people with special qualities?

IMPLICATIONS FOR ENTERPRISE DEVELOPMENT

If the profit motive remains the hallmark of the efficient business, this explains why so many businesses either are not true businesses or are destined to remain inefficient. This is a central theme of this book. Indeed, one important conclusion of this review of economic development theories is that the pace and mechanisms of innovation and economic development mean that economically productive firms are likely to be relatively rare, a finding that appears to be strongly supported by empirical evidence.

Business survival depends on the ability to control costs; business success may well depend on the ability to assess internal and external transactions costs reasonably accurately. To match any of the roles discussed in the previous sections, the entrepreneur must be expected to possess more than minimal financial and judgemental skills. It is interesting that the Bolton committee identified the importance of information use and retrieval as well as technological change as long ago as 1971, some time before the full impact of information technology. If anything, the need to manage efficiently in these areas has increased and, in the light of discussions on pp. 166–8, must represent areas of entrepreneurial management competence. Similarly, most small firms operate in known environments but entrepreneurs must be alert to new possibilities in the market, indeed must even be aware of new markets, so their marketing skills must be above average.

Management theorist Henry Mintzberg (1979) mentions that typical entrepreneurial firms have simple structures and are small, organic and innovative. This implies a flexibility towards the market yet he feels the entrepreneur will try to maintain tight, personal control. However, Vickery links an 'entrepreneurial' approach to equity finance with more concern about access to appropriate finance and *de facto* decision-making control than with fear of loss of ownership control (a common small business fear). Once again, this raises the issues of delegation, entrepreneurial management styles and the well-recognised reluctance on the part of most small business owners to part with equity in their firms (Bolton, 1971; Wilson, 1979; Hutchinson and Ray, 1986; Vickery, 1989). The fact that business is a social process suggests again that it is the entrepreneurs' well-developed social skills which are of prime importance. Most definitions of the entrepreneur (from Cantillon to Schumpeter) stress the ability to organise and combine as the key feature. This conclusion is supported by the influential management writer Peter Drucker (1985) who maintains that innovation no longer results from chance activities but is managed – whether in a big or a small firm – as an organised and systematic process. Indeed, there is some evidence from the management literature that entrepreneurs do not feel the need to seek help for organisational problems but are open to receiving outside help for marketing or financial problems (Flamholtz, 1986).

To some degree, the implication is that the era of the highly individual entrepreneur as a key economic actor may have come to an end as more cooperative or social forms of enterprise emerge (which would be ironic as 'the entrepreneur' is only now being recognised as an independent factor in economic development). Indeed, there is a growing body of evidence that modern entrepreneurial businesses succeed because of their social skills enabling them not only to obtain high performance from their employees inside the firm but also to network externally with other firms

(Amin *et al.*, 1986; Bamford, 1987; Lazerson, 1988; Cooke and Morgan, 1991; Curran and Blackburn, 1991). Certainly, successful entrepreneurs themselves identify their own social skills, their general power to communicate, as a key factor in their success. The important implication of entrepreneurs excelling in the directed use of their own social and organisational skills is that, as the ultimate aim of the enterprise culture is to promote successful entrepreneurs, the social skills side of enterprise training should not be ignored.

9 The future for small enterprise development

This book has drawn on a wealth of existing research from many disciplines and on its own original research to analyse, in economic and psychological terms, the function of the entrepreneur as both a target and an instrument of current development policies aimed at creating an enterprise culture. The key aspects of entrepreneurial development, and the part that enterprise culture policies have played in it, have been critically assessed. I hope it has been clearly established that the economic thrust of enterprise culture policies represented an alien culture to the vast majority of self-employed and small business owners. The psychological danger of the policies was to promote a culture of individualism which is inimical to the sustained development of enterprises and of the economy. The problems and potential solutions to Britain's socio-economic development crisis are extremely deep rooted and require long-term, innovative social and educational policies aimed at fostering an enterprising and cooperative culture rather than short-term, limited management skills training courses and advertising slogans aimed at promoting an individualistic culture of the *entrepreneur*.

In the terms of the central issues of this book, it must be concluded that it is difficult to make large numbers of people adopt a more entrepreneurial approach or establish sustainable enterprises which offer wider developmental or economic benefits to Britain (and to Europe) through the current management skills courses by relabelling them enterprise training. A wider development model that addresses issues beyond narrow economic or business concerns needs to be adopted and considerably more research needs to be conducted to establish the individual and social needs of enterprise development. However, the findings presented in this book are a first step, and cast light on some of these important issues. We can close by summarising their implications. First, the implications for enterprise training as an educative process will be discussed, then the political-economic implications for industrial policy of the theoretical and empirical bankruptcy of the enterprise culture model. Finally, some of the more important psychological considerations will be discussed concerning mainly motivation and how ideas generated through the constructivist and social representations approaches may yield more effective support methods for small firm and general economic development.

CAN ENTREPRENEURSHIP BE TRAINED?

In the sense that business-oriented people and groups share certain social representations about 'enterprise', it is meaningful to talk of an enterprise culture as a possible policy target and teaching target. There are no real problems about this at a theoretical level, as the discussions on the contributions of constructivism and social representations make clear. As Gerard Duveen and Barbara Lloyd point out, social representations change over time in any case (through a process they call *sociogenesis*) and the process of actually developing social representations, *ontogenesis*, 'is a process through which individuals re-construct social representations, and . . . in doing so they elaborate particular social identities' which become 'psychologically active for individuals' (1990: 7). Enterprise culture policies are about the transformation of social identities and the introduction of new cultural norms. As we have seen at various points throughout this book, this raises two important questions: is training the most effective form of intervention for securing these profound personal and social shifts and is management training of the type offered through enterprise training programmes the most effective instrument for achieving these goals?

Given the individual learning processes involved from early childhood in the development of most entrepreneurial characteristics, there are likely to be significant difficulties in replicating these processes among mature-age people on a mass scale. However, as we have argued throughout this book, there are also powerful social processes at work in shaping broad attitudes and responses towards work and in determining entrepreneurial behaviour. In the sense that training is often about the development of individual skills, it may not be an appropriate instrument for producing cultural change (indeed, if anything, this book has shown that the cultural values of the self-employed impede their acceptance of training). Within larger corporations and the public sector, higher management has been heavily influenced by human resource management ideas (Guest, 1987) to try to achieve internal cultural shifts (mainly in relation to self-management, quality issues, 'de-layering', etc.) through policies and processes where training may play only a minor part. Their approach often involves the empowerment of employees and affording a greater role for women. David McClelland (1968) believed that the development of a more self-confident, achievement-motivated personality lies in giving more power to women. He argued that mothers provide the kind of support likely to nurture achievement motivation at an early age while fathers can be too strict or competitive; therefore, women should be more empowered to rear children collectively.

Given the lack of prior information on family backgrounds, attitudes and rearing practices (let alone any reliable methodology for determining the actual effects of each individual's early family dynamics), it was beyond the scope of this book to investigate McClelland's views that mothers with high nAch tend to produce children who also exhibit high nAch but some support was found. Small enterprise owners who intend to grow are more achievement-motivated than the self-employed (who have higher nAch than the control groups) and they themselves are more likely to have parents from the same background (who, presumably, would also tend to have high nAch). Respondents who reported that their career choices were influenced by their mothers were more likely to be male and very growth-oriented. Most of these respondents, however, were not from self-employed backgrounds, which suggests that maternal attitudes and child-rearing practices have an effect independent of broader cultural effects. This not only provides some support for McClelland's views but also for the enterprise culture objective of encouraging cultural change. However, given the individualism that lies at the heart of enterprise culture ideology, it is unlikely that any proposal to provide collective support for child rearing would get a sympathetic hearing.

The weight of publicly available evidence and the findings of the surveys and repertory grids involving enterprise trainees strongly suggest that the enterprise training programmes of the 1980s were not successful either in imparting management skills of any depth or durability or in creating more positive attitudes towards 'enterprise' on a mass basis. Some of the enterprise training programmes achieved less lofty objectives such as removing people from the unemployment register and raising the awareness of training needs among certain self-employed and small firm owners; but in terms of economic and psychological development objectives their effects were minimal. As this book has shown, the real problem seems to lie in the inappropriateness of the policies chosen to transform non-business people into people who embrace these previously alien (to them) social representations. These problems multiply and perhaps even comprise different elements when the focus shifts to include only entrepreneurs as a special sub-set of business people.

A further complication for the designers of enterprise training arose from significant differences in the provenance of enterprise trainees, with the majority coming from two quite different economic and social starting points. The largest and least promising group are drawn from the large pool of the unemployed and a smaller group from paid employment. There are psychologically significant self-conceptual differences between the self-employed, the owners of small businesses employing other people, employees who work in large organisations and the short-term and long-term unemployed; this suggests that policy makers should explore different versions of enterprise training for each group, if not different specifically designed programmes. The present form of basic management training is of little value and makes little impact upon new start-ups from unemployment but may be more useful to either weak or expanding small firms, provided more suitable skills training is included in the course contents. The experiences of the OUBS's Startup Your Own Business course and the government's Firmstart courses also suggest that some people seeking to leave paid employment and start a self-employed career may use this type of training instrumentally, though those hoping to embark on a more serious business venture do not.

Although relatively few start-ups come directly from unemployment, a far higher proportion of enterprise trainees come from this source and it is reasonable to conclude that social policy objectives have obscured or diverted, in many cases, the economic development targets of enterprise culture policies. We have seen the enormous differences in the psychological profiles and expectations of the unemployed compared with the characteristics required for successful self-employment and, even more, management of a successful small enterprise. Unemployment is a traumatic experience for most people who have been made redundant and, as the period of unemployment increases, the symptoms – hostility, guilt, loss of self-satisfaction, loss of identity, feelings of rejection, low self-esteem, loss of self-confidence, and so on – become progressively more powerful (Stokes and Cochrane, 1984; Jahoda M., 1988). Consequently, very few unemployed who try self-employment or even successful EAS participants can expect to progress from the start-up stage to the survival stage, let alone the take-off stage (Gray and Stanworth, 1986). The economic implications of these differences extend not only to job search and labour market behaviour but will also impact on business behaviour and performance.

In order to replicate the process of ontogenesis, the unemployed will require programmes to boost their self-esteem before they can even contemplate running a successful business as opposed to managing to eke out a living for themselves and their families. For the traditional or 'artisanal' self-employed, who are generally resistant to external control and uncomfortable operating organisationally and who mainly prefer to have personal control over their own space but are not necessarily interested in extending it, official policies and exhortations in favour of growth will fall on deaf ears, unless they are seen as a way of protecting or strengthening that independence. Paradoxically, although the intense desire for personal independence that is so psychologically central for these people is clearly a key element in the concept of individualism, which is so central to the enterprise culture, current enterprise training does not address these issues. On the other hand, people already organising other people as a business seem more likely to welcome and benefit from support measures which enable them to organise and operate more efficiently but may not encourage them to become more growth-minded.

The entrepreneurial and non-entrepreneurial business owners surveyed in the more qualitative follow-up studies clearly have well-defined self-concepts and occupational concepts. To encourage more entrepreneurial growth-oriented behaviour among business owners of this type, training initiatives need to address individual concerns with appropriate learning objectives and course contents (not necessarily management skills) and business support policies with appropriate potential reinforcers need to be carefully defined for each group. To be successful on an appreciable scale, however, the social concerns also need to be addressed. The design of such initiatives will have to use the language and appeal to the expectations of each group, starting from an understanding of the social representations that these different types of small business owners hold about their own class or cultural groups. With overall economic growth and the establishment of growth-oriented, well-managed small businesses as central policy objectives throughout Europe, it is clearly vital that these differences in self-concept and, consequently, motivation be given full consideration. In the absence of long-term multi-focused enterprise or personal development training, socio-economic structural factors outside the control of enterprise culture policy makers seem likely to remain the main generator of new successful capitalists.

THE POLITICAL ECONOMY OF ENTERPRISE

From the beginning of this book I have made it clear that I have strong reservations about the theoretical underpinnings of the enterprise culture model applied in the 1980s as a development model, even at the level of its basic assumptions. Empirically, it is clear that no transformation of public attitudes has taken place and Britain's economic fortunes have not soared because of a reinvigorated small business sector or a renewal of the industrial fabric. However, this addresses the economic development issues according to the agenda proposed by enterprise culture policy makers. There is a strong critique of these policies on economic development grounds which points out that the removal of 'barriers to becoming entrepreneurial' is really a fig-leaf for a completely *laissez-faire* approach which jettisons any attempt at a coherent and planned industrial policy. As mentioned before, enterprise culture policies are not really about enterprise at all according to this view (supported by the evidence presented in this book) but about individualism and self-interest.

During the 1970s, industrial policy was mainly about trying to alter the markets in favour of encouraging particular types of firm or industry. This amounted to direct intervention to manipulate certain aspects of the current socio-economic structure. The capital markets can be manipulated by fiscal measures such as taxation exemptions or subsidised capital (Italy relies on several types of 'soft loans' – below base interest rates – to encourage the growth of small firms), both the capital and goods markets can be affected in one direction or another by authorising various allowances on new investment in capital goods, and the labour market can be affected, as mentioned above, by reducing employers' costs, by income support measures and by regulation (pay policies and freezes). The role of training in industrial policy was to upgrade the skills of workers and of managers in particular sectors and to improve the general skills of the workforce rather than the enterprise culture focus on enterprise management training. Enterprise culture policies only made use of fiscal policy to redistribute wealth to the employing classes and concentrated upon the labour market but as part of their social policy rather than their industrial policy, shying away from active and effective interventionist policies. Even the income support aspects of the EAS were rather limited in their scope and not directed at the entire labour force or at any particular industrial sector.

This leads on to a second issue. It is in the area of human resource management and development policies that advocates of industrial policy are now looking. Britain's record in all types of training at all levels has been abysmal and steadily declined during the enterprise culture years (NEDO, 1988; Cutler, 1992). The consequences in human and psychological terms has been to restrict employment choice and limit individual levels of aspiration, while on the economic front it has reduced the skills and the technology base, thus constraining entrepreneurial opportunities. There is a growing body of evidence that successful new small enterprises more capable of survival and growth are being started by several founders working together as a team (Dunkelberg and Cooper, 1982; Barkham, 1987; Storey *et al.*, 1989). This type of social activity takes the form of planned enterprises or, sometimes, of management buy-outs. It was spawned by recognition of new opportunities opened up by structural shifts in the economy or in the changing business strategies of larger corporations. The politics of individualism, which is such a fundamental part of enterprise culture policies and the ethos of many self-employed and traditional small firm owners, can stand in the way of this process and may be judged, consequently, as anti-entrepreneurial.

Business groups are clearly more aware of themselves as decision makers and appear to believe they have greater control over their own destinies than many other groups (including academics or personnel students). However, there are also clear signs that the self-employed tend to have significantly different self-concepts from those of small business managers. The greater importance placed on independence as a personal career motive and on lifestyle or status as business objectives among the self-employed, with the growing emergence of economic motives as the organisational size of the business increases, highlights these differences. The relative importance of achievement motivation, together with a stronger perception of internal locus of control among those intending to remain self-employed compared with potential small business managers, suggests that success among the self-employed is judged less according to business criteria and more in terms of personal autonomy and freedom from control. This would explain why so many self-employed prefer not to employ other people and why they set non-economic objectives for their 'businesses'. This is clearly an enormous internal contradiction in the enterprise culture policies that dominated Britain during the 1980s.

By contrast, the importance of independence seems relatively less strong among those who actually do employ other people. This suggests that independence for them is seen more in organisational terms and less as a part of personal individualism. This may also help to explain why there are only slight differences between them and the employees of large organisations in terms of their self-reported achievement motivation. However, the desire of potential small business owners to organise others and to take decisions is reflected in higher self-reported internal locus of control and achievement motivation than among the employees. Many of the potential managers were already operating businesses and their rather more realistic and calculated approach to business risks – they were less inclined to seek new challenges than the self-employed – suggests that an awareness of the imperatives of organisation and planning may temper their need for new or short-term achievements or that they had already attained their expectations. This generalised growth-aversion on the part of most self-employed and many small business owners obviously places serious constraints on the effectiveness of public policies aimed at developing the small firm sector.

From the detailed picture presented in this book of family and other cultural influences on the development of entrepreneurial small businesses, supporters of enterprise culture policies could argue that the effects of the massive growth of self-employment may not be felt in this generation but will have its full impact on the next generation, many more of whom will have a self-employed family background. Opponents may well argue that, as most self-employed operate as pre-capitalist elements in the secondary sector, their culture is not particularly entrepreneurial, especially as their educational standards and heritage has been considerably depleted. Instead, it could be argued that the higher cultural base and self-development inherent in a well-resourced broad educational system are more likely to lead to innovative and imaginative behaviour and the ability to organise the social forms of work that seem to be the true hallmark of entrepreneurial development. The evidence presented in this book tends to support the latter position but these issues were not addressed squarely and the argument here rests mainly on psychological grounds. The true empirical test is left to future historical judgement, as also is the question on whether the general enterprise culture approach has had long-lasting detrimental effects on other parts of the economy and the social fabric of Britain.

A number of related issues need to be addressed. These are, first, psychological and concern the effects of essentially non-entrepreneurial work motivation and low levels of aspiration among the self-employed, the unemployed and among many employees on business behaviour and participation in public policy initiatives. Attitudes towards and expectations of education and public policy are other areas of interest to social psychology while many issues of concern to developmental psychologists and cognitive psychologists have been raised at various points in this book. Second are the areas where economic and psychological research offer mutual benefits and new insights to each other, for example the areas of information gathering, usage and interpretation. Also, the strict concepts of economic motivation and rationality have been strongly questioned in this book and it may be that this area of inquiry should move to exploring new concepts of wealth and differential demand (as opposed to the neo-classical concept of effective demand). The third issue is more multidisciplinary and concerns the practical steps that may have to be taken in order to take into account the effects of cultural factors – class, education, family, peer group – initially in the self-employed career choice decision and later in continued growth orientation.

Taking the more psychological issues first, the prevalence of non-business work motivation needs to be taken into account in many areas of public policy. The behavioural ramifications of non-work motivation on business-related behaviour should provide a fertile field for psychological research and eventually support discussions on alternative policies designed to cater to a wider range of personal needs. It is evident that enterprise culture policies have totally failed to take into account the dominance of non-economic personal motives among their target groups, where there may be more interest in training to develop technical skills or social interactive skills which may have a business value but which are felt to be important because of linkages to other non-business areas of personal life. The demoralisation, poor self-esteem and low levels of aspiration – in short the characteristics of a fear of failure – prevalent among the unemployed and many of the new self-employed will clearly affect their attitudes towards business and their business behaviour. The other side of fear of failure, however, is also present among potential enterprise trainees and new start-ups – the dreamers who set themselves unrealistically high levels of aspiration. It is a tricky psychological and course design challenge to be able to identify both extreme types. The next, equally tricky challenge lies in devising strategies for boosting the self-confidence of the first group while gently discouraging the unrealistic aspirations of the second group. The clue may lie in providing longer-term pre-career and personal development choice programmes where self-employment is only one of several options. Courses helping the self-employed to use their business-related skills for other purposes may have the effect of raising the status of their working life in their own eyes and make them less apologetic and resistant to improvement.

As regards the areas where psychology can inform economic thinking and vice versa, this book has strongly questioned the appropriateness of economic rationality and the primacy of profit maximisation as the main motivation of small firm owners. The above discussion on the effects of different work motivations on business behaviour could be usefully extended to considering how and in what terms entrepreneurs define wealth. The high status given to 'lifestyle' as a business objective suggests that reducing wealth and reward to monetary or accounting values may run the risk of losing some of

Indeed, this book has shown that we should expect different behavioural patterns from owners of different types of firm. For instance, the essentially individualistic and non-entrepreneurial character of most self-employed, and the strong cultural influences evident in that milieu, have been discussed at some length throughout the book and are clearly present in the research findings we have discussed. It would be interesting to test the proposition that expectations among most self-employed are shaped directly by external structural factors and play little part in anticipating or planning future business behaviour. This is not to suggest that cultural determining factors are any less important to the self-employed. Indeed, the dominance of the need for autonomy or independence suggests that the picture of a strong anti-establishment consciousness among Marx's pre-capitalist formations may still hold true today. Instead of business plans, spontaneity and flexibility seem to be highly prized and the question of personal power over one's immediate affairs is clearly important. Some of the main differences between the self-employed and other small business owners with employees seem to spring from the fact that many small businesses have accumulated some assets which are put at risk by an injudicious decision – unlike many self-employed who essentially sell their labour (this reflects Kahneman and Tversky's (1982) framing effects in risk perception and endowment effects in economics). It is also clear from the discussions about the non-entrepreneurial nature of most self-employed that many of them have different cultural approaches towards participating socially in formal work environments or, more broadly, in capitalist society. These social elements are very important because they determine not only the different personal goals of the self-employed compared to small enterprise managers but also, in conjunction with perceived and objective opportunities and threats, they explain why they made their occupational choice. Small enterprise owners can also be flexible in their behaviour but may hold their expectations and perceptions of the external world more rigidly. This would conform to the high value that small firm owners place on maintaining their lifestyles and their limited or non-existent growth aspirations. There is a gap between the objective factors and their perception of them. An important overall aim of this book has been to identify which factors, whether objective or perceived, are important in the development of growth-oriented small enterprises and to explore whether these factors can be induced or nurtured where they were previously absent. As mentioned above, this implies that the owners or managers of such enterprises have a conscious intention of using their abilities to start and expand their businesses, further implying that they consciously set appropriate commercial and strategic objectives for their businesses.

It seems reasonable to hold that effective business judgement reflects the correspondence of individuals' perceived capacities, opportunities and threats with their objective possibilities and their ability (*competence*) to act upon that information. It is then not too difficult to interpret Timmons *et al.*'s (1977) list of common entrepreneurial characteristics in terms of business competence and the expected outcomes in terms of successful business growth and performance. Modern management theory is certainly moving in this direction and away from older hierarchical, scientific management or management-by-objectives models. In smaller enterprises, however, it remains an open question, not addressed directly in this book, whether business competence corresponds to the levels of individual capability and work effectiveness of small firm owners. Elliot Jaques (1976), who was one of the pioneers in applying cultural models to organisational behaviour in large firms, has argued that individual capacity in planning and work effectiveness (in effect, the capacity to plan for different time horizons) are the key determinants of the structure and career-path opportunities of bureaucratic hierarchies. It may be that similar individual capacities are also the main determinant of entrepreneurial small firm growth and success. The assumption that entrepreneurs must be more capable and competent as business managers than most self-employed and other small firm managers is supported by the findings of this book.

The main observable features of entrepreneurial behaviour are likely to be a stronger congruence between perceptions and reality, a greater emphasis on opportunities, the dominance of work motivation and the way feedback directly affects expectations (which then proactively determine the setting of appropriate and clearly defined aims). The essentially social nature of a successful enterprise is also explicitly recognised in the importance accorded to the accurate perception of the capacities of self and others. It has been argued in this book that 'entrepreneur' is basically an economic concept which includes owners of independent businesses who are able to organise other people in successfully pursuing a business enterprise. In these terms, success is usually measured in terms of market success – market share, profit growth or the introduction of a significant and profitable product, process or organisational innovation. Both these criteria, particularly the second, would have the effect of boosting economic development and together they imply a positive psychological orientation towards the efficient growth of the business. However, this does not mean that the informational needs of expanding and innovative enterprises will remain constant or that their growth and development will continue and flourish under the control of a single individual entrepreneur. There is nothing in this model which stipulates that sustained growth must be an outcome (indeed some entrepreneurs switch from one opportunity to another in search of revenue or profits, unencumbered by any sense of maintaining assets in the form of permanent staff or premises). In some cases, however, growth is an outcome and the policy challenge remains that of how to encourage this to occur more often and more significantly.

DEVELOPMENT OF AN 'ENTERPRISE CULTURE'

Throughout this book various references have been made to the importance of cultural influences on career choice and business behaviour. Edward

Tylor's (1874) definition of culture as the capabilities and habits formed by individuals as part of society has stood the test of time and remains valid, particularly in the light of the various discussions on the role of social representations; however, it is very broad and needs to be specified for any particular context to which it is applied. We have seen that the very concept of the 'entrepreneur' is a cultural construct that reflects the spirit and economic development of its times. We have also seen that, in today's advanced economies, the heavy promotion and encouragement of individualism that characterised the enterprise culture years is not likely to lead to the creation of a critical mass of innovative, growth-oriented enterprises. Yet the underlying rationale for the enterprise culture policies, namely that we need to create a milieu or even a whole class of entrepreneurs, still persists in business circles, as the following quote from the president of the CBI reveals.

> Unless we can build the entrepreneurs of the future, we will not have the dynamic new businesses, innovative new ideas and high value added products that will be the key to success in a world where we're unlikely to be cheapest but can certainly be smarter.
>
> (CBI, 1996: 11)

We have already commented on how the enterprise culture approach mutated into a more management and human resource developmental approach. This quotation suggests that a new approach is now favoured by larger corporations, a sort of 'network approach' that stresses the links between small, medium and large enterprises and between them and government or parastatal agencies. There are also elements of a 'technology-driven' or high-skills approach emerging in recent British and EU development thinking that has strong resonances with Schumpeter's ideas. Even so, the cultural considerations we have discussed need to be taken into account when training policies for the development of small enterprises, the self-employed and entrepreneurs as groups in today's advanced economies. The status of different industries and occupations needs to be taken into account, as this will affect not only career choice but also the values and organisational forms of all types of enterprise, big and small. These factors may become even more important as the economies of Europe converge. We have already discussed how capitalism evolved differently from different medieval cultures in both east and west (Pirrene, 1937; Weber, 1984) and Hofstede's research reveals the power of different cultural norms as well as the dangers of being too 'culture-bound' when addressing different social and economic contexts.

Any attempt to foster values that support greater business cooperation and enterprising behaviour in the form of an 'enterprise culture' cannot afford to ignore the largest small business population – the self-employed. It has been established beyond reasonable doubt throughout this book that a need for independence (with related needs for autonomy and respect) is central to the value systems of most self-employed. It is clear that measures that can enable many self-employed to find more personal time without fear of a loss of income are needed. This book provides some support for those campaigners who advocate a reduction in red tape and form filling for the smallest firms. It may be that an acceptance of a national minimum wage for all people of earning age would enable the self-employed to earn up to certain levels without fear of fiscal penalty. This type of policy does not command universal political support and does not address directly the question of creating an enterprising culture.

It is hard to see how – even with messages and information crafted to appeal culturally to different categories of the self-employed – many self-employed will find time to consider their ways of earning their living more creatively or more rationally. One answer may lie in the content of enterprise training. Perhaps training related more to assertiveness and other social skills called for in business might be helpful. Another solution may lie (paradoxically given their staunch individualism) in a greater provision of universal social services relating to child care, education and communication. This approach would find support from McClelland's (1968) view that earlier socialisation and a greater emphasis on the 'mothering' side of personal development, coupled with reward for achievements among the very young, is the route to establishing a more achievement-oriented culture. Furthermore, refocusing on the social rather than the economic development of the self-employed may lead to a complete reappraisal of enterprise policy through recognising that entrepreneurial business behaviour need not require an individual entrepreneur and need not be confined to small independent firms. Increasingly, small autonomous units are being formed within larger organisations and many non-business organisations in the public and voluntary sectors can be extremely enterprising. The evidence and arguments presented above suggest that an enterprise culture is more likely to flow from the social interactions demanded of effective enterprise development policy than from any marketing campaign, no matter how effective. To repeat the point made on p. 180, one important implication to draw from the conclusion of this book – that the individualism so central to enterprise culture policies is also its fatal flaw – is that the unit of analysis, or the ultimate policy target, should not be the individual *entrepreneur* but instead the *enterprise* itself.

One policy option for addressing the cultural influences and for providing the new skills for addressing problems in dealing with competitors, contractors, customers and suppliers remains training. However, many of the skills required are technical rather than the more psychological aspects of developing positive feelings about 'enterprise'. This still leaves open other important questions about the role and content of 'enterprise' training. The book has already demonstrated convincingly that most of the basic business techniques courses provided under the rubric of enterprise training have failed to produce a skilled approach to business or to transform naive business owners or non-business people into effective innovating entrepreneurs. It was suggested that Gary Becker's (1964) *human capital theory* provided a useful economic rationale for analysing the effect of training and the attitudes of small firm owners towards it. Becker's theory links participation in training to the expectations of increased future reward as a result of new skills, experience or qualifications.

Whether financial incentives or status/career improvements could induce the acquisition of the right range of staff and management skills to support more effective enterprises is ultimately a political decision outside the scope of this book. However, it can be said that the portents are not good. The question still returns to cultural influences and how highly education, development and training are valued. A great deal of attention has already been paid by present enterprise culture supporters to finding good exemplar case studies of firms that have prospered following training. Their efforts have not been crowned with evident success. According to Becker's theories, enterprise owners are too aware of the obvious costs in time, money and lost opportunities to risk investing in staff improvements when faced with the prospects of uncertain reward. This may strengthen the case for compulsory training levies so that enterprise owners seek to recoup at least some of their outlay and try to ensure that training works.

One of the most important issues that needs to be addressed if enterprise policy is to be about the development of enterprises, not just of entrepreneurs, is how to drive the early founder-managers along the stage development curve. Another related problem is how to provide them with acceptable exit routes so that they can leave a viable enterprise with the feeling they have been properly rewarded for their initial hard work and vision. This may be the way to attract more people like Roger McKechnie to apply their experience and talents to running their own businesses rather than someone else's. Once again, this seems to be the role of fiscal policy by giving successful retiring owners tax incentives – income tax, sales tax and inheritance tax. Local development banks or local stock exchanges could also offer markets in local firms enabling owners to sell or to move out gradually. They would also have an incentive to ensure that their firm was left in a healthy and profitable state. These ideas have been aired by various commentators and some have found their way into the small firms policies of various political parties. They are not of direct concern to this book. Rather, the human behavioural aspects of encouraging successful business founders to raise their levels of competence and satisficing behaviour remains as the central issue. The focus is slightly different and the concept of an enterprising culture does not contain the unfortunate attack on the 'dependency culture' that current enterprise culture policies do. The 'enterprise culture', where individual changes in attitudes were expected to transform existing cultural norms, may be better viewed as a 'culture of enterprise' that shapes individuals' values, perceptions and behaviour as part of a progressive and developing society and active local community.

References

Advisory Council on Science and Technology (ACOST), Cabinet Office (1990) *The Enterprise Challenge: Overcoming Barriers to Growth in Small Firms*. HMSO. London.

Allport G. (1937) *Personality: a Psychological Interpretation*. Holt, Rinehart and Winston. New York.

Allport G., Vernon P. and Lindzey G. (1951) *Study of Values*. Houghton Mifflin. Boston.

Amin A., Johnson S. and Storey D. (1986) 'Small firms and the process of economic development: explanations and illustrations from Britain, Italy and the United States'. CURDS Research Working Paper 4. University of Newcastle upon Tyne.

Anderson C. (1977) 'Locus of control, coping behavior and performance in a stress setting: a longitudinal study'. *Journal of Applied Psychology* 62: 446–51.

Antonides G. (1991) *Psychology in Economics and Business*. Kluwer Academic Publishers. Dordrecht.

Argyle M., Furnham A. and Graham J. (1981) *Social Situations*. Cambridge University Press. Cambridge.

Atkinson J. (1957) 'Motivational determinants in risk-taking behaviour'. *Psychological Review* 64: 359–72.

Atkinson J. and Feather N. (1966) *Theory of Achievement Motivation*. Wiley. New York.

Bamford J. (1987) 'The development of small firms, the traditional family and agrarian patterns in Italy', in Goffee R. and Scase R. (eds) *Entrepreneurship in Europe*. Croom Helm. London.

Bandura A. (1991) 'Perceived self-efficacy in the exercise of personal agency'. *The Psychologist: Bulletin of the British Psychological Society* 10 (October): 411–24.

Bannister D. and Fransella F. (1986) *Inquiring Man: the Psychology of Personal Constructs*. Croom Helm. London.

Bannock G. (1981) *The Economics of Small Firms*. Basil Blackwell. Oxford.

Bannock G. and Daly M. (1990) 'Size distribution of UK firms'. *Employment Gazette* (May). HMSO. London.

Bannock G. and Peacock A. (1989) *Governments and Small Business*. Paul Chapman. London.

Bannock G. and Stanworth J. (1990) *The Making of Entrepreneurs*. SBRT Monograph. Small Business Research Trust. Milton Keynes.

Barkham R. (1987) 'Regional variations in new business size, financial structure and founder characteristics: NEP survey results'. Discussion Paper 32 in Urban and Regional Economics. University of Reading.

Barry B. (1980) 'Human and organizational problems affecting growth in the smaller enterprise'. *Management Review* 5(4): 14–16.

Bates S. and Wilson P. (1989) 'Turning points in business growth: implementing management development in small businesses'. Paper presented to 12th National Small Firms Policy and Research Conference. London.

Baumol W. (1968) 'Entrepreneurship in economic theory'. *American Economic Review* (May): 64–71.

Bechhofer F. and Elliott B. (1976) 'Persistence and change: the petite bourgeoisie in industrial society'. *Archives of European Sociology* XVII: 74–99.

Beck U. (1992) *Risk Society*. Translated by Ritter M. Sage. London.

Becker, G. (1964) *Human Capital*. National Bureau for Economic Research. New York.

Begley T. and Boyd D. (1986) 'Psychological characteristics associated with entrepreneurial performance'. in Ronstadt *et al.*, *op. cit.*

Bellofiore R. (1985) 'Marx after Schumpeter'. *Capital and Class* 24.

Berryman J. (1983) 'Small business failure and bankruptcy: a survey of the literature'. *International Small Business Journal* 1(4): 47–59.

BiC *see* Business in the Community.

Binks M. (1991) *Investment Behaviour in Small Firms*. SBRT. Milton Keynes.

Binks M. and Jennings A. (1986) 'Small firms as a source of economic rejuvenation', in Curran *et al.*, *op. cit.*

Binks M. and Vale P. (1984) 'Constraints on the new firm'. Nottingham University Small Firms Units. Discussion Paper 3.

Binks M. and Vale P. (1990) *Entrepreneurship and Economic Change*. McGraw-Hill. London.

Blanchflower D. and Oswald A. (1990) *British Social Attitudes*. Social and Community Planning Research. London.

Blythe S., Granger B. and Stanworth J. (1989) *On Course for Business*. SBRT. Milton Keynes.

Bolton J. (1971) *Small Firms – Report of the Committee of Inquiry on Small Firms*. Cmnd 4811. HMSO. London.

Bonnett C. and Furnham A. 1991 'Who wants to be an entrepreneur?' *Journal of Economic Psychology* 12(3).

British Business (1987) 'Registrations and deregistrations for VAT UK, 1980–86'. DTI. London.

British Overseas Trade Board (1987) *Into Active Exporting*. Occasional Papers. BOTB. London.

British Social Attitudes (November 1990). Social and Community Planning Research. London.

British Statistics Office. (1987) *Business Monitor*.

Brockhaus R. (1977) 'Locus of control and risk-taking propensity as entrepreneurial characteristics: a comparative study'. *Dissertation Abstracts International* 37, 12-A (part 1) (June).

Brockhaus R. (1980) 'Risk taking propensity of entrepreneurs'. *Academy of Management Journal* 23(3): 509–20.

Brockhaus R. (1982) 'The psychology of the entrepreneur', in Kent *et al.*, *op cit.*

Brockhaus R. and Horwitz P. (1986) 'The psychology of the entrepreneur', in Sexton and Smilor, *op. cit.*

Brown D. and Brooks L. (1984) *Career Choice and Development*. Jossey-Bass. San Francisco.

Brown R. and Myers A. (1987) 'Progress report on English Graduate Enterprise Programme 1985/86'. Paper presented to the 10th UK Small Firms Policy and Research Conference. Milton Keynes.

Brusco S. and Sabel C. (1981) 'Artisan production and economic growth', in Wilkinson F. (ed.) *The Dynamics of Labour Market Segmentation*. Academic Press. London.

Burns P. and Dewhurst J. (eds) (1989) *Small Business and Entrepreneurship*. Macmillan. London.

Business in the Community (1986) *Small Firms: Survival and Job Creation*. BiC. London.

Caird S. (1990) 'Self-assessment of participants on enterprise training'. *British Journal of Education and Work* 4(3).

Caird S. (1993) 'What do psychology tests suggest about entrepreneurs?' *Journal of Managerial Psychology* 8(6): 11–20.

Campbell M. and Daly M. (1992) 'Self-employment into the 1990s'. *Employment Gazette* (June). HMSO. London.

Cantillon R. (1756) *Essai sur la nature du commerce en général*. Gyles. London.

Carland J., Hoy F., Boulton W. and Carland J.C. (1984) 'Differentiating entrepreneurs from small business owners: a conceptualisation'. *Academy of Management Review* 9(2): 354–59.

Carswell M. (1987) 'Management training needs of small firms: a study of the engineering and clothing & textile industries'. Paper presented to the 10th UK Small Firms Policy and Research Conference. Milton Keynes.

Casey B. and Creigh S. (1988) 'Self-employment in Great Britain: its definition in the Labour Force Survey, in Tax and Social Security Law and in Labour Law'. *Work, Employment and Society* 2(3): 381–91.

Cassidy T. and Lynn R. (1989) 'A multifactorial approach to achievement motivation: the development of a comprehensive measure'. *Journal of Occupational Psychology* 62: 301–12.

Casson M. (1982) *The Entrepreneur: an Economic Theory*. Martin Robertson. Oxford.

CBI *see* Confederation of British Industry.

CEDAT (Centre for Educational Development and Training). (1988) *Investing in the Future: SMEs, New Technology and Training*. Manchester Polytechnic. Manchester.

Chell E. (1985)'The entrepreneurial personality: a few ghosts laid to rest?' *International Small Business Journal* 3(3): 43–54.

Chell E. (1986) 'The entrepreneurial personality: a review and some theoretical developments', in Curran *et al.*, *op cit.*

Chell E. and Adam E. (1994) 'Exploring the cultural orientation of entrepreneurship: conceptual and methodological issues'. Discussion Paper in Management 94–7. University of Newcastle upon Tyne.

Chell E., Haworth J. and Brearley S. (1991) *The Entrepreneurial Personality: Concepts, Cases and Categories*. Routledge. London.

Chisnall P. (1986) *Manchester Business School New Enterprise Programme Participants Survey: 1977–1983*. MBS. Manchester.

Churchill N. and Lewis V. (1983) 'The five stages of small business growth'. *Harvard Business Review* 61: 30–51.

Coase R. (1937) 'The nature of the firm'. *Econometrica* 4 (November): 386–405.

Cockcroft J., Frank A. and Johnson D. (1972) *Dependence and Underdevelopment*. Doubleday. New York.

Cole A. (1949) 'Entrepreneurship and entrepreneurial history', in *Change and the Entrepreneur*. Harvard University Press. Cambridge, Mass. Pp. 94–6.

Cole A. (1968) 'The entrepreneur – introductory remarks'. *Papers and Proceedings, American Economic Review* 58.

Collins O., Moore D. and Unwalla D. (1964) *The Enterprising Man*. University of Michigan Press. Lansing.

Confederation of British Industry. (1986) *Management Training for Small Businesses*. CBI. London.

Confederation of British Industry (1996) *Generating Growth: an SME Policy Checklist and Agenda*. CBI. London.

Constable J. and McCormick R. (1987) *The Making of British Managers*. BIM/CBI. London.

Cooke P. and Morgan K. (1991) *The Network Paradigm*. Regional Industrial Research Report 8. Cardiff.

Cooper A. and Dunkelberg W. (1987) 'Entrepreneurial research: old questions, new answers and methodological issues'. *American Journal of Small Business* 11(3).

Coopersmith S. (1967) *The Antecedents of Self Esteem*. Freeman. San Francisco.

Creigh S., Roberts C., Gorman A. and Sawyer P. (1986) 'Self-employment in Britain: results from the Labour Force Surveys 1981–84'. *Employment Gazette* (June). Department of Employment. London.

Cromie S. and Johns S. (1983) 'Irish entrepreneurs: some personal characteristics'. *Journal of Occupational Behaviour* 4: 317–24.

Cross M. and Payne G. (eds) (1991) *Work and the Enterprise Culture*. Falmer Press. London.

Curran J. (1986) *Bolton Fifteen Years On: a Review and Analysis of Small Business Research in Britain 1971–1986*. Small Business Research Trust. London.

Curran J. (1988) 'Training and research strategies for small firms'. *Journal of General Management* 13(3): 24–37.

Curran J. and Blackburn R. (1991) *Paths of Enterprise: the Future of the Small Business*. Routledge. London.

Curran J. and Burrows R. (1988) *Enterprise in Britain: a national profile of small business owners and the self-employed*. Small Business Research Trust. London.

Curran J. and Stanworth J. (1981) 'A new look at job satisfaction in the small firm'. *Human Relations* 34(5): 343–65.

Curran J. and Stanworth J. (1989) 'Education and training for enterprise: some problems of classification, policy, evaluation and research'. *International Small Business Journal* 7(2).

Curran J., Burrows R. and Evandrou M. (1987) *Small Business Owners and the Self-Employed in Britain: an analysis of General Household Survey Data*. SBRT. London.

Curran J., Stanworth J. and Watkins D. (eds) (1986) *The Survival of the Small Firm*. Gower Publishing. Aldershot.

Curran J., Blackburn R., Kitching J. and North J. (1996) 'Establishing small firms' training practices, needs, difficulties and use of industry training organisations'. DfEE Research Studies. HMSO. London.

Curwen P. (1976) *The Theory of the Firm*. Macmillan. London.

Cutler T. (1992) 'Vocational training and British economic performance: a further instalment of the "British labour problem"?'. *Work, Employment and Society* 6(2): 161–83.

Daly M. (1991) 'The 1980s – a decade of growth in enterprise'. *Employment Gazette* (March). HMSO. London.

Daly M., Campbell M., Robson M. and Gallagher C. (1991) 'Job creation 1987–89: the contributions of small and large firms'. *Employment Gazette* (November). HMSO. London.

Davidsson P. (1989a) *Continued Entrepreneurship and Small Firm Growth*. Economic Research Institute. Stockholm.

Davidsson P. (1989b) 'Entrepreneurship and after? – a study of growth willingness in small firms'. *Journal of Business Venturing* 4: 211–26.

Deal T. and Kennedy A. (1982) *Corporate Cultures: the Rites and Rituals of Corporate Life*. Penguin. Harmondsworth.

Deci E. and Ryan R. (1985) *Intrinsic Motivation and Self-Determination in Human Behavior*. Plenum Press. New York.

Denicolo P. and Pope M. (1989) 'Towards an enterprise culture: a personal construct psychology approach to professional development in education'. Paper presented at the 9th International Congress on Personal Construct Psychology, Assisi, Italy.

Department of Employment (various years) *Census of Employment.* HMSO. London.

Department of Employment (various years) *Labour Force Surveys* (LFS). HMSO. London.

Department of Employment (various years) *Labour Market Quarterly Reports* (LMQR). HMSO. London.

Department of Employment (1986) *Building Businesses . . . Not Barriers.* HMSO. London.

Department of Employment (1988) Written reply, Secretary of State for Employment to Parliamentary Question, 19 July. HMSO. London.

Department of Employment (1989, 1992) *Small Firms in Britain.* HMSO. London.

Department of Trade and Industry (various years) *Annual Census of Production. Industrial Analysis of Employees and Self-Employed.* HMSO. London.

Department of Trade and Industry (1991) *Constraints on the Growth of Small Firms.* HMSO. London.

Department of Trade and Industry (1996) *Small Firms in Britain.* HMSO. London.

Dignam J. (1990) 'Personality structure: emergence of the five-factor model'. *Annual Review of Psychology* 41: 417–40.

Donckels R. and Dupont B. (1987) 'New Entrepreneurship and Labour Market Conditions'. *International Small Business Journal* 5(4).

Doyle J. and Gallagher C. (1986) 'The size-distribution, potential for growth and contribution to job-generation of firms in the UK, 1982–84'. Research Report 7. University of Newcastle upon Tyne. Newcastle.

Drucker P. (1985) *Innovation and Entrepreneurship: Practice and Principles.* Harper and Row. New York.

Duesenberry, J. (1949) *Income, Saving and the Theory of Consumer Behavior.* Harvard University Press. Cambridge, Mass.

Dunkelberg W. and Cooper A. (1982) 'Entrepreneurial typologies', in Vespers K. (ed.) *Frontiers of Entrepreneurial Research.* Babson College, Massachusetts. Pp. 1–15.

Durkheim E. (1898) 'Représentations individuelles et représentations collectives'. *Revue du Métaphysique et de Morale* 6: 273–302.

Duveen G. and Lloyd B. (1990) *Social Representations and the Development of Knowledge.* Cambridge University Press. Cambridge.

Eggertsson T. (1990) *Economic Behavior and Institutions.* Cambridge University Press. Cambridge.

ENSR (1993, 1995) *The European Observatory for SMEs.* EIM. Zoetemeer, Netherlands.

Erickson E. (1959) 'Identity and the life cycle'. *Psychological Issues* 1.

Etzioni A. (1987) 'Entrepreneurship, adaptation and legitimation: a macrobehavioural perspective'. *Journal of Economic Behavior and Organization* 175–89.

European Commission (1996) *Employment in Europe.* Directorate-General V, EC. Brussels.

Evans D. (1987a) 'Tests of alternative theories of firm growth'. *Journal of Political Economy* 95(4): 657–74.

Evans D. (1987b) 'The relationship between firm growth, size and age: estimates for 100 manufacturing industries'. *Journal of Industrial Economics.* XXXV(4): 567–81.

Eysenck H. (1967) 'Personality patterns in various groups of businessmen'. *Occupational Psychology* 41: 249–50.

Farr R. 'Heider, Harre and Herzlich on health and illness: some observations on the structure of *"représentations collectives"'*. *European Journal of Social Psychology* 7(4): 491–504.

Farr R. (1977) 'On the nature of attributional artefacts in qualitative research: Herzberg's two-factor theory of work motivation'. *Journal of Occupational Psychology* 50: 3–14.

Farr R. and Moscovici S. (eds) (1984) *Social Representations*. Cambridge University Press. Cambridge.

Fiedler F. (1967) *A Theory of Leadership Effectiveness*. McGraw-Hill. New York.

Fine B. (1975) *Marx's 'Capital'*. Macmillan. London.

Fine B. (1980) *Economic Theory and Ideology*. Arnold. London.

Fineman S. (1979) 'The achievement motive construct and its measurement: where are we now?'. *British Journal of Psychology* 68: 1–22.

Flamholtz E.G. (1986) *How to Make the Transition from Entrepreneurship to a Professionally Managed Firm*. Jossey-Bass. London.

Fleishman E. (1953) 'Leadership climate, human relations training and supervisory behavior'. *Personnel Psychology* 6: 205–22.

Frank A.G. (1978) *Dependent Accumulation and Underdevelopment*. Macmillan. London.

Fransella F. (1984) 'Kelly's constructs and Durkheim's representations', in Farr and Moscovici, *op. cit.*

Fransella F. and Bannister D. (1977) *A Manual of Repertory Grid Technique*. Academic Press. London.

Freeman C. (1974) *The Economics of Industrial Innovation*. Penguin. London.

Frey B. (1992) *Economics as a Science of Human Behaviour*. Kluwer. Boston.

Frey B. and Heggli B. (1989) 'An ipsative theory of business behaviour'. *Journal of Economic Psychology* 10(1): 1–20.

Furnham A. (1986) 'Economic locus of control'. *Human Relations* 39: 29–43.

Furnham A. (1990) *The Protestant Work Ethic: the Psychology of Work Related Beliefs and Behaviours*. Routledge. London.

Furnham A. (1992) *Personality at Work: the Role of Individual Differences in the Workplace*. Routledge. London.

Furnham A. and Lewis A. (1986) *The Economic Mind: the Social Psychology of Economic Behaviour*. Wheatsheaf Books. Brighton.

Galbraith J.K. (1969) *The New Industrial State*. Penguin. London.

Gallagher C. (1991) 'Introduction' in *Small Firms in Britain*. Employment Department, HMSO. London.

Ganguly P. (1985) *UK Small Business Statistics and International Comparisons*. Harper and Row/SBRT. London.

Gasse Y. (1982) 'Elaborations on the psychology of the entrepreneur', in Kent, *op. cit.*

Gecas V. and Seff M. (1990) 'Social class and self-esteem: psychological centrality, compensation and the relative effects of home and work'. *Social Psychology Quarterly* 53(2): 165–73.

Geertz C. (1973) *Interpretation of Cultures*. Basic Books. New York

Giannola A. (1986) *Industria Manifatturiera e Imprenditori del Mezzogiorno*. Guida Editori. Naples.

Gibb A. (1983) 'The small business challenge to management education'. *Journal of European Industrial Training* 7(5): 1–41.

Gibb A. (1987) 'Enterprise culture – its meaning and implications for education and training'. *Journal of European Industrial Training* 11(2).

Gibb A. and Ritchie J. (1981) 'Influences on entrepreneurship: a study over time'. Paper presented to the Small Firms Policy and Research Conference. London.

Gill J. (1985) *Factors Affecting the Survival and Growth of the Smaller Company*. Gower. Aldershot.

Goldthorpe J. with Llewellyn C. and Payne C. (1987) *Social Mobility and Class Structure in Modern Britain*. Clarendon Press. Oxford.

Gordon J. (1983) *A Diagnostic Approach to Organisational Behaviour*. Allyn and Bacon. Boston.

Goss D. (1991) *Small Business and Society*. Routledge. London.

Gray C. (1987a) 'Construal of course contents as a clue to success on a Business Management Programme'. Paper presented to the 12th Colloquium of IAREP. Ebeltoft, Denmark.

Gray C. (1987b) 'Enterprise training as a development strategy: evidence from southern Italy'. Paper for the 10th National Small Firms Policy and Research Conference. Cranfield School of Management. Milton Keynes.

Gray C. (1988) 'Open learning and the small business sector'. Paper presented to the first MSC Regional Enterprise Consortium Conference in the East Midlands. Girton College, University of Cambridge.

Gray C. (1989) 'From unemployment to self-employment: a manageable change?' Paper presented to the 4th West European Congress of the Psychology of Work and Organisation. Robinson College, Cambridge, England.

Gray C. (1990) 'Some economic-psychological considerations on the effects of the EAS'. *Piccola Impresa* 1: 111–24.

Gray C. (1992a) 'Enterprise Trainees' Self-Construals as Entrepreneurs'. *International Journal of Personal Construct Psychology* 5(3): 305–20.

Gray C. (1992b) 'Entrepreneurial motivation and the smaller business', in Lea *et al.*, *op. cit.*, pp. 214–42.

Gray C. (1994) 'Individualism as a barrier to British SME participation in the Single Market'. Paper for the 39th Annual World Conference of the International Council for Small Business. Strasbourg, France.

Gray C. and Bannock G. (1988) 'The growing small businesses of Britain: trends in quarterly profiles of growing small firms 1984–88'. Paper presented to the 11th UK Small Firms Policy and Research Conference. Cardiff.

Gray C. and Stanworth J. (1985) *The London Enterprise Programme: a Follow-up Research Study*. PCL. London.

Gray C. and Stanworth J. (1986) *Allowing for Enterprise: a Qualitative Assessment of the Enterprise Allowance Scheme*. SBRT. London.

Greiner L. (1972) 'Evolution and revolution as organizations grow'. *Harvard Business Review* (July–August): 37.

Guest D. (1987) 'Human resource management and industrial relations'. *Journal of Management Studies* 24(5).

Haahti A. (1993) *Interstratos: Internationalisation of Strategic Orientations of European Small and Medium Enterprises*. EIASM. Brussels.

Hakim C. (1988) 'Self-employment in Britain: recent trends and current issues'. *Work, Employment and Society* 2(4): 421–50.

Hakim C. (1989) 'Identifying fast growth small firms'. *Employment Gazette* (January): 29–41.

Hampson S. (1988) *The Construction of Personality* (2nd edn). Routledge. London.

Handy C. (1985) *Understanding Organisations*. (3rd edn) Penguin. Harmondsworth.

Handy C. (1987) *The Making of Managers*. NEDO. London.

Harre R. and Secord P. (1972) *The Explanation of Social Behaviour*. Basil Blackwell. Oxford.

Hebert R. and Link A. (1988) *The Entrepreneur – Mainstream Views and Radical Critiques*. Praeger. New York.

Heider F. (1958) *The Psychology of Interpersonal Relations*. Wiley. New York.

Herzberg F. (1966) *Work and the Nature of Man.* World Publishing. New York.
Hirsch F. (1977) *The Social Limits to Growth.* Routledge. London.
Hofstede G. (1980) *Culture's Consequences.* Sage Publications. Beverly Hills, Calif.
Hofstede G. (1991) *Cultures and Organizations: Software of the Mind.* McGraw-Hill. Maidenhead.
Hofstede G. and Bond M. (1984) 'Hofstede's cultural dimensions: an independent validation using Rokeach's Value Survey'. *Journal of Cross-Cultural Psychology* 15: 417–33.
Holland J. (1973) *Making Vocational Choices: a Theory of Careers.* Prentice Hall. New Jersey.
Holland J. (1985) *Making Vocational Choices: a Theory of Vocational Personality and Work Environments.* Prentice-Hall. New Jersey.
Hughes A. (1990) 'Industrial concentration and the small business sector in the UK: the 1980s in historical perspective'. Small Business Research Centre, Working paper number 5. University of Cambridge. Cambridge.
Hughes J. (1988) 'The body of knowledge in management education'. *Management Education and Development* 19(4).
Hutchinson P. and Ray G. (1986) 'Surviving the financial stress of small enterprise growth', in Curran *et al., op. cit.*
Ichheiser G. (1949) 'Misunderstanding in human relationships: a study in false social perception'. *American Journal of Sociology* LV, special supplement: 1–72.
Institute of Employment Research (1987) *Review of the Economy and Employment 1987.* University of Warwick. Coventry.
Jahoda G. (1988) 'Critical notes and reflections on social representations'. *European Journal of Social Psychology* 18: 195–209.
Jahoda M. (1979) 'The impact of unemployment in the 1930s and the 1970s'. *Bulletin of the British Psychological Society* 32: 309–14.
Jahoda M. (1988) 'Economic recession and mental health: some conceptual issues'. *Journal of Social Issues* 44(4): 13–23.
Jaques E. (1976) *A General Theory of Bureaucracy.* Heinemann. London.
Javanovic B. and Rob R. (1987) 'Demand-driven innovation and spatial competition over time'. *Review of Economic Studies* LIV: 63–72.
Jennings D. and Zeithanl C. (1983) 'Locus of control: a review and directions for entrepreneurial research'. *Proceedings, Academy of Management*: 417–21.
Jennings R. and Morris P. (1991) 'Pathways to the top: talking to those who have made it'. Paper presented to the Annual Conference of the British Psychological Society, April 1991. Bournemouth.
Johnson C. (1991) *The Economy under Mrs Thatcher 1979–1990.* Penguin. London.
Johnson P. (1986) *New Firms: an Economic Perspective.* Allen and Unwin. London.
Johnson P. and Thomas B. 'Training means (small) business: an economic evaluation of the New Enterprise Programme'. *Employment Gazette* (January): 17–22.
Johnson S. (1989) *Employment Change in UK Small Businesses.* Report to Employment Department, Institute for Employment Research, Warwick Business School, Coventry.
Jung C. (1953) *The Integration of Personality.* Farrar and Ruchart. New York.
Kahneman D. and Tversky A. (1979) 'Prospect theory: an analysis of decision under risk'. *Econometrica* 47: 253–91.
Kahneman D. and Tversky A. (1982) 'The psychology of preferences'. *Scientific American* 246: 136–42.
Katona G. (1964) *The Mass Consumption Society.* McGraw-Hill. New York.
Katona G. (1975) *Psychological Economics.* Elsevier. New York.
Keat R. and Abercrombie N. (1990) *Enterprise Culture.* Routledge. London.

Keeble D. (1987) 'Entrepreneurship, high-technology industry and regional development in the United Kingdom: the case of the Cambridge phenomenon'. Paper presented to the seminar on Technology and Territory. Istituto Universitario Orientale, University of Naples. Italy.

Kelly G. (1955) *The Psychology of Personal Constructs*. Norton. New York.

Kent C., Sexton D. and Vespers K. (eds) (1982) *Encyclopedia of Entrepreneurship*. Prentice-Hall. New Jersey.

Kets de Vries M. (1977) 'The entrepreneurial personality: a person at the crossroads'. *Journal of Management Studies* 14(1): 34–57.

Kets de Vries M. (1980) *Organisational Paradoxes*. Tavistock Publications. London.

Keynes J. (1936) *General Theory*. Royal Economic Society. London.

King J. (1990) *Labour Economics* (2nd edn). Macmillan. London.

Kirzner I. (1973) *Competition and Entrepreneurship*. University of Chicago Press. Chicago.

Kirzner I. (1982) 'The theory of entrepreneurship in economic growth', in Kent *et al.*, *op. cit.*

Knight F. (1921) *Risk, Uncertainty and Profit*. Harper and Row. New York.

Labour Market Quarterly Report (March 1988; August 1990; February 1991). Employment Department. Sheffield.

Lave J. (1988) *Cognition in Practice*. Cambridge University Press. New York.

Lazerson M. (1988) 'Organisational growth of small firms: an outcome of markets and hierarchies?' *American Sociological Review* 53(June): 330–42.

LBS *see* London Business School.

Lea S., Tarpy R. and Webley P. (1987) *The Individual in the Economy*. Cambridge University Press. Cambridge.

Lee B. (1987) 'The use of appropriate theory in management education'. *Management Education and Development* 11(18): 4.

Lefcourt H. (1966) 'Internal versus external control of reinforcement: a review'. *Psychological Bulletin* 65: 206–20.

Lefcourt H. (1976) *Locus of Control*. Lawrence Erlbaum. New Jersey.

Legal and General Assurance Society Ltd (1985) *The Self-Employed Report*. London.

Leibenstein H. (1976) *Beyond Economic Man*. Cambridge University Press. Cambridge.

Levinson H. (1973) 'Multidimensional locus of control in psychiatric patients'. *Journal of Consulting and Clinical Psychology* 41: 397–404.

Lewin K. (1938) *The Conceptual Representation and the Measurement of Psychological Forces*. Duke University Press. Durham, NC.

LMQR *see Labour Market Quarterly Report*.

Lofquist L. and Dawis R. (1969) *Adjustment to Work*. Prentice-Hall. Englewood Cliffs, New Jersey.

London Business School (LBS) (1987) 'A study to determine the reasons for failure of small businesses in the UK'. September 1987. Stoy Hayward. London.

Lynn R. (1969) 'Personality characteristics of a group of entrepreneurs'. *Occupational Psychology* 43: 151–2.

Lynn R. (1991) *The Secret of the Miracle Economy*. The Social Affairs Unit. London.

McClelland D. (1961) *The Achieving Society*. Van Nostrand. New York.

McClelland D. (1968) 'The achievement motive in economic growth', in Hoselitz B. and Moore W. (eds) *Industrialisation and Society*. UNESCO. Paris.

McClelland D. (1987) 'Characteristics of successful entrepreneurs'. *Journal of Creative Behavior* 21(3): 219–33.

McClelland D. and Winter D. (1971) *Motivation and Work Behaviour*. Free Press. New York.

Mangham I. and Silver M. (1986) *Management Training: Context and Practice*. ESRC/DTI. London.

March J. (1988) *Decisions and Organizations*. Basil Blackwell. Oxford.

March J and Shapira Z. (1987) 'Managerial perspectives on risk and risk-taking'. *Management Science* 33: 1404–18.

Marris R. (1964) *The Economic Theory of 'Managerial Capitalism'*. Macmillan. London.

Marshall A. (1920) *Principles of Economics*. Macmillan. London.

Marx K. [1848] (1964) *Pre-Capitalist Economic Formations*. Lawrence and Wishart. London.

Marx K. [1867] (1930) *Capital*. Everyman's Library, Dent and Son. London.

Marx K. (1969) *Theories of Surplus Value*. Lawrence and Wishart. London.

Marx K. (1973) *Grundrisse*. Penguin Books. London.

Maslow A. (1954) *Motivation and Personality*. Harper and Row. New York.

Mason C. (1989) 'Explaining recent trends in firm formation in the UK: some evidence from south Hampshire'. *Regional Studies* 23: 331–46.

Mason C and Harrison R, (1991) 'The small firm equity gap since Bolton', in Stanworth and Gray, *op. cit.*

Mead G. (1934) *Mind, Self and Society*. University of Chicago Press. Chicago.

Meager N., Kaiser M. and Dietrich H. (1992) *Self-Employment in the United Kingdom and Germany*. Anglo-German Foundation. London.

Mill J. (1848) *Principles of Political Economy with Some of Their Applications to Social Philosophy*. Parker. London.

Miller G. (1970) *The Psychology of Communication*. Pelican. London.

Mingione E. (1991) *Fragmented Societies: a Sociology of Economic Life beyond the Market Paradigm*. Basil Blackwell. Oxford.

Mintzberg H. (1979) *The Structuring of Organizations*. Prentice-Hall. New York.

Mischel W. (1968) *Personality and Assessment*. Wiley. New York.

Morgan D. and Schwalbe M. (1990) 'Mind and self in society: linking social structure and social cognition'. *Social Psychology Quarterly* 53(2): 148–64.

Moscovici S. (1988) 'Notes towards a description of Social Representations'. *European Journal of Social Psychology* 18: 211–50.

Murray H. (1938) *Explorations in Personality*. Oxford University Press. New York.

Myrdal G. (1970) *The Challenge of World Poverty*. Pantheon Books. New York.

NEDO (1986) *External Capital for Small Firms: a Review of Recent Developments*. NEDC. London.

Oakey R. (1987) 'Entrepreneurship and regional industrial growth in small high technology firms'. Paper presented to a seminar on Technology and Territory. Istituto Universitario Orientale, University of Naples. Naples, Italy.

O'Guigan T. and Shrum L. (1991) 'Mass-mediated social reality: the social cognition and ecology of economic norms'. Paper presented to the 1991 Colloquium of International Researchers in Economic Psychology. Frankfurt.

Ormerod P. and Worswick G. (1982) 'Unemployment in inter-war Britain'. *Journal of Political Economy* 90(2): 400–36.

Osipow S. (1983) *Theories of Career Development*. Prentice-Hall. New Jersey.

Patel P. and Pavitt K. (1989) 'A comparison of technological activities in West Germany and the United Kingdom'. *National Westminster Bank Quarterly Review* (May). London.

Pettigrew A. and Whip R. (1991) *Managing for Competitive Success*. Basil Blackwell. Oxford.

Phares J. (1976) *Locus of Control in Personality*. General Learning Press. New Jersey.

Pirenne H. (1937) *Economic and Social History of Medieval Europe*. Harvest/HBJ. New York.

Pope M. and Keen T. (1981) *Personal Construct Psychology and Education*. Academic Press. London.

RBL (1987) *Enterprise Allowance Scheme Evaluation: Three Year National Survey.* Research Bureau Limited. London.

Rokeach M. (1968) *Beliefs, Attitudes and Values.* Jossey-Bass. San Francisco.

Ronstadt R., Hornaday J., Peterson R. and Vespers K. (eds) (1986) *Frontiers of Entrepreneurship Research.* Babson College. Wellesley, Mass.

Rosch E. (1978) 'Principles of categorization', in Rosch E. and Lloyd B. (eds) *Cognition and Categorization.* Erlbaum. New Jersey.

Rostow W. (1962) *The Stages of Growth.* Cambridge University Press. Cambridge.

Rothwell R. and Zegveld W. (1982) *Innovation and the Small and Medium Sized Firm.* Frances Pinter. London.

Rotter J. (1966) 'Generalised expectancies for internal versus external control of reinforcement'. *Psychological Monographs* 80(609).

Rubery J. (1994) 'The British production regime: a societal-specific system?'. *Economy and Society* 23(3): 335–54.

Saunders P. and Harries M. (1987) 'Firmstart at Cranfield 1986–1987'. Paper presented to the 10th UK Small Firms Policy and Research Conference. Milton Keynes.

Say J.-B. (1817) *Catechism of Political Economy.* Carey and Son. Philadelphia.

SBRT *see* Small Business Research Trust.

Scase R. and Goffee R. (1982) *The Entrepreneurial Middle Class.* Croom Helm. London.

Schein E. (1981) *Organizational Psychology.* McGraw Hill. New York.

Schumacher E. (1973) *Small is Beautiful.* Blond and Briggs. London.

Schumpeter J. (1934) *Theory of Economic Development.* Harvard University Press. Cambridge, Mass.

Schumpeter J. [1942] (1976) *Capitalism, Socialism and Democracy.* George Allen and Unwin. London.

Schwartz S. and Bilsky W. (1990) 'Toward a theory of universal content and structure of values: extensions and cross-cultural replications'. *Journal of Personality and Social Psychology* 58: 878–91.

Schweder R. and Levine R. (1984) *Culture Theory: Essays on Mind, Self and Emotion.* Cambridge University Press. New York.

Sexton D. and Smilor R. (1986) *The Art and Science of Entrepreneurship.* Ballinger. Cambridge, Mass.

Silver M. (1984) *Enterprise and the Scope of the Firm.* Martin Robinson. Oxford.

Simon H. (1955) 'A behavioral model of rational choice. *Quarterly Journal of Economics* 69: 99–118.

Simon H. (1956) 'Rational choice and the structure of the environment'. *Psychological Review* 63: 129–38.

Simon H. (1957) *Models of Man.* John Wiley. New York.

Simon H. and Bonini C. (1958) 'The size distribution of American firms'. *American Economic Review* 48: 607–17.

Skinner B. (1957) *Verbal Behaviour.* Appleton-Century-Crofts. New York.

Small Business Research Trust (1985–96) *The NatWest/SBRT Quarterly Survey of Small Business in Britain.* Volumes 1–12. SBRT. London.

Smith A. (1776) *An Inquiry into the Nature and Causes of the Wealth of Nations.*

Smith N. (1967) 'The Entrepreneur and his Firm'. Occasional paper. Bureau of Business and Economic Research. Michigan State University.

Stanworth J. and Bannock G. (1990) *The Making of Entrepreneurs.* SBRT. Milton Keynes.

Stanworth J. and Curran J. (1973) *Management Motivation in the Smaller Business.* Gower Publishing. Aldershot.

Stanworth J. and Gray C. (eds) (1991) *Bolton 20 Years on: the Small Firms in the 1990s*. Paul Chapman/SBRT. London.

Stanworth J., Purdy D. and Kirby D. (1992) *The Management of Success in 'Growth Corridor' Small Firms*. Small Business Research Trust. Milton Keynes.

Stewart V. and Stewart A. (1981) *Business Applications of Repertory Grid*. McGraw-Hill. Maidenhead.

Stigler G. (1961) 'The economics of information'. *Journal of Political Economy* 69: 213–25.

Stokes G. and Cochrane R. (1984) 'A study of the psychological effects of redundancy and unemployment'. *Journal of Occupational Psychology* 57: 309–22.

Storey D. (1986a) 'Entrepreneurship and the new firm', in Curran *et al.*, *op. cit.*

Storey D. (1986b) 'New firm formation, employment change and the small firm: the case of Cleveland county', in Curran *et al.*, *op. cit.*

Storey D. (1990) 'Evaluation of policies and measures to create local employment'. *Urban Studies* 27(4): 669–84.

Storey D. (1992) 'Should we abandon the support to start up businesses?'. Paper presented to the 15th National Small Business Policy and Research Conference. Southampton.

Storey D. (1994) *Understanding the Small Business Sector*. Routledge. London.

Storey D. and Johnson S. (1987) *Job Generation and Labour Market Change*. Macmillan. Basingstoke.

Storey D. and Strange A. (1992) *Entrepreneurship in Cleveland 1979–89: a Study of the Effects of the Enterprise Culture*. Department of Employment. London.

Storey D. and Westhead P. (1994) 'Management training and small firm performance'. Working paper 18. SME Centre, Warwick University. Coventry.

Storey D., Watson R. and Wynarczyk P. (1989) 'Fast growth small businesses: case studies of 40 small firms in northern England'. Research Paper no. 67. Department of Employment. London.

Storey D., Wynarczyk P. and Johnson S. (1987) 'The high tech entrepreneur and his business'. Paper presented to the seminar on Technology and Territory. Istituto Universitario Orientale, University of Naples. Naples.

Super D. (1957) *The Psychology of Careers*. Harper and Row. New York.

Super D. (1980) 'A life-span approach to career development'. *Journal of Vocational Behavior* 16: 282–98.

Tajfel H. (1981) *Human Groups and Social Categories*. Cambridge University Press. Cambridge.

Taylor F. [1910] (1947) *Scientific Management*. Harper and Row. New York.

Thurstone L. (1931) 'A multiple factor study of vocational interests'. *Personnel Journal* 10: 198–205.

Timmons J. (1989) *The Entrepreneurial Mind*. Brick House Publishing. Andover, Mass.

Timmons J., Smollen L. and Dingee A. (1977) *New Venture Creation*. Irwin Homewood, Ill.

Triandis H. (1989) 'The self and social behavior in differing cultural contexts'. *Psychological Review* 96(3): 506–20.

Tylor E. (1874) *Primitive Culture: Researches into the Development of Mythology, Philosophy, Religion, Language, Art and Custom*. New York.

Vale P. and Binks M. (1990) 'An alternative approach to the theory of entrepreneurship'. Paper presented to the 13th National Small Firms Policy and Research Conference. Harrogate.

Valentine E. (1982) *Conceptual Issues in Psychology*. Allen and Unwin. London.

Vespers K. (1980) *New Venture Strategies*. Prentice Hall. Englewood Cliffs, NJ.

Vespers K. (ed.) (1982) *Frontiers of Entrepreneurial Research*. Babson College, Mass.

Vickery L. (1989) 'Equity financing in small firms', in Burns and Dewhurst, *op. cit.*

Vroom V. (1964) *Work and Motivation*. Wiley. New York.

Vyakarnam S. and Jacobs R. (1993) 'Teamstart – overcoming blockages to small business growth'. Paper presented to the 16th National Small Business Policy and Research Conference. Sheffield.

Wainer H. and Rubin I. (1969) 'Motivation of research and development entrepreneurs: determinants of company success'. *Journal of Applied Psychology* 53(3.1): 178–84.

Wallace A. (1970) *Culture and Personality*. Random House. New York.

Watkins D. (1983) 'Development, training and education for the small firm: a European perspective'. *European Small Business Journal* 1(3): 29–44.

Weber M. (1930) *The Protestant Work Ethic and the Spirit of Capitalism*. George Allen and Unwin. London.

Weber M. (1947) *The Theory of Social and Economic Organisation*. Free Press. New York.

Weber M. (1984) *Confucianism and Taoism*. Translated by Alter M. and Hunter J., abridged by Morishima M. London School of Economics. London.

Weiner B. (1985) 'An attributional theory of achievement motivation and emotion'. *Psychological Review* 92: 548–73.

Weiner M. (1981) *English Culture and the Decline of the Industrial Spirit*. Cambridge University Press. Cambridge.

Williamson O. (1985) *The Economic Institutions of Capitalism*. Free Press. New York.

Wilson Report (1979) *The Financing of Small Firms. 1979. Interim Report of the Committee to Review the Functioning of Financial Institutions*. HMSO. London.

Wolk S. and Ducette J. (1973) 'The moderating effect of locus of control in relation to achievement motivation variables'. *Journal of Personality* 41.

Wright G. (1975) 'A review of research investigating the internal–external (I–E) control construct'. Working report 75-2. Brunel Institute of Organisation and Social Sciences. Uxbridge.

Index

achievement motivation model 75–7
acorns to oaks thesis 23
Advisory Council on Science and Technology (ACOST) 19
Advisory Group on Enterprise Training (AGET) 61
agency theory 78, 90
alienation 84, 85–6, 88, 104–5
allocentric 103
Allport-Vernon-Lindzey scale 152
Amin, A. *et al.* 45, 170
Antonides, G. 130, 157, 159
Atkinson, J. 136, 152, 166; and Feather, N. 109, 127, 129, 134, 136–7
attribution theory 104

Bamford, J. 170
Bandura, A. 156, 157, 167
Bannister, D. and Fransella, F. 101, 151
Bannock, G. 4, 18, 32, 33; and Daly, M. 35, 51, 60, 61; and Stanworth, J. 49, 105
Barkham, R. 176
Bates, S. and Wilson, P. 25
Baumol, W. 90
Beck, U. 93, 94
Becker, G. 28, 145, 161, 187
behavioural theories: of enterprise development 180–4; of the firm 77–9
Bellofiore, R. 89
Bentham, J. 11, 131, 147, 151
Binks, M. 142; and Jennings, A. 33, 43, 52, 58, 65; and Vale, P. 77, 78
Blanchflower, D. and Oswald, A. 95, 104
Blythe, S. *et al.* 27, 64, 138

Bolton, J. 10, 11, 18, 49, 65, 105, 107, 108, 110, 117, 123, 133, 137, 138, 140, 169
Bolton Report (1971) 7, 137
British Business magazine 34
British Leyland 9
British Social Attitudes surveys 30, 59, 95
British Steel Corporation 2, 9
British Venture Capital Association 37
Brockhaus, R. 15, 90, 134, 136, 142, 143, 158; and Horwitz, P. 132
Brown, R. and Myers, A. 64
Burrows, R. 105
Business in the Community 67, 68
business cycle 12, 52
business ethic, negative perception of 11
Business Links 67, 74
business services sector 42

Caird, S. 69, 154
Camden Enterprise 4
Campbell, M. and Daly, M. 39, 64, 96
Cantillon, R. 146
capitalism 15–16, 147; emergence of 7; improving efficiency of 6; Marxian view 82–8, 131, 151
career choice 123, 126–7, 130–1
career development: humanist/self-awareness theory 123, 124; and inheritance of occupation 125–6; and push/pull factors 126; and structural factors 123–4; theories 123–5; trait and factor theory 123–4
Carland, J. *et al.* 49, 121, 132
Carswell, M. 66, 180
Casey, B. and Creigh, S. 38, 44, 50
Cassidy, T. and Lynn, R. 134, 182

Lightning Source UK Ltd.
Milton Keynes UK
UKOW06f1800150616

276381UK00011B/204/P